SUCCESSFUL AGRIBUSINESS MANAGEMENT

For Jill, Karla, and Maija
with love

Successful Agribusiness Management

Edited by
JOHN FREIVALDS
Founder and Editorial Director,
Agribusiness Worldwide magazine

Gower

© John Freivalds, 1985.

HD9000.5
S78

Published by
Gower Publishing Company Limited,
Gower House, Croft Road, Aldershot, Hants GU11 3HR,
England

Gower Publishing Company,
Old Post Road,
Brookfield,
Vermont 05036,
USA

British Library Cataloguing in Publication Data

Successful agribusiness management.
   1. Farm management
   I. Freivalds, John
   630'.68   S561

Library of Congress Cataloging in Publication Data

Freivalds, John
   Successful agribusiness management

   1. Produce trade--management--case studies.
2. Food industry and trade--management--case studies.
3. Agriculture industries--management--case studies.
I. Title
HD9000.5.F735   1984   630'.68   84-24739

ISBN 0-566-00802-5

Contents

Contributors   viii

Introduction   x

PART I AGRIBUSINESS STRATEGY

1. The Rise and Fall – and Rise Again – of IBEC   1

2. Maximizing Quality in Processed Foods: Green
    Giant's International Sourcing Approach   12

3. International Multifoods' Strategy in Venezuela   18

4. Pillsbury's Involvement with the Saudi Arabian
    Flour Mills   24

5. The Explosive Growth of the Brazilian FCOJ Industry   32

6. Progress on the Plantation: The Growth Strategies
    of Sime Darby   39

7. White Elephant Tales: Venezuela's Cassava
    Processing Plants   47

8. Jamaica Soya Products Industries: A Troubled
    Joint Venture   53

90-17S062

9.   The Growth and Integration of Jamaica Broilers   63

10. Trinidad's Poultry and Feed Industries   70

11. The Pride of the African Beef Industry:
     Botswana Meat Commission   76

12. Marketing Commodities: New Types of Export
     Contracts   82

13. Organizing Commodity Trading Groups   93

14. Airfreighting High Value Perishables:
     Flowers from Colombia   101

15. Sabritas' Backward Integration into
     Agricultural Production   108

16. A Lobster Tale: The Collective Marketing
     of Brazilian Seafood   116

17. How 'Chiquita' Helped United Fruit   122

PART II AGRICULTURAL AND LIVESTOCK PRODUCTION

18. Farming Failures: The Fate of Large Scale Agri-
     business in Iran   133

19. The Moldavia Tomato Project   147

20. Amazonia Agro-forestry: Projeto do Jari   152

21. Tapping Alaska's Agricultural Potential:
     The Delta Project   162

22. Rice Production at Big Falls Ranch   169

23. Hummingbird Farm: Hershey's Hope for More
     Abundant and Improved Cocoa   175

24. Contract Growing of Flue-cured Tobacco in Jamaica   182

25. Puerto Rico's Agricultural Diversification Program   189

26. The Kufra Production Project   197

27. The Kenana Sugar Project in Sudan   203

28. Starting a Feed Industry: The Crucial Ingredients 213

29. Jamaica's Attempts to Develop its Dairy Industry 222

30. Eggs for Haiti: Poultry Project Brings Modern Technology to Peasant Farms 229

31. Protein for Panama: Financing Cattle Production 238

Contributors

Dr. Everett Blasing is an internationally known feed consultant.

Thomas Craig is a consultant at Agribusiness Associates, Inc., a firm specializing in commodity systems analysis.

Tony Doran is Research Assistant, Department of Economics, University of Durham, England.

John M. Fox, currently an agribusiness consultant, was the executive in charge of reorganizing all banana operations for United Fruit.

John Freivalds, President of Freivalds & Associates, an international communications firm, is the founder and Editorial Director of Agribusiness Worldwide magazine.

J. Michael Harker is Assistant Professor and Resource Economist, Cooperative Extension Service, University of Alaska, Fairbanks, Alaska, USA.

Curt Harler is editor of the largest farm weekly newspaper in the USA.

Austin Hayden, Vice President of Experience, Incorporated, a Minneapolis-based consulting firm, was previously in charge of

Green Giant's agricultural sourcing operations.

Dennis A. Johnson is a free-lance writer.

David Levy, formerly an international commodities trader, writes on international trade topics.

Robert G. Lewis is a free-lance journalist specializing in international topics.

Carol M. Morgan is President of Morgan Public Relations/Marketing, Minneapolis, Minnesota, USA.

Richard J. Strohl is a plant and animal science entrepreneur.

David Toht is editor of a publication bringing company news to the employees of DeKalb AgResearch, Inc.

Dr R.J.A. Wilson is professor, Department of Economics, University of Durham, England.

Introduction

I will never forget the scene. Outside, a huge irrigation project was being built, and I was sitting next to a man who had just leased 10,000 hectares of it. His investment was in the millions of dollars, and he was visiting the site to get the project underway. This was my first job in agribusiness, and I wanted to know what grand strategy this renowned California farmer would use.

'What's the first thing you will do?' I asked.

'Buy a desk,' came the reply.

That thought has remained with me. Success in agribusiness comes from three factors: attention to detail, doing tasks in sequence, and recognizing the interconnected relationships in the agribusiness system. The California farmer was following the steps precisely.

It is always possible to draw a lot of graphs to explain how the system is supposed to work, but until you experience it, you cannot really understand it. The examination of a range of international agribusiness case studies comes as close as possible to providing one the experience without his having actually lived it.

When Agribusiness Worldwide magazine was begun in 1979, it represented something new: an attempt to present case histories of agribusiness projects to international agribusiness decision makers in order to help them do a better job. Now 25,000 subscribers around the world use the magazine as one of their management tools. The cases have been reprinted in other journals, used as study materials in seminars, quoted in government publications, and incorporated into a television documentary.

The enthusiastic response to the timeliness and lasting quality of the cases has led us to put the best of <u>Agribusiness Worldwide</u> into book form. In this format we hope to expand its editorial reach into academia. New agribusiness managers are constantly being trained, but to teach them effectively, the examination of real life situations is necessary. The case studies presented herein have been carefully selected to provide the touch of reality sometimes lacking in academic environments.

Many of the cases illustrate what happens when the system breaks down because it is easier to learn a lesson from failure than from success. Moreover, even though many projects started out as failures, some were eventually rehabilitated and made into something useful.

The cases are grouped into two sections for ease of analysis and reference. Part I includes case studies concerning agribusiness strategic planning, marketing and finance. Many of these cases involve processing operations, the first way station for raw agricultural products. The success or failure of a particular project seems to depend largely on the degree of coordination it achieved with its farmer/suppliers, and the innovations in marketing and finance that were utilized.

'Nothing happens until you make a sale' is an axiom of successful marketing, and many agribusiness marketers have made that sale only by coming up with new and unusual marketing strategies.

Money is also needed to develop agribusiness, and 'financial packaging' has become a key concept in undertaking new agribusiness projects. Money is indeed available for projects if someone is ingenious enough to put all the pieces together. The international financial system has begun to respond to the needs of agribusiness by creating special packages for it, and it is common for the investment or the merchant banker to play the role of financial banker. 'Every deal is different,' notes one banker friend of mine, and he is right.

Part II comprises case studies in the areas of agricultural and livestock production. Everything starts with the seed, and these studies examine farming projects both new and old, how they were started, how they matured, and their degrees of success.

With incomes rising around the world, more and more grain is being consumed in the form of meat, eggs, milk and cheese. The growth in livestock production in the developing countries promises to be explosive. Maintaining animal health will be a paramount management challenge in these countries.

Examination of successful agribusiness projects reveals that their management was able to deal with all the variables involved in developing and operating the project: production, processing, financing, and distribution, not to mention the influences of politics and technology.

Too often agriculture connotes only production, with little effort placed on understanding the various influences upon it or how production fits in with the total food system. While the term 'agribusiness' was coined to indicate a more integrated approach to agriculture, it is not universally understood by all. I recall a meeting with the executive of General Mills in charge of the firm's flour milling business. 'We are not in agribusiness; we are a packaged goods company,' he maintained. It seemed to me a strange comment for a man who oversaw grain buying and shipping and flour milling and distribution.

Farm leaders now realize that successful farming depends as much the dollar/yen exchange rate as on the use of the correct herbicide. The venerable 'old salt' who concentrated on only one area is rapidly becoming obsolete; he is being replaced by a modern manager who integrates and even tries to control all the variables affecting his particular operation.

I have flown over 400,000 miles since Agribusiness Worldwide was founded in 1979, and each time the plane landed, I encountered a new story. Particular thanks go to the many companies and government agencies that provided me with access to their files, even for their projects that were less than successful.

The development of the case studies in this book was made possible by the many advertisers that have supported Agribusiness Worldwide. Paul Green, Publisher of Intercontinental Publications, deserves special recognition for the courage he showed in getting the magazine off the ground when no one else would try. Sean Hawe, Gordon Blair, Norman Green, Rollie Boynton, Marc Gueron, Debbie Frost, and Charlotte O'Donnell, all of Intercontinental, also merit special praise. Morton Sosland and Mark Sabo of Sosland Publishing Companies continue to carry the original message envisioned by Agribusiness Worldwide.

Some members of the international agribusiness community have been particularly helpful. Walter Minger, former Senior Vice President of Agribusiness at the Bank of America, deserves special recognition for his insights and his help. David Flood at the World Bank, Jim Ferro at E.F. Hutton, and Dan Klingenberg at Chase Manhattan Bank also provided a lot of support. Robert Ross, President of LAAD, Daryl Natz at Continental Grain, Graham Williams at OPIC, and Wayne Anderson at Feedstuffs helped me often. Kit Codrington of the Asian Development Bank was always ready with help, as was Gordon Booth in his charming cathedral near St. Albans. Bill Bursch and Ken Holt helped me try new directions, some of which fell short, but were nevertheless worth trying.

Others who deserve recognition include Jonathan Taylor of Ibec Inc; George Truitt, Nancy Truitt and Paul Rogers of FMME; Joe Kinney and Norm Youngsteadt of IMC; and Tom Veblen of Food Systems Associates.

My regular contributors were also invaluable: Dick Strohl, Carol Morgan, Robert Lewis, Ian Meadows, and Don Taylor, to mention a few. Bill Warne did an excellent job on book reviews; Beth Jackson worked on keeping us organized, timely, and neat; Thilo Westerhausen helped with research. Special thanks go to Lory Tischer for her careful preparation of the book's manuscript. Susan Freivalds coordinated the book's production.

Part I
Agribusiness strategy

1 The rise and fall – and rise again – of IBEC

ROBERT G. LEWIS

During the Cancun conference in October, 1981, several world leaders advocated that private enterprise take a lead role in promoting agricultural development in the Third World. Although some journalists hailed this as a 'new approach,' International Basic Economy Corporation (IBEC) had launched such a program in Latin America nearly 35 years earlier.

The unique venture that was IBEC was begun by the late Nelson Rockefeller, former Vice President of the United States and grandson of the fabled oil tycoon, John D. Rockefeller, Sr.

IBEC was merged in 1980 into Ibec Inc, jointly owned by the Rockefeller family and Booker McConnell PLC, an English company with worldwide interests in agriculture, agribusiness, engineering, food distribution, spirits and liqueurs, and shipping.

Whether IBEC should best be characterized as a pioneering business venture or a bold social experiment – or some of both – still bemuses observers of the international business scene. Whether it should be judged a success or a failure in either of the two categories – or in both – also remains a matter of debate. But there is no argument that IBEC was both a pioneer and a force to be reckoned with in the international economy, particularly in South America.

IBEC's main contributions probably could not have been accomplished as efficiently, if at all, by any existing or now imaginable national or international governmental agency. Not

1

the least of them is that its experience illustrates the great value to the human society that can be contributed by the multinational corporate form of enterprise.

The first seed of the IBEC idea was planted early in 1937 when Nelson Rockefeller, then a director of the Creole Petroleum Corporation, visited the company's oil properties in Venezuela. The young Rockefeller formed a life-long interest in and commitment to Latin America during that visit. When he returned to the US he advocated the need for private enterprise to assume broader social responsibilities in underdeveloped countries, and in 1940 he formed the Compania de Fomento Venezolana, SA, one of the first private development companies in the continent.

WARTIME EXPERIENCE

Fomento's first project was the construction of a hotel in Caracas. After a slow beginning, the hotel became successful, and other business projects were planned. But World War II intervened. Rockefeller was appointed coordinator of the Office of Inter-American Affairs by USA President Franklin D. Roosevelt late in 1940, and Fomento became dormant.

One of Rockefeller's central concerns as Coordinator of the temporary wartime agency was the development of food supplies. A key unit called the Basic Economy Department was occupied with improvement of existing production, storage, transportation, and marketing facilities. Rockefeller became impressed with the need to go beyond the short run expedients imposed by wartime constraints. He believed that more fundamental innovations and change in the basic economic, social and political structures in the Latin American countries would be needed to remedy the economic instability arising from one-crop or one-product economies, political adventurism, and social tension created by inequalities between social classes, ethnic conflicts, inadequate educational systems, and widespread poverty.

At the war's end, the agency was terminated. Rockefeller's final report stressed the necessity 'to depend upon responsible private interests and agencies in carrying on the Inter-American program.'

Rockefeller was determined to find a way whereby private interests could continue work on the most vital aspects of the wartime agency's program, particularly those of its 'Basic Economy Development.' Some social needs, such as health and sanitation, fit readily into the traditional functions of philanthropic organizations or government agencies, but others seemed to require the creation of new economic entities, which philanthropic foundations rarely if ever had undertaken to do.

Moreover, Rockefeller himself (and many others) disliked the idea of governments getting into business activities.

This objection to governmental intrusion into activities which in the United States were traditionally reserved for the private sector was not a merely academic issue.

Franklin Roosevelt's 'New Deal' administration, inaugurated in the depths of the Great Depression before World War II, had instituted a veritable revolution in life in the USA by extending the reach of the federal government into almost every aspect of the private economy through measures to foster recovery from the depression and to satisfy many social needs formerly left to private responsibility.

PRIVATE INITIATIVE

Many political opponents of the 'New Deal' appeared to the US electorate to be simply insensitive or uncaring about the suffering, deprivation, and insecurity of the people to whom such measures as social security, rural electrification, agricultural price supports, public housing, public works, and others were addressed. Nelson Rockefeller had developed a strong commitment to alleviation of exactly such social needs in Latin America, and elsewhere. But although his wartime appointment had been made by Roosevelt, Rockefeller was of the opposing Republican party, and it was there that his own political future would be found. Moreover, his personal and family loyalties were with the business community in its conflicts with and antagonism toward the Democratic 'New Deal.' Reflecting both his personal and political identification with private business in the central political issue of the time, Rockefeller's efforts leading to the formation of IBEC can be seen as an attempt to mobilize private business as an effective rival of government in producing remedies for social problems and thereby winning the allegiance of the people.

This was an ambitious goal for the aspiring young politician, and it was one whose full realization eluded him to the end of his life. Nelson Rockefeller never was able to dispel the suspicions of hard-line leaders in his own party, and his personal and political commitment to alleviating social needs marked him as a 'New Dealer' in disguise, despite his ardent championship of the primacy of private business in economic affairs. He did, however, win great nationwide popularity and was twice elected Governor of New York, the nation's largest state. He became Vice President of the United States by appointment, but even then, his party denied him its nomination for election to a second term.

By the end of 1945, Nelson Rockefeller had devised a first

approach to his vision of fostering private businesses that would begin to satisfy social needs in Latin America. With financing primarily from the Rockefeller family, the American International Association for Economic and Social Development (AIA) was formed to set up 'small, efficient, profitable business projects' to demonstrate the practicality of using modern science and technology in developing countries to develop basic resources, raise nutritional levels, improve health, train and educate workers, and promote international goodwill and understanding.

However, as Rockefeller's proposal put it, 'No profits will ever be realized by the subscribers to the Association,' and it concluded: 'Once projects are well established and operating on a sound basis, it shall be the policy of the Association to sell or give away its equity in them to private or governmental agencies which have demonstrated clearly their sympathy for the aims of the Association...'

This dichotomy of purpose, for both philosophical and practical reasons, soon forced AIA's founders to the realization that another kind of company had to be formed to undertake the profit-making role.

IBEC IS BORN

The catalyst was the opportunity that arose to combine AIA's experimental seed project in southern Brazil with a small but growing Brazilian maize seed company called Agroceres Limitada. To carry on this and other profit-making ventures, IBEC was formed in 1947. The company's mission was expressed in the preamble of its Certificate of Incorporation: 'To promote the economic development of various parts of the world; to increase the production and availability of goods, things, and services useful to the lives or livelihood of their peoples; and thus to better their standards of living.'

During its initial nine years, IBEC's activities were confined to Venezuela and Brazil. A Venezuelan subsidiary (VBEC) set up a farming company (PACA), a fishing company (PESCA), a wholesaling and food supermarketing company (CADA), and a milk company (INLACA). In Brazil, IBEC set up five key companies designed to provide specialized services to farmers rather than itself engaging in production. They were a hybrid maize seed company (SASA), a hog production company (SAFAP), a grain storage company (CAGSA), a helicopter crop-dusting company (HELICO) and a mechanized agricultural service company (EMA) for clearing virgin land for cultivation. Later IBEC started an investment banking operation jointly with the Chase National Bank which lasted only four years, but which led to creation of a Brazilian mutual fund, later to become one of

4

IBEC's most important development efforts.

A study by the National Planning Association completed in 1967, found that:

> IBEC's overall financial gains were not substantial in this first period. During most of these early years, the company as a whole lost money. Yet several individual companies, especially the hybrid maize seed company, the milk company, and the supermarkets were financially profitable and fulfilled the IBEC goals of upgrading the living standards of the people.... By the end of (the) period, IBEC had proved an important 'cutting tool' for economic development.

EXPANSION

Major expansion was initiated beginning in 1956 when stock was offered to the public. New activities were begun in mutual funds, housing, soluble coffee, manufacturing, and poultry. Operations were expanded into 33 countries by 1965. Net profits, although modest, were reported for each year.

During the next five years, IBEC's operations expanded vigorously. Its profitability rose to a peak in 1970, and the number of its affiliated and subsidiary companies rose to 147. At that time, IBEC's new president and chief executive officer (since 1968) reviewed the company's purposes and achievements in an article published in Harvard Business Review ('Turn Public Problems to Private Account,' January, 1971). He was Rodman C. Rockefeller, eldest son of Nelson Rockefeller.

Rodman Rockefeller endorsed the basic idea of IBEC's founders that:

> Business will profit by assuming a more aggressive leadership role as an innovative force capable of exercising social judgment, consciously initiating change, and shaping the overall environment. Such an approach means that profit is valued as an essential discipline and measurer of economic stress, not as the sole corporate goal.

He went on to declare that IBEC was making the idea work successfully:

> We have made money by meeting human needs in an efficient and business like way. Over the past ten years, for example, our total revenue has nearly tripled and our stockholders' equity has more than doubled. Last year (1969) we earned US$1.72 per share

5

on a total revenue of US$256 million and the results so far this year lead us to expect even further improvement. (IBEC's 1970 profits reached US$1.96 per share.)

Rodman Rockefeller attributed IBEC's successes to four guidelines:

1. Attempt to identify a human need in a particular market, usually a developing area.
2. Try to develop fresh, innovative ways to meet that need in that market.
3. Subject any concrete proposal to a searching analysis in order to determine if it will meet standard financial criteria of a workable business enterprise, and if local management is capable of success.
4. Satisfy ourselves that the new venture does not violate the cultural, social, and economic values of the people for whom it is intended.

These four guidelines would seem to be remarkably novel business doctrine for the time of IBEC's founding 22 years before. But on close analysis today, they do not seem uncommon. Each can be interpreted as a routine maxim by which modern practical businesses guide their operations.

However, it is the very relevance to the contemporary business mentality that reveals the greatest distinction of the business doctrine that was conceived for IBEC a half-century ago. It was 'ahead of its time' – and thereby it contributed to the progress of private business to the greater sensitivity and sophistication in relating social and political problems to business operations that is exemplified by successful modern international corporations of today.

This contribution is recognized with fine perception by Jean Crouzet, who was Director of Marketing of IBEC's Food and Housing Division for nearly ten years until 1977. He says:

Today's international business manager of vision combines the objective of profits for his company with the objective of social benefits for the people of the countries in which he operates. IBEC's strong motivation to achieve social benefits was the precursor of the business motive that emerged more generally during the 1970s and predominates in the doctrines of almost all successful international businesses today. The modern businessman must recognize the necessity to satisfy the critical modern public that his operations are consistent with the

6

social interest if he is to succeed, or ultimately
even to survive.

IBEC'S DECLINE

As a business operation, however, IBEC's fortunes declined
drastically after 1970. Huge losses (as much as US$16 million
in 1975) were reported for several years, and annual profits
were never large. Losses during the nine years until the
merger with Booker McConnell exceeded profits by nearly US$44
million. IBEC sold its interests in many of its wholly-owned
and affiliated companies, reducing their number from a peak of
153 (in 1972) to only seven distinct entities by the time of
the merger in 1980.

During all of its 33 years of operations, IBEC never paid a
dividend.

Some of the causes of IBEC's decline were similar to the
risks that confront all businesses, and actually spelled the
doom of many others during the same period.

The 1970s were a period of drastic economic disruption and
political upheaval which exceeded any business manager's
ability either to forecast or to control. In order of their
importance to IBEC and their effects upon its earnings, they
were: the abrupt elimination of subsidies for low-cost housing
in the United States and Puerto Rico; the rise of nationalism
and changing political conditions in much of Latin America;
the oil embargo and its economic consequences; and the Iranian
crisis which crippled the IBEC subsidiary, Development and
Resources Corporation. These events cost IBEC dearly.

IBEC's own management recognized also that the company had
overextended its activities into too many and overly diverse
enterprises, exceeding its capacity to support them
adequately. This was indicated by the company's belated and
costly efforts to divest unpromising activities and to
retrench during the 1970s.

IBEC'S SUCCESSES

Yet IBEC had many business successes to its credit. Its milk
enterprise in Venezuela was the first in Latin America;
despite initial mistakes, it became highly profitable, and was
sold (primarily in response to political pressures) at a
profit. The supermarkets in Venezuela were sold similarly
after achieving high profitability and exerting lasting
beneficial influences upon agribusiness operations in that
country.

The hybrid maize seed enterprise in Brazil owes much of its

7

outstanding success to IBEC's initiative and financial support, and is now one of the world's foremost companies in its field; it too was sold at a profit. Tremendous contributions were made to the housing industries in Puerto Rico, Peru, and Brazil, although many of IBEC's housing enterprises incurred substantial losses, particularly in the United States and Puerto Rico.

IBEC's poultry operations, first as a partner and later as sole owner of Arbor Acres, exerted a tremendous influence upon the world's poultry industry, and became highly profitable. Together with Nicholas Turkey, Arbor Acres remains the cornerstone of IBEC's successor company, Ibec Inc.

IBEC's most serious mistakes accompanying its misfortunes in housing were made in nonagricultural enterprises. Small manufacturing companies which had been successful on the domestic scene in the USA were overexpanded in the international arena and became big losers.

IBEC's successes and failures were not completely unlike the experiences of many other companies engaged in similar businesses during the same period. However, there seems to have been another, unique factor also at work in IBEC's business decline. Perhaps it is linked directly to the unique motivation that distinguished IBEC from the 'ordinary' business enterprise.

A QUASI-GOVERNMENTAL APPROACH

IBEC's unique and original approach was to view social problems as market opportunities. By responding to those 'Market opportunities,' IBEC sought both to make a profit and to contribute toward solving the underlying social problems.

IBEC's origin corresponds with the beginning of an era of widespread consciousness of social problems and high motiviation to promote social objectives. The power and scope of the problems ordain that those who act upon them are sure to encounter enormous complexity and to be made to endure risks and difficulties not ordinarily faced by traditional business. Many viewed government as the appropriate agency for undertaking such risks and difficulties. IBEC's approach engendered an ambivalence in how IBEC was viewed from the outside, and more importantly, in how it was viewed from the inside, by its own people. IBEC seemed to be taking on a quasi-governmental role.

The ambivalence in IBEC's self-perception appears to have affected its performance. In fact, many of the enterprises launched by IBEC, like those launched by governments at the same time, lacked in some degree the harshly constraining discipline upon managers of traditional businesses to make a

Table 1.1
Operating Results of IBEC, 1955 to 1980

Year	Number of Subsidiaries[a]	Return per Share Outstanding	Net Profit (Loss) for Year
1955	NA	NA	US$ (1,086,088)
1956	34	NA	553,167
1957	37	NA	1,214,891
1958	36	NA	724,531
1959	38	NA	2,008,837
1960	61	NA	3,930,772
1961	64	NA	3,247,038
1962	57	NA	1,901,330
1963	52	US$0.26	1,202,489
1964	103	0.35	1,527,301
1965	115	0.67	2,723,007
1966	106	0.88	3,572,119
1967	109	0.23	936,547
1968	113	1.03	4,225,134
1969	110	1.72	7,122,000
1970	147	1.96	8,146,000
1971	143	0.52	2,177,000
1972	153	(3.34)	(13,835,000)
1973	141	0.56	2,301,000
1974	124	0.43	1,757,000
1975	97	(3.66)	(16,674,000)
1976	68	0.52	2,674,000
1977	61	(2.59)	(13,231,000)
1978	18	0.15	784,000
1979	18	(1.91)	(9,716,000)
1980	NA	NA	7,000,000[b]

Notes:
a. Includes companies in which only a minority interest was owned by IBEC.
b. Reported by IBEC, Inc, as 'in excess of $7,000,000 from operations.'

Source: SEC form 10-K, for the years 1955-1979. Data for 1980 supplied by IBEC, Inc.

profit. The price of failure for a government enterprise was increased public debt. The price of failure for an IBEC enterprise was more subtle - the bleeding of good projects to pay for bad; the erosion of capital; the decline in prestige among the business community.

Because many of the problems tackled both by IBEC and by governments were fraught with greater challenge and risk than those tackled by 'ordinary' businesses, it would not be fair to measure the success or failure of either strictly by the standards of 'ordinary' business.

Yet IBEC must be credited with some outstanding business achievements, and outstanding achievements for business. IBEC demonstrated the reality of business opportunities where none had been perceived before. Imitators followed its example, profited from its experience, and thereby contributed to economic growth and welfare. IBEC created companies (which it long ago divested) that continue to grow and to contribute importantly to their societies and the world economy. IBEC pioneered in the conception and demonstration of a social ethic for international business which is suited to the modern human environment and is being widely adopted by other 'ordinary' businesses.

THE 'NEW' IBEC INC

Two well known US-based poultry genetics companies are the 'jewels' of the newly formed Ibec Inc, created by the merger of IBEC and the English-owned Booker Agriculture International (BAI).

That is how Jonathan Taylor, the company's president who headed BAI before the merger, sees it.

The two companies are Arbor Acres Farm, Inc., of Glastonbury, Connecticut, and Nicholas Turkey Breeding Farm, Inc., Sonoma, California. Both were owned by IBEC before the merger.

Arbor Acres is the leading supplier of breeding stock to the broiler industry of the United States, and accounts for over one-fourth of the worldwide market. The company also markets the Harco strain for brown shell table egg production. Nicholas Turkey is the foremost breeder of heavy white turkeys. Both companies have extensive international sales.

Taylor anticipates that the two poultry genetics companies will be prominent elements in the 'new' Ibec Inc's activities in the years ahead. Ibec Inc. 'will be more tightly focused than the old IBEC, concentrating on poultry breeding, agricultural management and consulting, fish farming, and the like,' Taylor said. 'We are selling off the old nonagribusiness investments, such as shopping centers, in order to concentrate on the basic agricultural business,' he added.

The 'new' Ibec Inc's other main interest will be the activities that had been the leading enterprises of BAI, including the development and management of cane sugar projects, other agricultural enterprises, consulting, farm management, and fish farming.

BAI was owned by Booker McConnell PLC, a leading British international company with annual revenues approaching US$2 billion. Its other principal interests are engineering in the United Kingdom and overseas, food distribution in the UK, health products and pharmacies, spirits and liqueurs, shipping, and copyrights.

Booker McConnell's agricultural interests (represented by BAI) were consolidated with the Rockefeller family's IBEC to form Ibec Inc. Booker McConnell owns about 45 percent of the stock and the Rockefeller family the remaining 55 percent in the merged company. Each owner is represented equally on Ibec Inc's board, with Booker McConnell accorded primacy in operating decisions. Rodman Rockefeller is chairman of the board, and is responsible for long range company planning.

2 Maximizing quality in processed foods: Green Giant's international sourcing approach

AUSTIN HAYDEN

'We have reached the point that we are now sure of our markets,' commented a former Green Giant official, 'but we are never sure of our crop.'

This fact has led Green Giant, a major international processor of vegetables, to develop an international sourcing strategy in order to achieve its goal of maximizing profits through maximizing the quality of its product. The company, a subsidiary of Pillsbury (which had sales in 1980 of US$3.3 billion) can then sell its high quality products at premium prices.

Since there are only a few hours in the life cycle of a maturing vegetable when it should be harvested and processed for maximum quality, a very sophisticated system must be followed to allow for a continuous fast flow of the perishable product to the food processing plant during this short processing season.

Green Giant has accomplished this through harvesting at peak quality as determined by a cumulative heat unit system; by immediate processing of the harvested product; and by selecting processing plant sites internationally to minimize processing costs while allowing for optimum use of facilities, equipment and personnel.

BACKGROUND

The basic processes used by Green Giant are canning with brine and freezing (taking product to 0°C or less). Green Giant is also studying foil retort pouches as the packing medium of the future.

The major vegetable products which Green Giant processes are grown on farms of 30 to 60 hectares. Green Giant annually harvests about 100,000 hectares of vegetables, primarily over a 90 day period. These products are delivered to 13 plants in the USA, Canada, and France. The major seasonal vegetables are peas, sweet maize, asparagus, and green beans. In addition, mushrooms, carrots, lima beans, broccoli, brussel sprouts, cauliflower and spinach are also processed on a much smaller scale. Vegetables in California are processed on a year round basis. Prepared products with rice, cheese, and meats have been added in recent years.

Approximately 40,000 hectares of vegetable land are directly leased, with the company carrying out all of the agricultural activities on that land. The remaining 60,000 hectares are under signed contract agreements with selected vegetable growers in order to use large scale, modern equipment and to provide a continuous flow of product to the processing plants. Usually, the company agrees to harvest, since it is necessary to utilize the latest harvesting equipment and to maintain extremely close control over delivery of these perishables.

PINPOINT HARVESTING

The loss as a result of timing of harvest can be as much as US$240 to US$360 per hectare per day. In the case of peas, sweet maize, and green beans, if the crop is not harvested within a six hour period of the life cycle of the vegetable, less than maximum profits will result. Of course, if the product is left in the field, many times this amount can be lost, especially if it results in the loss of supermarket shelf space after company overhead and advertising have already been committed.

In addition to 'pinpointing harvesting,' most of the products are processed within three hours of harvest. At the rate of 1,200 hectares per day during the height of the season, there is a real need for tight scheduling and the closest coordination of raw product deliveries.

The major purpose of this pinpoint scheduling and harvesting is to obtain the highest percentage of maximum quality products possible and to provide for full utilization of equipment, facilities, and personnel. Mobile pea combines alone now cost US$130,000 a unit and generally harvest about

160 hectares per year in a long season. With this type of overhead, there is very little room for variance of opinions or changes in plans. Plans must be detailed, confirmed and completely coordinated at all levels, since without this, either quality or profits will suffer.

HEAT UNITS

The entire scheduling program is based on the heat unit cropping system originally designed and developed by Green Giant in the early 1930s. Each vegetable is planted and harvested through the detailed utilization of this system. Cultivation, insect control, and other activities related to the crop are also tied into the program. Calendars are used only for developing plans, after which the management works with the variables of the season on a heat unit basis.

Peas, for example, after the seeds have swollen, will begin growing at 40°F (5°C). Each degree Fahrenheit above 40°F on the average for 24 hours is called a heat unit. If the daily average temperature is 50°F (10°C), that would be ten heat units. At harvest time when the average daily temperature is 71°F, there would be 31 daily heat units.

Each variety of peas has its own unique number of heat units from planting to maturity, ranging from 1,200 to 1,900. For any given variety, planting is spaced by projected daily heat units at harvest. If that is 30 heat units, then the crop to be harvested on a particular day (for example, July 1), would have to be planted over a 30 heat unit period, which might be from one day to six days, depending on the weather at planting time.

The harvest schedule is developed based on daily processing plant capacity. These daily hectarage requirements spread across the planting season by variety form the planting schedule.

QUALITY GRADING

Sweet maize is another volume processed vegetable in which the same heat unit system applies, with a further sophistication at harvest time. As harvest approaches, statistical field sampling begins before the predicted hour to determine the exact hour of harvest. Once the intensive field samples indicate that harvest is 12 to 36 hours away, the progression to the exact harvest hour is predicted from the best available weather forecasts.

Figure 2.1 illustrates the maturity progression of sweet maize immediately preceding harvest. The final processed

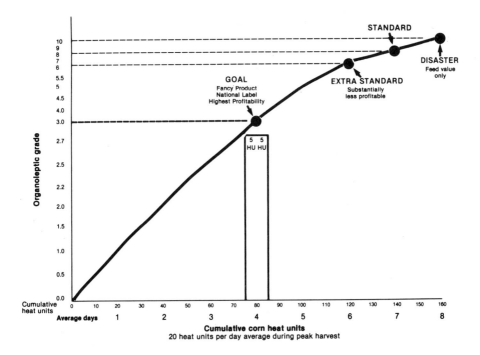

Figure 2.1 Processed Sweet Corn Profitability by Maturity
Progression.

product is divided into organoleptic quality grades. This is a
subjective test through mouth feel whereby the canned or
frozen product is graded into tenths of grades. In effect,
there are 100 different organoleptic grades from 0.0 to 10.0.

The maturity progression varies by organoleptic grade
bracket and is not directly proportional for each one-tenth of
a grade. It requires many more heat units to mature the crop
in the lower range than it does in the target or goal areas.
This is due to the fact that in the early stages, the cobs are
filling out and uneven areas of the field are coming into the
average. Once this is completed, maturity progresses much
faster in the target area.

To miss the target area by five hours can reduce the value
of a hectare of sweet maize by US$360. Earlier harvest will
reduce recovery and increase cost substantially. From the
target day on, the maturity and value of the product decreases
until after a few days, the product is not worth harvesting at
all.

For the heat unit system to work, weather forecasts,
including five-day, three-day, daily and six-hour forecasts,

15

are essential to maximize adherence to preplanned schedules. Green Giant's network of 300 two-way mobile radios and base stations does much to assist in following weather patterns, as well as to carry out changing plans to work around rain patterns.

Even with the heat unit system, fields are still checked closely during the last several days of maturity progression to determine the final six-hour period in which the crop is to be harvested. Soil type variations, changing weather conditions, and specific field areas can cause differences in maturity. Once the product is harvested and arrives at the processing plant, it is still subdivided by maturity and other characteristics for profit maximization and product uniformity.

PROCESSING SITE SELECTION

The highly perishable nature of Green Giant's raw materials makes processing plant site selection of critical importance. As part of its international sourcing strategy, Green Giant is constantly looking for new production and processing sites. In recent years, areas in Costa Rica, Ecuador and other Andean countries, and Korea have been investigated. Production and processing have actually begun in Taiwan, France, and Canada, in addition to the US.

Prior to going to full scale production, the company runs plant trials for three or four years to determine quality and quantity of output. The factors examined include costs compared to competing crops, evaluations of local farmers, analysis of special climatic conditions, and availability of qualified labor.

Site selection for food processing plants is critical. Once the plant is built, it is extremely uneconomical to abandon the site. Gradually changing unfavorable economic forces due to poor site selection mean excessive costs will be incurred.

Among the factors considered in site selection by Green Giant are:

1. Freight rate structure and cost to target market. Except for a strictly local market, freight rates must be evaluated thoroughly. Rate structures are often illogical, depending upon the direction of traffic, the relative size of load, back haul opportunities, time of year, and type of product and associated services.

2. Raw product recovery. Each cropping area has its characteristic advantage in raw product recovery. The smoother, the more symmetrical, and the more normal the individual fruits and immature seeds are, the greater chance

there is for improved product recovery. Hilly areas are not as good as flat or gently rolling land for maximum product recovery.

3. Population patterns and migration trends. Before investing in plant construction and equipment, the ultimate consumers must be identified as well as determining where they will be located some years hence, while the heavy depreciation bill is still being paid.

4. Product mix and its effect on overhead costs. In site selection, an attempt should be made to allow for as many products as possible to provide maximum utilization of equipment, people, money and time. This applies both to the agricultural operation and the plant operation.

5. Labor. The availability of adequate labor, as well as costs of housing, transportation, and payment for non-working hours, must be considered.

6. Evaluation of weather and other risks. A natural disaster that takes the plant out of production after the crop is contracted for could result in economic death for the venture.

7. Water, utilities, and waste disposal. Water and utilities need to be available at a reasonable cost. Waste disposal can be a problem except where the plant is adjacent to extremely sandy soils. For the plant to be located in such an area can make for a substantial cost advantage.

8. Availability of complementary industries. A site in which utilities, equipment, and seasonal personnel, as well as specialized year-round personnel, can be used in conjunction with another industry is extremely attractive.

9. Tax rates. Long term advantageous tax rates for both the industry and the individuals working in the industry are essential in order to be competitive with other areas of the world where such tax incentives are provided.

10. Availability of storage facilities. In addition to facilities that are fully utilized during the entire year, there is a need for temporary storage to handle peak loads because of the nature of the variable supply of vegetables.

11. Degree of urban encroachment. Because of the substantial investment in a modern processing plant and the need for expansion and placement of service facilities, as well as environmental insulation from population centers, the closest urban area must not be able to close in on the site. The price of adjacent land will increase rapidly once the plant is in place, so to purchase additional land at a later date may be prohibitively expensive.

3 International Multifoods' strategy in Venezuela

DENNIS A. JOHNSON

When MONACA, an International Multifoods wholly-owned subsidiary, began grain milling operations in Puerto Cabello, Venezuela, in 1958, Andre Gillet, then general sales manager, was cautious in projecting the future of the new undertaking. At the time, both MONACA and the Bunge Corporation were rushing to get their roller mills operating. What had been a lucrative export market in Venezuela for foreign flour millers was quickly becoming a competitive field for flour production and distribution.

Venezuela's search for a national identity had taken the form of high tariffs and import duties directed toward forcing more manufacturing to be conducted within Venezuela. Richard Troxel, a partner with Peat, Marwick, Mitchell & Co. who lived in Venezuela during this era, recalls:

> The effect on foreign flour millers was obvious. To remain in the flour market in Venezuela, it was necessary to open local milling capacity – and while one might convincingly argue as to the relative economy of shipping wheat rather than milling in the USA and shipping flour – the fact remained that there was only one choice.

Fast-paced industrialization propelled the new Multifoods subsidiary to expand its operations rapidly, and within a few short years the company was operating three industrial flour mills and producing rolled oats for consumers.

With what Gillet now calls 'limited vision,' MONACA decided to build its first mill only large enough to handle its best year's export amount. Having underestimated market potential, the firm quickly acquired, through lease agreements with purchase options, two additional mills, one in Maracaibo and another in La Guaira. 'Within two short years we were running our own facility and two others, and we were able to merchandise all of the production,' said Gillet. By 1961, another plant was obtained in Cumana.

In 1962 Gillet became managing director, the same year MONACA's share of the family flour market burgeoned to 50 percent. The next year the company diversified into animal feeds. In fact, the company's growth was such that between 1968 and 1973, International Multifoods' pre-tax earnings from international operations (primarily Venezuela) grew by over 125 percent.

The track record of MONACA is impressive, and highlights International Multifoods' developing country gamble. The numbers, however, are only a scorecard of its development over the past two decades. The real story behind MONACA lies in the strategy that Gillet and his team used in converting a grain export market to one including flour production and distribution.

'We were pioneers; we were the first ones there,' said Gillet, now President of International Multifoods. An examination of MONACA's history offers insights into the successful establishment of a new business in a developing country.

MARKET RESEARCH

MONACA management's willingness to experiment when solving problems or tackling new projects enhanced its ability to penetrate new markets. When the firm first decided to move into family flour production, several significant US and Canadian competitors, including General Mills, Pillsbury and Quaker, dominated the market. A market survey, however, uncovered consumer dissatisfaction with some of the imported brands.

'One of the biggest complaints was that bugs got into the flour during the shipment,' said Gillet. 'We knew we could manufacture bugless flour, so we asked ourselves how we could convince the people of that,' he added. A clear plastic wrapper or window to allow shoppers to inspect the flour themselves was tested to see if this packaging would cause mold or other problems. Within a year MONACA had its Robin Hood brand on the market in polyethylene bags. Competing brands were packaged in paper.

'Within a year of launching a television, newspaper, radio and in-store advertising promotion, we had 30 percent of the total family flour market,' Gillet said, pointing out that MONACA gained 50 percent of the market in two years. Eventually, paper bags were discarded by competitors in favor of polyethylene. Said Gillet, 'We were on our own and without any constraints. We were able to do things a lot faster than we could do otherwise. It turned out to be very healthy.'

EMPLOYEE RELATIONS

MONACA established close ties with the local community by opening a school at Puerto Cabello to teach the employees. Since this was Venezuela's first flour mill, there was nobody who knew much about running it. A system of afternoon and evening classes was developed within the plant.

Managers were encouraged to join various social clubs in the community, and blue-collar workers were encouraged to form their own unions.

'That was unheard of before. We told them that in the long term they would be better off,' said Gillet, explaining that each plant has its own union which is affiliated with a national labor organization.

One requirement MONACA had was for all staff members to speak and understand Spanish so that they could participate in the local community. 'We also made it a point for each and every one of us to know some people in the federal government,' said Gillet. 'I would personally meet with several of the ministers and discuss with them the problems of industry in general and ours in particular,' he explained.

The company also shared its expertise with the government. 'We made our people available to the Venezuelan government. For example, the man in charge of our lab became a permanent member of the government agency that established quality norms for flour,' said Gillet. 'I think that gave us an opportunity to have access to government people, and perhaps a way to anticipate and understand better what their thinking was and what the direction was going to be,' he said.

MARKETING PROGRAM

When developing its marketing and distribution system, MONACA tapped an existing network of small agents located throughout the country which later became the national sales force. They also provided the means for improving customer service, an important goal of the company.

'We had to prove ourselves and overcome the feeling in developing nations that anything made locally is not as good as the imported product,' Gillet said. 'We set out to show our flour was better; it was cleaner and fresher, and that made an impact. Instead of hiding the difference between local and imported, we advertised it.'

Promotional efforts covered the advertising spectrum: television, newspapers, radio, delivery truck and in-store displays. MONACA also used more subtle methods.

One institutional campaign began, explained Gillet, when he and others attempted to enhance flour sales during the Christmas season when consumption typically declined. 'A national pastime at Christmas is to make "ham bread",' said Gillet, explaining the bread is a maize cake with bits of bacon inside. MONACA bakers developed a new recipe incorporating a special grade of flour. 'We tried it in everything from neighborhood bakeries to large scale operations,' he said.

Once satisfied with the product, the company went incognito and devised a promotional drive encompassing everything from radio announcements to colorful street penants. 'It attracted a lot of curiosity, and no one knew who was doing it,' said Gillet.

The firm followed with letters to businesses suggesting that they inlcude 'ham bread' with the food baskets they traditionally gave to employees during the holiday season. The letters suggested they contact a designated bakery in their neighborhood. Gillet said, 'The idea worked. The next year we advertised and said it was a special Christmas message from MONACA.'

Since the campaign was started in the early 1960s, boasted Gillet, 'ham bread' has become a revived tradition in Venezuela.

EXPANSION FAILURES

Not all of MONACA's ventures, however, have been so successful. An experiment from 1964 to 1967 to grow sorghum, a feedgrain which can survive extreme climatic conditions, and a brief attempt to export maize flour to the United States and Puerto Rico, were projects later abandoned.

The three year, US$900,000 sorghum project was undertaken to develop a local source of grain for animal feed milling. Relying on recommendations from a consultant, explained Gillet, MONACA went ahead and acquired tractors, combines, and other necessary equipment, and leased 6,000 hectares of land near Barinas. After much experimentation, the firm developed a strain of sorghum that would grow in the region.

21

Once the project was underway, however, problems developed. 'We found out the soil wasn't quite right (the leased land was highly acidic); the insecticides weren't working as well as we expected; and rice birds invaded the crop,' Gillet said. 'We realized it was far too large a venture for International Multifoods to tackle.'

'Today there is a substantial amount of sorghum grown, and we played an important part in developing that,' Gillet said. MONACA published a book outlining its early experiences with sorghum and presented the findings to the Venezuelan government.

Another experiment was exporting maize flour for ethnic groups in the USA. 'We tried it for a very short period, hoping we could turn it into something,' said Gillet, 'but our plants were taken up with local production, and we didn't think politically it would be right with shortages of maize in Venezuela.'

SUCCESSFUL DIVERSIFICATION

Although those attempts at expansion failed, MONACA successfully diversified into other areas including animal feed, precooked maize flour, and bakery mixes.

'Because flour milling was so new in the country, very few people had been exposed to its byproducts,' said Gillet. 'Well, we had a problem on our hands. The mill feed was piling up in the yards, and we didn't have a place to store it.'

Relying heavily on guidance from International Multifoods' Supersweet Feeds division, MONACA assembled a sales force to promote formula feeds. A plant was built in Valencia and the slogan 'Improve Yourselves with Super S' was coined. MONACA has reached production capacity at Valencia and now plans to construct a second feed mill.

The Multifoods subsidiary also diversified into precooked maize with the acquisition of DAMCA in 1968. Worried about its vulnerability to government controls, MONACA wanted a business based on locally produced raw material.

Gillet entered negotiations with DAMCA to purchase its plant at Carabobo, and eventually the mill at Acariqua (1970). Since those operations have come into International Multifoods' fold, production capacity at both plants has doubled, giving DAMCA roughly 20 percent of the market.

GOVERNMENT INTERVENTION

Government policy has affected some of MONACA's ventures more than others. During the past two years a ceiling has been placed on the price of maize sold to the consumer. The price controls have eroded the profitability of precooked maize sales to the point that DAMCA is cutting costs by no longer advertising.

Government intervention also cut heavily into MONACA'S profits during 1974 when price controls on bread products were frozen despite significant increases in the cost of imported wheat.

Gillet attributed those problems to attempts to hold down consumer prices during the presidential election. 'It was a lousy profit picture,' Gillet complained, explaining that eventually subsidized prices for wheat and other raw materials were offered by the government. Gillet said a systematic program to reduce expenses in all of MONACA's operations was implemented. 'It was a calculated gamble, but we were able to maintain our sales and marketing positions and, at the same time, keep morale high,' said Gillet, who looks back on the experience as a test of surviving the worst possible economic conditions.

MONACA TODAY

The firm's current operations are divided evenly between agricultural, industrial and consumer products. Growth during the past ten years has continued impressively: From 1973 to 1978 the firm increased personnel by nearly a third (from 717 to over 1,000 employees); in 1977 MONACA introduced another item to its consumer line, 'Misia Juana,' a maize package mix, and new varieties of animal feeds and specialty flours.

Gillet does not point to any one factor for MONACA's success in Venezuela. However, he does emphasize, 'We became involved with local politics. We also got involved with and attempted to understand the host government.'

Equally important was not trying to force methods, ideas or ways upon the country that may have been successful in other places. 'Don't ever assume that's good. Forcing those things which are successful in your own country is not good. That shows a lack of understanding of the tastes that makes them different.'

4 Pillsbury's involvement with the Saudi Arabian flour mills

DENNIS A. JOHNSON

The dedication of Saudi Arabia's largest flour and feed milling plant in October, 1979, by King Khaled trumpeted his country's success in revolutionizing grain processing from the primitive hand grinding used by nomadic tribes to modern industrial methods.

In less than a decade, Saudi Arabia laid down the cornerstone of a new era in agribusiness and, in some ways, surpassed the milling industry in the United States and Canada, the two major wheat exporters to the Kingdom. By combining the experience of Pillsbury Holdings (Canada) Ltd., a subsidiary of the Pillsbury Co., USA, with equipment from two leading European manufacturers, the Saudi Arabian Grain Silos and Flour Milling Organization established three mills and constructed grain storage for a six month supply.

Within five short years, Saudi Arabia revolutionized its cereal processing industry, abandoning stone grist mills for modern roller milling methods. For approximately US$261 million, the Saudis constructed:

1. A flour and feed mill in Riyadh with storage capacity for 80,000 MT. The flour mill has a 24-hour processing capacity of 540 MT and the feed mill has an 8-hour capacity of 100 MT. At a cost of US$61.4 million, the plant employs approximately 200 workers.

2. A flour and feed mill in Damman, as well as storage facilities for 80,000 MT. The Damman plant, which has the same

flour and feed milling capacities as the Riyadh operation, cost US$71.3 million. The labor force is approximately 200.

3. A flour and feed mill and grain storage silos at Jeddah. The plant has a 24-hour flour processing capacity of 1,080 MT and an 8-hour feed milling capacity of 100 MT. Grain storage capacity is 120,000 MT. With a labor force of approximately 250, the plant cost US$112.9 million to construct.

4. A grain elevator of 20,000 MT capacity at Quasseem. The cost of the facility was US$25.4 million.

The Saudis' remarkable feat is not without its paradoxes, however. Pillsbury, one of the oldest flour millers in the United States and a major consumer foods products company, was contracted as design engineer and consultant, despite its unfamiliarity with that business. What started as a joint venture ended as a Saudi government owned project. Tracing the trials and errors of this developing country's experience offers some insight into the practicality and profitability of such an undertaking.

BEFORE THE MILLS

The seeds of this agribusiness venture go back to the mid-1960s when a small trade delegation was sent from the United States to scout potential commercial ties with the Mideast oil producer. Reports following the mission were overwhelmingly optimistic: unlimited opportunities for profitable enterprise were there for the taking. The Saudi Arabians welcomed the visitors with open arms.

In 1967, one year after the delegation returned to the United States, the consulting firm Arthur D. Little Co., USA, was contracted by Saudi Arabia to do a feasibility study on reorganizing the Kingdom's grain trade. At that time the Saudis were importing second clears - a coproduct of milling a high patent flour - and using it as finished flour. There was much waste and spoilage when unloading and storing the flour. A lot of the flour arrived in dingy tramp vessels, further worsening the quality.

These problems were intensified since much of the population had come to rely on this flour for making a round, cake-like flat bread. The Saudis had quickly developed a taste for wheat bread and had moved away from rice as their main cereal. The Saudis also experienced disruptions in the flow of flour during the Suez Canal closure in 1956 and, fearful of future cutoffs, sought long term storage capabilities.

Arthur D. Little Company delved into these and other questions in its exhaustive study. Its report recommended that a flour miller, not a plant manufacturer, should negotiate the primary contract with the Saudi Arabian governmental agency, the Grain Silos and Flour Milling Organization. The study also suggested financing the project as a joint venture between the milling firm and the Kingdom. Subsequently, eight firms were investigated, and eventually five companies entered bids. General Mills stayed out of the bidding because the project was so far away and the engineering staff was needed at home, according to a spokesman.

PILLSBURY'S INTEREST

Pillsbury was interested on the basis of its 20 year association with Saudi Arabia in importing flour, cake mixes and other consumer products. The company also had similar overseas experience, having participated in other joint ventures, such as in Jamaica and Venezuela. One competitor stated that during this era, Pillsbury had 'smokestack fever': it wanted to put up mills wherever it could.

Between 1967 and 1969, negotiations changed radically; the Saudis were interested in developing storage capacities beyond 30, 60 or 90 days. The capital investment required for such storage was enough to absorb any profit margin a firm like Pillsbury could expect. Eventually, discussions with Pillsbury broke off, leaving the Saudis to pursue the project with other likely firms.

The following year the Kingdom embarked on the first of its five year development plans. Agricultural growth from 1970 to 1975 was projected at 4.6 percent annually, nearly three times the growth rate during the 1960s. Prior to the first development plan, agriculture was characterized by subsistence crops planted by the Bedouin tribes which roamed the deserts. Agribusiness was nearly nonexistent; combined agricultural products (primarily wheat, alfalfa, sorghum, barley, dates, and livestock) represented only six percent of the Gross Domestic Product in 1971.

During the first five year plan, the Saudis continued to press forward with their plans to industrialize flour milling. Those entering bids included three US-based companies, Seaboard Allied Milling Corp., Continental Grain Co. and Pillsbury, as well as one firm from Sweden and another from France.

One executive from Seaboard Allied said the Saudis 'had very definite ideas how they wanted things done.' At one point they expected the consulting firm to monitor manufacture of the milling equipment to insure expected quality standards. The Saudis suggested independent tests on the carbon content of the steel rollers to be used in the mills.

Seaboard Allied considered that idea, among others,

unreasonable. 'They (the Saudis) may have been talked out of those tests, but that was the kind of conversation they gave,' the executive added.

After several trips to Saudi Arabia, Seaboard Allied dropped out of the negotiations. By one account, the negotiations came down to Continental and Pillsbury. Both sent representatives to Riyadh. During these final negotiations, the two men spent their days at the various ministries arguing their cases and then met at night to play cards.

THE FIRST CONTRACT

While Pillsbury wanted to construct the mills to enhance its position in the Saudi consumer products market, Continental Grain — more of a commodities firm — saw an opportunity to expand its grain operations. But it was Pillsbury that was asked to continue talks and by 1972 a contract, estimated at US$3 to 5 million, was tendered to the conglomerate. Pillsbury would act as project consultant in charge of design, evaluation, coordination and personnel training. Instead of a joint venture, Saudi Arabia would finance the entire project, which had soared from an original estimate of US$90 million to US$261 million.

Pillsbury officials declined to discuss any details of their contract. However, responsibilities included supervising the plant design, evaluating bids from equipment manufacturers, supervising on-site construction, training plant supervisors and assisting in plant management for four years following the start of operations.

Persons close to the project pointed out that Pillsbury had the experience to undertake the work but not the experience to develop a consulting contract. 'They got into something way over their heads,' one observer said, describing Pillsbury as a production and sales firm, not a consulting engineer. Difficulties, however, did not stop there. Pillsbury was accustomed to moving directly from one phase to another, while the Saudis' style was slower paced.

Backtracking resulted when a number of changes were made, as when two separate contracts were negotiated. The first included construction of a mill at Jeddah, a port on the Red Sea, and a plant at Damman on the Arabian Gulf. The plants would include feed mills, grain unloading equipment and storage silos. The second contract incorporated a mill at Riyadh, the capital, as well as expanding storage facilities at Jeddah and Damman.

Progress was circuitous in other phases as well. Construction of the feed mills got underway before completion of a product market study to determine demand for camel, goat, sheep and poultry feeds. The mills turned out to be smaller than the market required and some redesign was necessary.

THE TRAINING PROGRAM

Pillsbury, however, had greater control over the training program. In 1974, two years after the first contract was signed, 15 Saudis arrived in Minneapolis, USA, to begin an intensive training program as plant superintendents. The students first enrolled in a 14-week course at the University of Minnesota to study English. Later the students were divided, some attending the Canadian International Grains Institute at Winnipeg, Canada, and the others studying at schools throughout the USA. Next, the Saudis received on the job training at various mills operated by Pillsbury in the USA.

The training program continued for two and one-half years followed by orientation sessions by equipment suppliers in England and Italy. Those students who departed the US in February, 1977, were trained as silo/feed mill supervisors and as flour millers.

Concluded one company official about the training program, 'Pillsbury was able to significantly impact the project by training the Saudis over here. So many projects don't work because you get the infrastructure up and nobody knows how to run it. This is where we felt we were able to make a large contribution.'

During the training phase, construction of all three plants was underway. The plant at Riyadh was erected first with construction begun in November, 1975. Building at the other sites began in 1976.

PROBLEMS DEVELOP

Timing of the project was critical given the enormity of the venture. Pillsbury kept close track of changes and the effects they had on other parts of the project. Penalty clauses were written into the contracts to keep construction on schedule. Still, changes caused disruptions.

'If there was a change in delivery date of an important component, we had to go ahead and adjust all of the other factors,' an engineer said. Other times materials arrived ahead of time, but without other necessary parts, construction could not continue.

'There were times we had lots of steel we couldn't use. It was like building from an erector set, but some of the parts were missing,' one engineer said.

In an attempt to offset scheduling problems, Pillsbury used

'critical path planning,' a method establishing time limits for each construction phase. The plants were built as if a new car were traveling along an assembly line. Each step was planned according to the next. When a change occurred, subsequent steps were adjusted accordingly.

'It reached the point where all changes were major,' one engineer said. A former Pillsbury executive who was involved with the project concurred. 'The logistics were overwhelming. The greatest problem was trying to get everything to arrive on time,' he said. According to Buhler-Miag, the firm that supplied most of the milling equipment, its biggest problem was to comply with the specifications of US engineers using European-manufactured parts.

UNDERDEVELOPED INFRASTRUCTURE

A number of other problems further complicated matters. The Saudi Arabian infrastructure was still highly underdeveloped. Telephone communication to the Riyadh site was not available during the first year of construction, so messengers were required. Contractors had to build roads and other amenities at the site, as well as supply their own sources of power. In order to reach water at Riyadh, a well over 1,400 meters deep was drilled.

Congestion at the two major ports affected the project also. In December, 1975, offloading at Jeddah was delayed up to four months while offloading at Damman took up to three months. A critical shortage of cement for Riyadh forced the Saudis to use helicopters to unload the needed supplies.

Construction workers were imported from the Middle and Far East. Laborers and craftsmen came from Jordan, India, Yemen, Iran, Iraq, Korea, Pakistan, Lebanon, Palestine and Sudan, creating a language barrier that was almost insurmountable at times.

'Language was very limiting when trying to inspect the work that was done,' one American said. Sign language, interpreters and broken English were used.

Linguists aside, temperament was the cause of some issues. The Italians were easy to work with and adapted well to Saudi specifications, whereas the Swiss were less inclined to change their ideas, one official commented.

Housing shortages plagued the Kingdom, and rent was exorbitant. In Riyadh, Pillsbury officials paid US$12,000 a year for rent, payable three years in advance. Other prices were exceedingly low, such as gasoline at US$0.18 per gallon.

Cultural differences between the East and West also accounted for some difficulties, observers noted. In accordance with religious law, Islamic workers laid down their tools during ritual prayers at mid-morning, noon and midafternoon. The public prayers were monitored and enforced by Mutawwa, holy men carrying long canes who patrol public areas.

Construction of the three mills boosted the Kingdom's combined grain milling capacity to over 2,000 metric tons per day, proving the Saudis are capable of meeting their long range objectives of accelerating industrial development. The only limitation, according to the introduction to the second five year plan, is 'the Kingdom's capacity to organize and to implement its programs and policies.'

A MOST AMBITIOUS UNDERTAKING

Industry experts consider the Saudi grain processing venture the most ambitious undertaking by a single country to date. The three plants, all better equipped than mills in the US, give Saudi Arabia the potential eventually to export flour.

There are a number of reasons the Saudis cite for the project: to generate additional employment and income; to improve the balance of payments; to utilize technological advancements; and to experience savings from importing bulk grain instead of flour. Industrialization of grain processing represents a step towards diversifying the Kingdom's economy which relies so heavily on oil exports.

Additionally, the Kingdom is striving to overcome a dependence on importing grain. The Director General of the Grain Silos and Flour Milling Organization, Dr A. Shinawi, has stated that Saudi Arabia expects to produce 50 percent of its wheat requirement by 1980.

To help achieve this goal, heavy government participation in financing and marketing is expected. 'To be able to buy local grain, the government is building country silos for receiving and storing. Thus, mechanization is becoming a tool in the agricultural development plan,' Dr Shinawi says.

These goals are in sharp contrast to past Saudi experience. In 1971 only 74,000 metric tons of wheat were produced within the Kingdom, compared to imports of 237,000 metric tons.

THE STRATEGIC IMPORTANCE OF DOMESTIC MILLING

Dr. Ahmed Shinawi, Director General of GSFMO, explains what the domestic milling capacity has meant to his country:

1. The projects have provided food security to the country by stockpiling a six month supply of local and imported wheat.
2. The mills have assured a continuous supply of fresh, high quality flour at a stable price.

3. All locally produced flours are enriched with vitamins and iron, thereby improving their nutritional contribution to Saudi diets.

4. The project has promoted agricultural development in two areas: increased wheat cultivation through provision of crop storage facilities and stable prices; and encouragement of animal husbandry by providing improved feed.

5. Savings to the government totalled approximately US$100 million in 1979, since the cost of the locally produced flour and bran is about half that of importing these products.

6. The introduction of a new industry into Saudi Arabia resulted in the acquisition of grain processing technology and new labor skills. Grain processing activities could expand to include pasta, cake mixes, frozen dough, etc.

7. Saudi Arabia is now almost self-sufficient in grain milling. With the completion of three more mills under construction, the country will be completely self-sufficient in flour and feed production.

Saudi Arabia has utilized the experience of technically advanced countries to propel itself into a new era of mechanized cereal processing. The experience, however, was less profitable for the consultant. Excluded from financial participation, Pillsbury's only source of income was possible profit was its consultant fee which, industry observers note, was exceedingly low for a project this complex.

Pillsbury's export market to Saudi Arabia has been eroded as well. Both flour and feed product sales have suffered since the new plants went into operation. Although Pillsbury has been credited with building the best possible mills, its own interests were sidestepped.

One former official of Pillsbury called its participation in the project a 'financial disappointment.' Another ex-Pillsbury staffer noted, 'You can judge the success of this project by the fact that Pillsbury won't do another one.' Pillsbury failed to anticipate the amount of work that needed to be done and the impact of inflation on the dollar value of the contract. William Spoor, Pillsbury's Chairman, was more sanguine and noted, 'I am very proud of our relationship with the Saudis and the manner in which we were able to work together and build the flour and feed mills there. Based on that relationship, we'd be delighted to enter into a similar contract in the future.'

An executive from Seaboard Allied concluded, 'Of all the people who tried to put this project together, I think Pillsbury was the best equipped to give the Saudis what they wanted. They were a large enough company and they had the personnel. I think the Saudis made the right choice with Pillsbury.'

31

5 The explosive growth of the Brazilian FCOJ industry

RICHARD J. STROHL

Spurred by frosts in Florida's vast citrus groves, the Brazilian citrus industry is now number one in world production of frozen concentrated orange juice (FCOJ). While the industry is still growing, its fortunes are alternately plagued and revitalized by Florida's weather. For example, in December, 1980, Brazil had 200,000 tons of FCOJ that it could not sell at US$500/ton. The next month, frost hit Florida's orange crop and Brazilian FCOJ jumped to US$1,000/ton: it was another stimulus for Brazil's citrus industry. The worry is now that the industry will be overstimulated and more FCOJ will be produced than can be marketed.

THE BEGINNINGS

Brazil's earliest FCOJ plant squeezed its first orange in 1962. Today Brazil's output of 490,000 tons of 65° Brix (65 percent solids) FCOJ exceeds Florida's production by more than 100,000 tons and the gap is widening. Brazil's orange production from 140 million trees is increasing rapidly, while Florida's continues to decline. Whereas Florida had 267,000 hectares in oranges in 1970, it now has 50 million trees on 233,000 hectares.

The bulldozers have been busy. Urban sprawl, Cape Canaveral and Walt Disney World are taking over orange groves and pushing up the price of land. Florida orange growers cannot afford to keep their land in citrus groves, while Brazilian growers just keep planting. In any case, the world's FCOJ industry now has two producing areas (one balanced in Florida around 28°N 82°W; the other firmly placed in Sao Paulo, Brazil, at 22°S 48°W), but only one major consuming area, North America.

The Brazilian FCOJ industry is characterized by an abundance of oranges; the wherewithal to increase orange production; an efficient processing sector, well supplied with the latest equipment; a high degree of government support and intervention in promotion and stabilizing the industry; and an almost total reliance on the export market. Ninety-five percent of Brazil's FCOJ output is exported, 20 to 40 percent to the U.S. The export market has been subject to wide price fluctuations due to frosts in Florida and surplus production in Brazil.

So the challenge which now faces the Brazilian FCOJ industry is that of devising a plan that keeps the industry prosperous during years of good orange crops in both Brazil and Florida and that also can take maximum advantage of high prices when Florida's oranges freeze. Brazil wants a minimum price of US$1,400/ton for its FCOJ, but present markets are not able to absorb its annual production at that price.

THE PROCESS

To make FCOJ, the orange juice is first separated from the rind by squeezing, crushing and reaming out the rind. The juice is then screened to remove seeds, pulp, and other extraneous matter, and put through a vacuum evaporator which concentrates fresh orange juice from around 12° Brix (12 percent solids) to as high as 70° Brix. All of Brazil's production is exported at 65° Brix.

To maintain a uniform product, every batch of concentrate is blended with concentrate from every harvest period and orange variety to correct differences in sugar-acid ratios. All concentrate must also be flavored with a bit of fresh unconcentrated orange juice and some orange peel oil and pulp to restore any flavor lost in the evaporation process.

Most of Brazil's FCOJ is stored and transported in 200 liter polyethylene-lined drums as a frozen slush, but cheaper bulk transport in tank trucks and tank ships is gradually replacing drum transport. When 65° Brix FCOJ reaches the USA, it is cut back to 41.8° Brix - the US standard for retail FCOJ - with fresh orange juice, then canned or frozen. In Europe, Brazilian FCOJ is either canned, frozen, or reconstituted and sold at full strength.

One hundred kilograms of fresh oranges yield around four

kilograms of 65° Brix FCOJ, that is, approximately 25:1. FCOJ, however, is not the only source of revenue from the orange groves.

CITRUS BYPRODUCTS

There are four main byproducts of the FCOJ industry: D-limonene, essential oils, essence oils, and citrus pulp pellets. D-limonene is a liquid with a lemon-like fragrance that is recovered from citrus molasses which, in turn, is made from peel sugars. D-limonene is used in many products including solvents, wetting agents, dispersing agents, perfumes, and resins. It is also put back into concentrated orange juice to enhance the taste.
   Essential oils are obtained from orange peels, and essence oils are recovered from the water vapor produced in the evaporation process. These oils are used for food and beverage flavoring and in soaps, plastics and the textile industry. A minor albeit lifesaving byproduct, also from orange peels, is hesperidin, which is used to stop leaks which occur in human blood vessels.
   Citrus pulp pellets (CPP), used as cattle feed, are made from all of the residues of orange juice production - peels, pulp, seeds, etc. - with citrus molasses added for palatability. The residue is first dried to 12 percent moisture content and then pressed into pellets. One hundred kilograms of fresh oranges yield about five kilograms of CPP, in addition to the four kilograms of FCOJ. These pellets sell for around US$120/ton in European markets, which take over 500,000 tons annually from Brazil.

PROCESSORS AND EXPORTERS

There are giants in Brazil's orange juice business: four firms account for over 90 percent of FCOJ exports. Sucocitrico Cutrale is the largest and has been so for over ten years. Citrosuco Paulista and Citrosuco Limeira are close seconds. Frutesp, owned by the Coopercitrus Cooperative of Coffee and Citrus Growers which controls 40 percent of Brazil's citrus production, is rapidly increasing production of FCOJ, with output in 1981 of 87,500 tons of FCOJ, plus over 100,000 tons of citrus pulp pellets.
   Cargill Ind. Ltda. and Cargill Agric. S.A. together export ten to fifteen percent of Brazil's FCOJ production for fourth place, and also handle a large share of the citrus pulp pellets. Cargill pioneered in the bulk sea shipment of FCOJ by tankers.

Oranges have been grown in Brazil since 1540; however, commercial production did not get underway until the end of the 19th century. Portugal had citrus fruit of its own and could readily get more from Spain, so there was little demand in Europe for Brazilian citrus. Consequently, the first exports of fresh oranges from Brazil did not occur until 1916.

Fresh orange exports grew rapidly thereafter until 1939 when 5.6 million boxes (40.8 kg/box) were shipped from Brazil, mostly to Europe. World War II put a stop to this growing trade and although exports of fresh oranges rebounded after the war, they have never reached pre-war levels due to the competition in European markets from Mediterranean and South African oranges.

Nevertheless, the orange growers in the regions of Bebedouro, Araraquara, Limeira, Pirassununga and Sao Jose do Rio Preto of Sao Paulo state have always been eager to take more land out of grass pastures and plant oranges. Orange trees just looked more profitable to them than beef, and they were right. The citrus business was slow during the 1950s and early 1960s, since it depended mainly on local and export demand for fresh oranges.

In anticipation of an export market for FCOJ, a small concentrating plant was built and began concentrating orange juice in Bebedouro in 1962. Demand for this FCOJ was not long in coming.

FLORIDA'S DECLINE

A severe frost in the heart of Florida's citrus groves in December, 1962, caused a shortage of oranges for Florida's flourishing FCOJ industry. The subsequent sharp rise in the price of frozen orange juice encouraged buyers to look abroad for FCOJ. The newly operating plant in Bebedouro was able to supply some FCOJ and contracted for more. The Brazilian citrus business expanded to meet this new demand for its oranges and has been growing explosively ever since.

In 1963 Brazil exported 735 tons of FCOJ to the USA and several hundred tons to other countries from its single concentrating plant. In that same year, a more modern and larger plant was constructed in Araraquara, 285 kilometers northwest of the city of Sao Paulo.

Today there are 15 processing plants in Sao Paulo state, one of which has the world's largest single evaporator with the capacity to evaporate 80,000 kilograms of water per hour. Most of the equipment used in these plants is of US manufacture. The juice extractors are leased from US companies and much of the other equipment is sold and installed by the same US companies which have been supplying Florida's FCOJ equipment

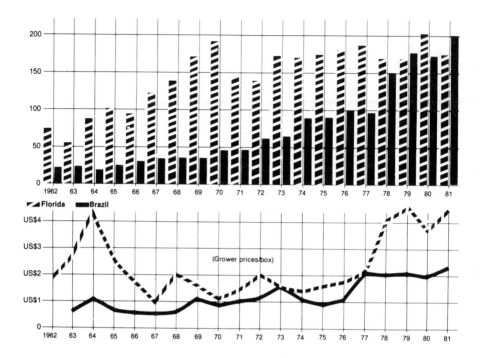

Figure 5.1 Orange Production 1962-81
    Millions of boxes (40.8 kg/box)

needs. In addition, all but two of Brazil's processing plants
have installed the equipment necessary to recover and produce
the entire range of citrus byproducts.

Cold storage tanks of 400,000 liter capacity are used at
most plants to make blending juice from several harvest
periods possible. Furthermore, they enable processors to lower
costs by dispensing with the traditional 200 liter
polyethylene-lined drums for transport in favor of bulk
transport on both land and sea.

BRAZIL'S GROWTH

In 1962, Brazil had 20 million trees producing 850,000 tons of
oranges, not an inconsequential amount by any means. But by
1970, the number of trees had more than doubled to 50 million,

and production had risen to two million tons of fresh fruit. In 1980, there were over 140 million orange trees in Brazil producing seven million tons of oranges, and FCOJ became the eighth largest export.

Brazilian growers are optimistic about their industry's future, and there is ample room for more orange trees in and around the present growing areas. Furthermore, tree yields are expected to rise as irrigation systems are installed in the groves. The current average yield per tree in Brazil is two boxes (40.8 kg/box). This will rise to three boxes in a few years, and along with production from recently planted trees now starting to bear, twice as many oranges will be produced in Brazil in 1985 as in 1980.

At present, the price of FCOJ is high, and strong demand for Brazilian oranges is expected until Florida's production recovers in two or three years. Brazilian growers have come to expect regular frosts in Florida to boost their orange prices.

Brazil's orange trees are seldom damaged by frost. However, yields are sometimes hurt by prolonged dry spells because most of Brazil's citrus depends on rainfall alone. Irrigation systems are being installed in many groves to supplement rainfall and increase yields.

Growers are willing to invest in their groves because they have been making money. The cost of establishing orange trees is around US$1,500/hectare. This includes all costs of growing the trees for the first four nonbearing years except land costs, which average US$2,000/hectare for prime citrus land. Operating costs during the bearing years are around US$650/hectare, so when the price per box is over US$2.00, as it was in 1977, 1978 and 1981, the growers are making money and investing in more trees.

GOVERNMENT INTERVENTION

The only brake on this spectacular expansion is the federal government. In 1980 it stopped financing new plantings, put a declining export tax on FCOJ of US$210/ton, cancelled its export subsidy for FCOJ, and required processors to store 50 percent of all FCOJ produced. All the programs it had initiated to encourage production it is now dismantling.

Obviously, the federal government thinks that Brazil is producing all the orange juice that can be sold at a profit. In fact, when both Florida and Brazil have bumper crops, present markets will not absorb all the FCOJ produced. To keep the price up, Brazil has to cut production, store a lot of FCOJ between freezes in Florida and find new markets for FCOJ and its byproducts.

The government has intervened to accomplish the first two

goals rather than allowing market forces to achieve the same ends. It hopes to avoid disruption in the industry by keeping export prices artificially high in times of surplus through storing FCOJ for frost markets. Last year's frost in Florida took care of Brazil's surplus, but similar conditions might not occur again for ten years. Brazil cannot afford to store 200,000 tons of FCOJ each year for even half that time, nor can it turn off the trees (as OPEC turns off its oil wells) to limit production. More oranges, FCOJ, and byproducts must be marketed. To do this, Brazil must tap that reservoir of talent which has made it premier in production to make it premier in sales.

BRAZIL'S MARKETS

So far, in addition to the large US market, Canada, Europe, Japan, and Venezuela have become good customers for Brazilian FCOJ, while Europe buys most of Brazil's citrus pellets. Markets in Mexico and neighboring South American countries are also gaining importance, and attempts are being made to sell FCOJ in the Soviet Union and several nations in Africa.

No doubt more markets can be developed for Brazil's FCOJ and a greater quantity can be sold in the traditional markets. In the USA, FCOJ is considered a staple of the diet, and yet less than two kilograms per capita is consumed annually. Brazilians themselves will probably drink much more FCOJ in the future if present market development campaigns are successful. Today a population of 120 million in Brazil consumes only 20,000 tons of FCOJ annually.

In any case, Brazil's problem, unlike Florida's is too many oranges most of the time. To get rid of them, Brazilians may have to lower their price expectations or leave a few in the groves until more markets are developed. Nevertheless, Brazil will undoubtedly remain number one in FCOJ for many years to come.

6 Progress on the plantation: the growth strategies of Sime Darby

CAROL M. MORGAN

'Downstream processing' is a phrase often heard at Sime Darby, a major Asian agribusiness firm. Elsewhere referred to as 'forward integration,' the phrase means the same thing: upgrading your product in order to get as close to the final consumer as possible.

'The palm oil exporters have had an easy time exporting crude oil to the USA in recent years. But with continued increases in sales of sunflower and soybean oils, marketing problems will increase, not to mention the political ones of free access,' noted one US marketing expert. 'Final products from palm oil should not only make Sime Darby more money, but also make palm oil less of a political issue that it currently is.'

With this in mind, Sime Darby organized a one-day commercial conference in San Francisco in June, 1981. Over 100 US businessmen were enticed into attending the seminar to learn how they could join Malaysia's largest company in new downstream ventures. For the right project, Sime Darby is willing to invest up to US$400 million in cash or the equivalent in assets.

Attending the seminar were ten top Sime Darby executives, including the Joint Group Chief Executive, Tunko Dato Ahmad Yahaya. The seminar explored the scope and directions of Sime Darby, and included a slide show, panel presentations, and individual private sessions. Follow-up talks were held later in the month to discuss specific business proposals.

Sime Darby's San Francisco seminar stressed not only the company's compatability with industrial ventures, but its trading expertise in Asia as well. Although Sime Darby is not now in any processing joint ventures with companies, it serves as a marketing agent for several, and has recently concluded manufacturing joint ventures with Ford and B.F. Goodrich Philippines.

In coming to San Francisco, Sime Darby served as both a flag carrier for what Malaysia terms its 'new economic policy' and as a symbol of its commitment to free enterprise. Malaysia forecasts that over the next five years US$45 billion will be invested in its economy, and 70 percent of it will come from the private sector.

EXPAND OR PERISH

Sime Darby's tactics are the result of its belief in the philosophy of 'expand or perish.' Over the past several years, Sime Darby has pursued an aggressive policy of acquisition, with over 220 companies having been taken into the complex folds of its corporate garment. After relatively recent sales of stock, including its 25.9 percent holding in the Guthrie Corporation in 1980, the company is cash rich.

It came as no surprise, then, that at its San Francisco seminar, Sime Darby disclosed its interest in teaming up with US companies to exploit the vast potential in the downstream processing of palm oil, the petroleum industry, the timber and wood industry, and light and medium engineering.

To sustain its growth, Sime Darby must reduce its dependence on its traditional products, such as palm oil, and continue its expansion into manufacturing and distribution.

Sime Darby was founded in 1910 by three Scotsmen - two Sime brothers and H. M. Darby. It has survived the Japanese invasion of World War II and a struggle against Communist guerillas which took place before the formation of the independent state of Malaysia in 1963.

The management of Sime Darby has been mostly in Malaysian hands since 1976 with the appointment of Tun Tan Siew Sin, a Malaysian Chinese, as Chairman. At the present time, 30 percent of Sime Darby's stock is owned by the Malaysian government, and an additional 30 percent has slipped out of British control and is now owned by Malaysian investors.

Sime Darby's capital structure actually serves as an asset to foreign companies interested in investing in Malaysia. Sime Darby's participation in a joint venture would help an expatriate partner meet Malaysian requirements for certain levels of 'Bumiputra,' or indigenous race, ownership and management sharing.

Influential in the formation of modern Malaysia, Chairman Tan has made it clear that the Malaysian government does not intrude into the management of Sime Darby. He has been quoted to the effect that 'businesses run by governments are not very successful.'

Sime Darby has annual global sales of over US$1 billion. Its net income in 1980 before taxes was US$116 million, which gave a 14 percent return on shareholder's equity.

Today Sime Darby is involved in such diverse fields as plantation ownership and management, heavy and agricultural equipment distribution, and general and commodities trading (as well as associated financing and insurance operations). These activities are managed through its six divisions.

CORPORATE STRUCTURE

Sime Darby's Plantations Division employs over 21,000 people and owns and manages over 80,000 hectares of palm rubber and cocoa estates in Malaysia, and operates related processing facilities. The division also provides commercial tropical agriculture consulting services. Sime Darby markets the company's own palm products, rubber and cocoa, and is active in trading these commodities obtained from outside sources.

Raw materials produced by the Plantations Division are further refined and processed by the Commodity Refining Division. Employing about 500 people, it operates vegetable oil refineries in Malaysia and Singapore. Their output is concentrated on the production of bulk and branded cooking oils. This division is developing operations in steric acid and glycerine and the active ingredients for detergents.

Caterpillar heavy equipment and engines and Ford agricultural tractors and equipment are distributed by Sime Darby's Tractors Division. Employing more than 2,700 people, this division also provides sales and service support. It offers, in addition, a broad range of other agricultural and industrial implements and equipment.

The diversified Hong Kong Division has dealerships for several automobile manufacturers, including Alfa Romeo and BMW; is involved in property management and development; sells air conditioning systems; and imports industrial and consumer products. The Hong Kong Division is also active in general trading, rice trading, shipping and insurance brokerage. In addition, it operates a bus assembly plant in the People's Republic of China.

The activities of the ASEAN and Pacific Basin Division are also complex. It is involved in managing the company's investments in subsidiary and associated firms in the ASEAN region, as well as in Australia and the Mideast. Its operations include factory leasing, import and export activities, shipping, insurance brokerage and underwriting, and property development and management. It manufactures items ranging from paints to confectionery, security equipment to cartons.

Managing the company's activities in Britain, the rest of Europe, and North America, the Western Division employs nearly 800 people. This operation centers its activities in commodities trading in world markets. It is also involved in rice milling, tea estate ownership, and foreign exchange insurance activities.

THE FINANCIAL PICTURE

Together, the Plantations, Tractors, and Hong Kong Divisions make up 90 percent of Sime Darby's profits. The other three divisions contribute the remaining ten percent.

Fifty percent of Sime Darby's profits comes from its Plantations Division, which remains highly profitable. However, more than half of its land is used for palm oil, a commodity whose price has been depressed by the excess of vegetable oils on the market, including soybean crushings. In the last half of 1981, pretax earnings for Sime Darby's plantations fell 24 percent to US$28.7 million because of weaker palm oil prices. In contrast, the Tractors Division's pretax earnings rose 33 percent to US$22 million.

In 1980 Sime Darby lost ground in commodity refining. Its 1980 pretax return on sales in commodity refining dropped from 4.8 percent to 3.5 percent that year. Brushing these figures aside, Sime Darby moved to increase its dependence in 1980 on refining to 9.3 percent of total revenues, up from 7.3 percent in 1979.

With strong profits in plantations, Sime Darby sees that an increase in the quantity of processing and improvements in technique could prove to be a boon for business overall. In addition, the Malaysian government is highly interested in adding to the value of its nation's agribusiness by increasing its processing capabilities. These downstream activities would provide a hedge against fluctuating commodity prices.

Sime Darby is severely hampered in reaching its commodity refining goals because of its limited technical expertise. At the present time, its technology is primarily in tropical agriculture. Other than certain marketing skills, Sime Darby has, in the words of Tunku Ahmad, 'no basic technical know-how in manufacturing and chemicals.' Sime Darby's choices, as seen by Ahmad, are either to 'joint venture and buy it, or joint venture and rent it and hope we can put it all together.'

STRATEGY

Sime Darby is exploring four ways of acquiring the technology it needs. It is open to entering into a marketing agreement with US companies to sell US products in Asia, as it now does with Ford and Caterpillar, or to sell Sime Darby products in the United States. It is also interested in technical assistance and/or licensing agreements with US companies. Joint ventures in Asia with US companies as partners, as with Ford and B.F. Goodrich Philippines, are also attractive. With a large amount of cash at its disposal, Sime Darby is also open to purchasing some or all of the shares of US companies.

Sime Darby's intention to integrate its plantation operations further is a logical step. Today its Plantations Division owns and manages 80,000 hectares of oil palm, rubber and cocoa, an area larger than the island of Singapore. As one of Malaysia's largest producers of crude palm oil, the company's seven palm oil mills produced 250,000 MT in 1980, nine percent of the country's total production and seven percent of the world's total. As Tunku Ahmad pointed out at the seminar, the Plantations Division is clearly Sime Darby's 'anchorman.'

Ten years ago, Sime Darby saw a pressing need for diversification. At that time, its main crop was rubber, but Sime recognized palm oil's growing potential. Major replanting programs were begun to alter the plantation's crop mix.

A switch to oil palm was made, and it now accounts for 60 percent of Sime Darby's planted hectarage. Rubber constitutes 35 percent, with cocoa making up the remaining five percent of total planted area.

GREATER INTEGRATION

At the same time, Sime Darby planned a major expansion program into downstream processing of palm oil and embarked upon acquisitions in Malaysia, Singapore, and Australia. It was convinced that a 'womb to tomb' processing division would bring greater overall stability to the commodity business. The first of these ventures was the acquisition in 1972 of Edible Products Limited (EPL), a vegetable oil refinery in Singapore.

EPL processes cooking oils from palm, corn, soya, high quality ghee (a hard cooking fat) and other oils. EPL's current annual sales of US$70 million - 90 percent of which are in overseas marketing - are up 600 percent from 1972.

EPL's cooking oils are packaged for consumers and marketed in Africa and Asia. The company is presently developing markets in Japan and the United States, the latter of which is of particular interest to Sime Darby.

43

Two years ago EPL doubled its edible vegetable oil refining capacity to 25,000 tons a year. A new refining plant, designed by Lurgi of Germany, was installed at a cost of US$1.3 million. The new plant incorporates the latest available processes and machinery, and its design emphasizes refinery efficiency and versatility. 'Our packing capability was greatly expanded and made more efficient with the introduction of automation to the packing lines,' says Kenneth N. Eales, Sime Darby's Group Director-Projects.

In 1977, Kempas (Malaya) Berhad, a plantation-owning subsidiary of Sime Darby, acquired 70 percent interest in a small palm oil refinery in Malaysia. The refinery, Kempas Edible Oil Sdn. Bhd. (KED), is on the Pasir Gudang Industrial Estate, located in the southern Malaysian state of Johor.

KED produces bulk neutralized bleached deodorized olein, ghee, neutralized palm oil, crude stearin and acid oil. These products are shipped to packers in Singapore, India, Pakistan, Japan, the USA, West Asia and Africa. Apart from these overseas markets, a significant portion of the products produced by KED is sold to its sister company, EPL, in Singapore.

KED's annual sales in 1982 were US$60 million. In 1979 and 1980 KED expanded, adding two new refining plants, which tripled its total processing capability to 150,000 tons a year. KED's new Alfa Lipofrac fractionation plant can handle 200 MT of crude palm oil per day. The new vegetable ghee plant has a daily capacity of 50 tons.

As part of its expansion program at KED, Sime Darby also commissioned an effluent treatment plant. KED is believed to be the first vegetable oil refinery in Malaysia to install such equipment. 'As with many process plants, effluent treatment is a major concern of ours. Sime Darby has been a leader in this field in staying well below the maximum effluent discharge standards set by the Malaysian and Singapore Governments,' says Eales.

NEW PRODUCTS

Sime Darby's program of integration continued when, in 1978, it bought Surfactant Services Ptd. Ltd., an Australian company specializing in the production of detergent surfactants made from vegetable oils, primarily coconut and palm oils.

Based in Sydney, Surfactant Services Ptd. Ltd. is a leading producer of biodegradable detergent concentrates. These concentrates, in liquid and powder forms, are essential ingredients in the manufacture of household and industrial detergents, shampoos, and foaming products for the bath. Because the products are based on vegetable oils, they dissolve readily in water, causing fewer industrial effluent disposal problems than petroleum based products.

Sime Darby's newly acquired expertise in the production of surface-acting agents from vegetable oils has been transferred to Singapore. There a Sime Darby subsidiary, Surfactants Pte. Ltd., now produces detergent products for export to the ASEAN region and elsewhere.

In 1981 Sime Darby made yet another pioneering move in its plan to diversify downstream from its tropical agriculture base. It moved into the field of fatty acid distillation by acquiring the only plant of this type in Singapore, which now operates under the name of Sime Darby Oleochemicals Limited (SDOL). SDOL is located on a one and one-half hectare site in Singapore, in close proximity to the DPL plant in Jurong, Sime Darby's first venture into diversification.

SDOL produces distilled fatty acids, stearic acid and glycerine from fatty acid oils, which are byproducts of the group's two vegetable oil refineries, Edible Products, Ltd. and Kempas Edible Oil. Stearic acid is used in the manufacture of rubber, plastics, pharmaceuticals, waxes and lubricants. Glycerine is used as a moisturizer in cosmetics, as a food sweetener, and in the manufacture of pharmaceuticals and explosives.

The SDOL refinery has a raw material processing capacity of nearly 10,000 tons a year. Its process plant, built by Lurgi, is well up to world standards in its technology.

Ken Eales believes that the acquisition of SDOL represents a significant new step in Sime Darby's program of diversification downstream. 'SDOL has given Sime Darby new products, new capabilities, and new markets,' he says. 'It will broaden our downstream capability and link our downstream businesses strongly. It can take more than 60 percent of its raw material from our other two refineries.

'Obviously, complete integration does not always make good business sense. We have established sources of supply from the more than 40 refineries that have been set up in Malaysia over the last ten years,' Eales adds. 'World demand for stearic acid and glycerine is growing strongly. We expect to find good markets in the industrialized countries and in Asia.'

OUTLOOK

It was clear from the seminar held in San Francisco that Sime Darby is intent on going even further downstream into more sophisticated products. It is currently discussing the possibility of expanding its range of oleochemicals and hard fats with US companies.

For example, exploratory discussions have been held with two

US companies, Energy Industries Incorporated, which is in the field of fatty acids and oleochemicals, and W.R. Grace, which has large cocoa manufacturing interests. Serious negotiations are underway with a major US agricultural genetics firm for the establishment in Malaysia of a shared venture in genetic experimentation in tropical agriculture which will benefit all the ASEAN countries. Through it, Sime Darby will have access to the latest in agricultural genetics technology. Negotiations should conclude by mid-1982.

Sime Darby sees a growing demand in the USA for attractively priced special grades of refined stearin for confectionery coatings: for use in the bakery trade; as an ingredient in plasticizers for the rubber and plastics industries; as a specialized lubricant in the metal trades; and in the pharmaceutical and cosmetic industries, as well as in a host of others.

'It is an attractive substitute for tallow in many applications and, at the right price, it could even be used as a substitute for diesel fuel, although that is unfortunately some way off yet,' Eales said.

In San Francisco, Eales warned the gathered US businessmen that the Japanese are now at the forefront of a new 'revolution' in the detergent and chemical industries:

> I am speaking of the switch from petroleum feedstocks to renewable vegetable oil feedstocks. The Japanese have ambitious plans for large methyl ester production units in Asia and are being closely followed by the more innovative Europeans, who are shortly going to establish plants for the production of amines and amides from palm fatty acids.

At the San Francisco seminar, Eales placed a heavy charge on the gathered businessmen:

> I believe it is significant that our group, the largest in Malaysia and heavily involved in palm oil production and processing, has yet to be approached by a North American chemical company for even exploratory talks in these areas. Where have you been?

7 White elephant tales: Venezuela's cassava processing plants

JOHN FREIVALDS

A Caracas businessman lamented:

> Sometimes I wonder if all this oil has been a benefit to Venezuela. We have had too much money and as a result have not spent it wisely. Worse, because we have the money, a lot of people in this country, including some of our bureaucrats, imagine themselves to be astute businessmen. You are here to look at the cassava plants, so you know what has happened.

These comments were made during a discussion of six cassava processing plants that were built in Venezuela in the early 1970s at a cost of US$20 million. All have failed - become 'white elephants.' In fact, one plant has never been uncrated and is rusting in the sun. The processing plants were purchased to dehydrate locally grown cassava for animal feed to replace imported feed grains.

The attempt to create a cassava processing industry in Venezuela illustrates the problems that a government can encounter in developing an agro-industry. It demonstrates that merely providing money for the purchase of plants is but one step in starting a viable industry. Considerably more care has to be taken regarding crop production costs, grain imports, government subsidies, farmer attitudes and demand.

Agriculture has not done well in Venezuela. In fact, in 1976 the country ran out of food. Miscalculations of domestic production and import needs led to a critical shortage. Meat was airfreighted into the country at great expense. As the air lift began, President Andres Perez vowed, 'We must become more self-sufficient.'

President Andres Perez faced the problem of food shortage from the time he took office in 1974. An increase in food supply was required to meet the rapid rate of population growth and to keep the price of food from rising too rapidly.

Imports filled the agricultural production gap. Grain imports which were 969,000 MT in 1969 grew to 1,800,000 MT by 1976. While the imports satisfied the needs of a growing urban population, President Andres Perez extended a series of benefits to farmers. First, under the Agricultural Debt Relief Law of 1974, farmers were in effect exonerated of all past debts owned to government agencies. New minimum prices were instituted by the 'Corporacion de Mercadeo Agricola' (CMA), the agency charged with providing the grower with minimum price levels for cereals and other basic food staples.

The government, with its increasing oil revenues (international reserves of U.S. dollars grew from US$1.1 billion in 1969 to US$8.5 billion by 1976), found itself playing a greater and greater role in the agricultural economy.

In May 1975, CORDIPLAN ('Oficina Central de Coordinacion y Planificacion' – Central Planning and Coordination Office) released its first draft of the country's fifth five year plan. The plan proposed to transform the agricultural sector into a 'modern, efficient, and financially sound activity that will serve as a base for the economic and social development of the country.' CORDIPLAN slated US$5 billion for the agricultural sector, and it was out of this money that the funds for the cassava processing plants came.

Unrealistically, the government planners hoped to reach a 12 percent average annual rate for growth in agriculture by 1979. Money was channeled to a number of agencies: Corpoindustrias, Corpozulia, Corpoandes, Corporiente, Corpoccidente; the list goes on and on.

Corporiente, just one agency, included the following projects for 1975: a plant to produce cocoa butter (US$1.6 million); a coffee processing plant (US$4 million); a grapefruit classification plant (US$2.1 million); a plant to process strawberries (US$235,000); a plant to process tamarind (US$404,000); a plant to process cashews (US$3 million); a vegetable processing and packaging plant (US$3.4 million); a tomato and catsup processing plant (US$913,000); a plant to process peanuts (US$6.2 million); a peanut oil extracting plant (US$2.5 million); a plant to produce precooked maize meal (US$9.3 million); a dairy products plant (US$8.4 million); and a cassava processing plant (US$3.2 million).

Money was being spent at a record pace, but little attention was paid to the management of all these projects. 'Some took the view that money could solve any problem,' commented one Venezuelan.

Given the large and growing level of feed grain imports and the fact that Venezuela had a history of cassava (called 'yuca' in Venezuela) production, interest grew to emphasize cassava processing plants.

Cassava is a starchy tuber which, when dried, can be used effectively as an energy source in animal feed formulae, serving basically the same function as sorghum or maize. According to the statistics available, Venezuela has consistently produced around 300,000 MT of cassava annually, most of it for direct human consumption. Average yields in Venezuela are seven MT per hectare.

In 1975 Venezuela consumed an estimated 1.4 million tons of mixed animal feeds. To produce this tonnage, feed manufacturers (Ralston Purina, Protinal and others) needed 800,000 MT of feed grains. Since local production was around 150,000 MT, Venezuela had to import huge quantities of feed grains. It was this import volume that the cassava plants hoped to replace.

As the orders went out for the cassava processing plants, agricultural commodity pricing was in flux. At the end of 1975, the government was working at cross purposes in its pricing policies. It sought to provide feed manufacturers with low cost subsidized imported feed grains so as to keep retail meat prices down. It succeeded, but at the expense of farmers. For example, the price of imported sorghum delivered to mixed feed manufacturers was US$142 while national sorghum was US$151. Feed manufacturers understandably preferred lower priced imported sorghum. Then in early 1976, the President announced a 30 percent increase in farmer prices which made for an even larger price discrepancy.

THE FEASIBILITY STUDIES

Given the large amount of money available for equipment and the huge imports of sorghum, Corpoindustrias, established by the government to provide credit assistance to small and medium scale industry, began buying plants. However, it is not as though Corpoindustrias and the regional development authorities did not study cassava processing through feasibility studies.

One of the most elaborate of these studies was done by the 'Corporacion de Desarrolo de la Region Zuliana' (Corpozulia). In 1976, this state development agency finished a 213 page feasibility study entitled 'Proyecto Agroindustrial: Elaboracion Harina de Yuca' (Project to Industrialize Yuca).

The project was not small in scope. The plant would produce 64,800 MT of dried cassava annually at a cost of US$6.6 million. Perhaps more importantly, the factory would create 637 jobs. The projected rate of return was low, even in the initial calculations. According to the study, after the tenth year the rate of return would be 11 percent; for the entire project, the internal rate of return would only be seven percent. Nonetheless, the project was approved. 'You have to remember that the return on investment in agriculture is below that of other sectors of the economy,' the planners rationalized.

Other benefits cited by the study were that 21,600 MT of cereal imports would be replaced and that marginal lands would be put into production; cassava can survive on poor soils where maize and sorghum cannot.

The study recommended that the most modern technology be used. The plants were to dry the cassava using #5 fuel oil instead of sun drying as in most of the world. The study recommended a purely integrated system utilizing machinery from leading manufacturers.

The equipment specified included imported storage tanks and prefabricated buildings, pelleting equipment, horizontal mixers and bucket elevators, truck scales, hammer mills, pneumatic conveyors, dehydrators, conveyers and feeders, IBM electronic and computerized control panels and automated boilers.

The report specified all sorts of details. For example, the number of chairs needed in the operation were listed, specifically whether they should be 'regular' or 'executive'; the precise number of file cabinets was given and whether they should have two drawers or four. The detail went on like this, but surprisingly only one page out of the 213 in the report was devoted to a discussion of the supply of fresh roots for the plant.

The planners seemed to feel that the statement that farmers in the area grew cassava was enough. No mention was made of competing uses of land, government price policies or import subsidies.

WHO'S IN CHARGE?

Any new business needs someone in charge but in the case of the cassava processing plants, there was no one. The equipment was purchased, but no farmers were organized. The assumption was that when the plants were built, the farmers would supply them with cassava.

With government financing available at only three percent interest, entrepreneurs with little or no experience in agro-industrial development became involved. As a result, the plants were built in locations either removed from a source of cassava or too distant from markets.

The 1981 status of the cassava processing plants was as follows:

1. Maturin (State of Monoagas). The installed capacity was ten MT per hour of fresh roots with end product capacity of three MT per hour of pellets using Brazilian equipment. The plant was operating sporadically to process feed, not cassava.

2. Cantaura (State of Anzotegui). Installed capacity was ten MT per hour using French equipment. The plant was operating sporadically to process feed.

3. Pariaguan (State of Anzotegui). With design capacity of ten MT per hour, this plant had never operated.

4. Upata (Amacuro Delta). With design capacity of ten MT per hour, this plant lay in crates for four years and was finally shipped to the Orinoco region.

5. Maracaibo (State of Lara). This plant had an installed capacity of 20 MT per hour. The plant was operating sporadically to process feed.

6. San Cristobal (State of Tachira). Same as Maracaibo.

One feed manufacturer noted in late 1980, 'The economic calculations that I have seen indicate that the cost of pellets from these plants is greater than the C.I.F. price for Thailand pellets placed in European ports!' Given the price structure of Venezuelan agriculture today and the processing costs for cassava, the plants can only pay US$40-45 per MT of fresh roots, yet farmers will not sell for less than US$75. And if you are a feed manufacturer paying US$150/MT of forghum, why would you buy dried cassava pellets costing US$250?

The farmers want to get the same price for cassava destined for animal feed as for the cassava they previously sold for human consumption. Although the economics were different, the farmers did not budge.

Failures like the cassava processing plants brought severe criticism to the Andres Perez administration. In his 1978 New Year's address, President Andres Perez cited increased food production as one of his administration's proudest achievements. However, the two major opposition parties citing his agrarian policy as expensive and wasteful published a rebuttal entitled 'Carlos Andres Perez: Zero in Agriculture.'

A surprising public statement was made in 1979 by the US Agricultural Attache as well:

> Those who subscribe to the philosophy that money can cure all should closely study the agricultural situation in this country. Credit has been liberally pumped into the rural economy for many years in an effort to stimulate farm output. It has been reported in the press that some of this credit may have been misplaced and poorly handled... Rural credit logically must be coordinated with other efforts, especially with sound technical assistance.

Today it is difficult to find anyone who knows who was in charge of the cassava processing program. Lack of leadership was a major problem in this tragic history. One current Venezuelan official believes the equipment suppliers could have spoken up as the plants were built. 'They knew the economics weren't here. If they could have helped us design this industry better and helped to make it work, they could have sold three times the equipment.'

When approached with this comment, one equipment manufacturer explained, 'We sold them three plants, but all through a broker in Miami. He made it clear we could deal only with him.'

Above all, the farmer was left out of all the planning. Everyone assumed he would provide the necessary raw material. Most of the plants went up without a corresponding increase in the amount of cassava grown in the area. In some cases farmers were willing to grow more roots, but technical assistance and organizational efforts were lacking.

Government planners in Venezuela now must realize that the purchase of expensive equipment is not sufficient to create an employment and revenue generating agro-industrial success. Now that Mexico has surpassed Venezuela in oil production, a Mexican agronomist confided, 'We are trying to avoid some of the problems Venezuela has had.'

8 Jamaica Soya Products Industries: a troubled joint venture

JOHN FREIVALDS

'Everything has gone wrong,' said the Jamaican government official to one of the few remaining private bankers that call on Jamaica as they sat and watched the Caribbean sunset.

The banker was curious; he had heard that this was a good joint venture, an example of what private companies and socialist governments could accomplish together. The official continued:

> First, all the Jamaicans left. The engineers that helped design the plant, the joint venture's first lawyer, and the first manager. They have all left the island. And then the chief Jamaican official on the Board of Directors allegedly misused monies from the State Trading Company and fled. Finally, the first plant engineer sent down from the States spent one day here and left without telling anyone. He didn't like what he saw.

No wonder the project is behind schedule. The banker was now relieved that his bank hadn't made the loan. The official said:

> That's just a part of it. Foreign exchange is tight, so getting spare parts is difficult. And as you know, the labor unions are very political and strikes are a constant problem. Some of the workers believe

sabotaging the plant is just another form of striking. The plant needs to operate at around 75 percent capacity to break even, but it is doing little better than half of that. Worse, no one in the government understands how a complicated plant like this should run. Well, the venture has been unique from the beginning.

Jamaica Soya Products Industries, Ltd. (JSPI), is unique not only in its composition, but also in that it is still operating in the face of Jamaica's economic and political difficulties. Whether it can continue to do so remains to be seen.

JSPI was established in 1974, a joint venture between the I. S. Joseph Company (Josco), a major multinational trading and processing firm, and Jamaica Nutrition Holdings, Ltd. (JNH), a Jamaican government agency set up in 1974 to improve that island nation's nutrition and food supply. In an era in which feelings of nationalism in developing countries are running high and when many private agribusiness firms are reluctant to invest or even operate in these countries, it is useful to analyze the joint venture that comprises JSPI.

JOSCO'S GOALS

The I.S. Joseph Company (Josco), headquartered in Minneapolis, Minnesota, USA, has a long history of involvement in the Caribbean. In the days when US trade with Cuba was permitted, it shipped substantial amounts of lard to that country. In the 1960s, it became involved in dairy and feed exports to Puerto Rico and in a commodity import operation in the Dominican Republic. In the 1970s, it began to export citrus pulp from Belize and import vegetable oil into Haiti, and started a new liquid bulk shipping company to serve the entire Caribbean. Josco executives found themselves stopping on all the islands, so permanent offices were established in the Dominican Republic and Haiti, while the US offices in Tampa, New Orleans, and Houston also contributed to the Caribbean business effort.

The idea of a soybean processing plant for the Caribbean had grown in the minds of Josco personnel, but they thought not in terms of Jamaica, but rather of Haiti. As opposed to Jamaica, Haiti had no animal feed industry, and it also imported substantial amounts of vegetable oil. In the period 1969-71, imports of oil had increased at 20 percent per year, and by 1980 per capital consumption was expected to have doubled. Josco believed that the creation of a new industry to process imported beans would:

promote the national interests of Haiti, increase trade and commerce, enlarge employment, decrease the need for imports, expand exports, enhance the development of related industry, bring about substantial new investments, increase the tax base, and in general modernize industry.

Josco's goals were severalfold: To establish an operation to maximize and utilize its existing Caribbean operations; to obtain a unique and exclusive position in processing oilseeds in Haiti; to achieve its profit and return on investment goals in a reasonable time frame; to play a key role in promoting agricultural development; and to use this project as a model to expand to other parts of the world.

Josco proposed to form a new company to process 315 short tons of soybeans every 24 hours. In addition to its investment in the plant, Josco also agreed to help establish a domestic farming operation to raise soybeans and other oilseeds. Given Haiti's state of development and erratic power supply, an extraction process plant (which does not have the explosion danger of a solvent plant) was chosen. A joint venture was formed with Josco the majority partner, but the project never got off the ground due to a government 'change of policy,' according to one US embassy official in Port-au-Prince.

JSPI was set up to construct a soybean processing plant in Jamaica, where imported and domestically grown soybeans would be processed into soymeal for use in animal feeds and soy oil for cooking. Future plans include upgrading the soymeal to textured vegetable protein and other high protein foods.

THE AGRICULTURAL SITUATION

Several developments in Jamaica during 1973 made the construction of a soybean crushing plant a good investment for the island's economy. Jamaica is a nation with 10,000 square kilometers of territory and a population of two million. Its main foreign exchange earnings come from tourism, as well as bauxite and sugar. Since international prices for these products are determined outside of Jamaica, its economy is at the mercy of outside forces.

To try to become more its own master, the government began to take over larger and larger segments of the economy. In 1973, it began to make plans to assume the responsibility for certain key imports, such as wheat, soymeal, maize, salt fish, and other products that are critical inputs into the low-cost mass diet.

Also, by this time, large livestock and poultry industries had been developed and were well established in Jamaica to satisfy the protein demand of the population and the expanding tourist industry; except for necks and backs, the island produced all its broiler meat and eggs. These industries created a need for a feed milling industry, and major feed companies like Central Soya, Ralston Purina, and Pillsbury established modern feed operations in Jamaica. But while there was a substantial domestic feed industry, all of the ingredients (soymeal, maize, and premixes) had to be imported, and due to the demand, soymeal imports soared. In 1968, imports were 2,000 tons, but by 1974 over 20,000 tons were being imported.

In addition to the demand for soymeal, there was an increasing demand for vegetable oils. Jamaica had formerly been self-sufficient in vegetable oil (mainly coconut oil), but had to start importing oil when lethal yellowing disease all but destroyed the coconut industry. From 1972 to 1975, annual coconut oil production had fallen from 14,000 tons to 4,000 tons. As the African tall coconut palm was being replaced with the Malaysian dwarf variety, many of the nuts produced were reaped green for an expanding trade in 'Jelly coconuts' (the liquid center of the green coconuts). Few nuts remained to be processed for oil for so many were pirated before they matured.

THE COMMANDING HEIGHTS

In response to all these difficulties, in 1973 the Jamaican government established Jamaica Nutrition Holdings, Ltd., as the focal point to improve nutrition. The nucleus of this operation was a school feeding program which supplied a fortified school children's milk and lunch pack. The initial program began with 110,000 children. One of its goals was to enrich locally available foods like cassava and banana flour with protein, one potential source of which would be soybeans in the form of textured vegetable protein, concentrates, or isolates.

Out of these developments grew the realization that a soybean crushing plant might offer advantages to the island's economy and food goals. The Ministry of Commerce and Industry assigned its agro-industrial specialist, Fred Anderson, to do a feasibility study. Mr. Anderson served as chairman of a study group which included leading industrialists and agronomists.

The studies done by this group indicated that Jamaica's economic situation would be improved by importing soybeans and processing them locally, rather than importing soymeal and vegetable oils. A crushing plant would provide a ready market for locally grown soybeans, and production of soybeans would offer a good opportunity to diversify economic activity from sugar. Since Jamaica is a member of Caricom, the Caribbean Common Market, members with more arable land like Belize and Guyana could ship their beans to Jamaica for processing; thus, foreign exchange could be saved throughout the region.

The plant was to be located so as to take advantage of existing infrastructure. Accordingly, the plant site near Port Esquivel was chosen so that an existing Alcan bauxite export dock could be used to off-load beans. This dock was already being used by the nearby Central Soya plant which was importing soymeal and maize.

In addition, the new crushing plant would provide the government with the facility for developing soy products for direct human consumption. Locally produced staples could substitute for costly imported wheat flour. Finally, the importation of beans combined with local processing was perceived as more economical than importing the processed products. (Figure 8.1 illustrates the various aspects that the plant was to encompass.)

Michael Manley, Prime Minister, had stated that his government was going to take hold of the 'commanding heights of the economy' and this project fit that category.

JOSCO'S APPROACH

Josco dispatched a trade mission to Jamaica in August, 1973, not knowing that the government had already begun its own feasibility study. Although members of the trade mission were warmly greeted by the Jamaicans, they quickly realized that the political climate would not allow Josco to have a majority of the equity in a plant. Josco did insist that it be responsible for managing the plant due to its expertise in this area.

In 1974, serious negotiations began between Josco and the Jamaican government with the result that Jamaica Soy Products Industries was formed. The key features of the agreement were:

1. The Jamaican government was to own 60 percent of the equity and Josco 40 percent.

2. Josco was to manage the plant and receive a management fee.

3. JNH was to market all the oil and meal while Josco was responsible for purchasing the soybeans.

4. Josco was to train Jamaicans so that they could take over the entire operation at the end of the ten-year management agreement.

5. The Board of Directors would be composed of four Jamaicans and three representatives from Josco.

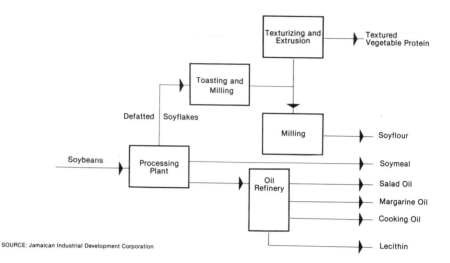

Figure 8.1 Schematic diagram of the market for soybean
products in Jamaica

6. No 'significant actions' involving JSPI could be
undertaken without consulting the Josco directors.

7. No further import of beans or soymeal would be allowed
except by JSPI.

8. Josco was to assist in training key management and
supervisory personnel.

9. A set crushing margin per ton of soybeans was agreed
upon.

The crushing margin is the total revenue realized from 21.6
kilos of soymeal and five kilos of crude soy oil, less the
cost of one bushel (27 kilos) of soybeans processed to obtain
these products. In practice, due to commodity price
fluctuations, the crushing margin is totally unpredictable. By
agreeing to a fixed margin, JSPI waived 'upside gains' to
eliminate 'downside risks.' There are many plants in the US
that have had negative crushing margins.

This last feature was essential, for everyone then knew in
advance how profits would be determined. Josco accepted the
margin and the profit forecast as set forth in the
government's own feasibility study, which provided for a
discounted rate of return of 12 percent after allowing for a
corporate profits tax of 45 percent.

The significant action clause was also crucial. Although
Josco was in a numerical minority on the Board of Directors,
the clause made its approval essential in most decisions

involving financing, dividends, and the hiring of key personnel. Although Josco accepted less than half of the financial stake in the enterprise, it was not about to take a minority management role. The significant action clause prevented that.

A budget of approximately US$7 million was developed to build a solvent extraction plant capable of processing 300 tons of soybeans per day. Merchant banks were to provide the loans with Jamaican government guarantees.

Josco was given the task of obtaining bids for the machinery and sought them from the United States, England, West Germany, and Sweden. One US company offered a good price, although not the best, but was able to deliver the equipment before all the other firms. It won the contract.

PROJECTIONS AND PROBLEMS

The projections called for JSPI to grow as indicated in Table 8.1. Table 8.2 shows estimated domestic consumption of soya products. These numbers demonstrate that almost half the meal produced and two-thirds of the oil would have to be exported.

Table 8.1
Projected Soybean Grind 1977-81
(Short Tons)

	Grind	Oil Production	Meal Production
1977	79,000	13,808	61,888
1978	89,000	15,540	69,721
1979	94,000	16,433	73,638
1980	97,000	16,958	75,988
1981	99,000	17,325	77,555

Table 8.2
Estimated Consumption 1977-79
(Short Tons)

	Soybean Meal	Once-Refined Oil
1977	46,000	5,000
1978	52,000	5,000
1979	58,000	5,000

The proposed export of oil was particularly upsetting to those connected with JSPI, since Jamaica was importing coconut oil. Anther quasi-government agency, Seprod, imported and refined vegetable oil and due to its economic and political strength, it resisted cooperating with JSPI. Seprod is part of the Coconut Industry Board, whose job it was to promote the cultivation and use of coconut oil. Seprod insisted that the Jamaican consumer wouldn't switch from coconut oil; the government's response was curt: 'If there's nothing but soy oil, they will switch.'

Faced with this and other marketing imponderables, Josco left all the marketing to Jamaica Nutrition Holdings. With price controls on everything sold in Jamaica and increasing amounts of state-to-state trading for export, it saw little marketing margin available. It chose to stay with the processing margin as its main source of income.

The plant was completed at a cost of US$6 million, or US$1 million less than originally projected. Operations commenced in mid-1977, which was later than anticipated, with full production achieved by April, 1978. JSPI even concluded a sale of meal to Cuba, which Josco could not have done directly. However, since July, 1978, production has fallen off due to labor disputes ('go-slows'), lack of foreign exchange for spare parts, and an unwieldy government bureaucracy.

The increasing government involvement in the economy has caused many of the initial managers involved with JSPI to leave the island, which has further hindered operations, and a scandal forced the individual in charge of marketing the oil and meal to flee. This convinced many workers that the managers were getting 'theirs' and they, by striking, hoped to get a piece of the 'thousands' the managers were making.

The foreign exchange problems symptomatic of Jamaica's economic difficulties have been particularly severe. The island ran short of hexane, the essential solvent in processing, when a major supplier decided not to ship to Jamaica without a letter of credit. In the past, it had kept an inventory in Jamaica, but now had to import from the USA.

Part of the difficulties have been caused by the failure of officials responsible for foreign exchange allocations to understand the integrated nature of the animal feed industry. It is not enough to allocate foreign exchange for maize and not premixes, or for soybeans and not maize. Similarly, you can't mix feed if the hexane required for oilseed processing is not made available. And if there is no inventory of spare parts, even simple things like belts, you can't operate. All the essential elements are needed at the same time.

The lack of spare parts has created innumerable delays in repairing breakdowns. After one breakdown, soymeal had to be imported because the plant couldn't keep up with demand. The domestic production of soybeans that was to complement imports has not yet developed to the point that it can supply significant amounts of beans, even though some soybeans yielded nearly five short tons per hectare on a double-cropped basis.

Recently, however, the plant has been in good operating condition and money has been available to purchase soybeans, but no foreign exchange was available for maize or premixes for animal feeds.

Another difficulty for Josco was that the constant erosion in the value of the Jamaican dollar meant that the allowable crushing margin got smaller in real terms. (In 1979, the Jamaican dollar was worth half of what it had been in 1974.) And few were the times when Josco and the Jamaican government could actually agree as to how far the value of the Jamaican dollar had fallen.

While the plant's future profitability is still dubious, it has dramatically affected Jamaica's import patterns from the USA, as Table 8.3 indicates.

Table 8.3
Imports from the USA
(Short Tons)

	1974	1978
Soybean Meal	36,000	15,119
Prepared Animal Feeds	17,000	0
Soybeans	0	44,110
Soy Oil	1,200	2,891

In addition, there has been a dramatic decrease in coconut oil imports. In 1976, 7,500 tons were imported; but one year later, imports had fallen to a nominal 600 tons.

LESSONS TO BE LEARNED

Although many lessons can be drawn from this joint venture, four stand out:

1. Private agribusiness and socialist governments can find a mutually satisfactory working relationship; whether it is profitable is another matter.
2. Although no enterprise can be insulated from the problems

61

of a suffering economy, a venture should be designed so as to mitigate the impact of overall economic problems. For example, this could be done by giving priority for foreign exchange for such items as spare parts and the raw materials needed to run the plant.

3. Involve all interested parties in the negotiations at an early date.

4. Give particular attention to the effects of inflation when calculating fixed processing margins.

In spite of all the difficulties the plant has had, the joint venture is intact. Josco, while disappointed with the progress to date, is committed to the project, as the over 50 trips to Jamaica by one of Josco's top executives show. The Jamaican point of view is expressed by Fred Anderson, who conducted the initial feasibility work and is now the managing director of JSPI: 'The project provided for the exchange of processes and techniques via the concept of joint venture, providing for greater utilization of technical services. It importantly demonstrates the possibility for cooperation between American private enterprise and a small developing country.' And it is because of that possibility that Josco is staying on.

9 The growth and integration of Jamaica Broilers

JOHN FREIVALDS

'We must become self-sufficient in basic foods, fruits and vegetables and we must start to look at the whole question of using imported grain as the sole source of raw materials in our animal feed industry,' says David Wildish, Managing Director of Jamaica Broilers.

Wildish believes that when locally grown sorghum replaces imported maize, Jamaica Broilers will have achieved almost total integration. It already produces its own chickens, controls the grow-out operations, runs the largest feed mill in Central America and the Caribbean, maintains processing plants and refrigerated trucks for distribution, and is starting to produce its own feed ingredients. Without hesitation, Wildish notes, 'Local raw materials are the key to our future.'

What makes this tremendous growth of Jamaica Broilers all the more outstanding is the fact that it was achieved despite serious obstacles ranging from strikes to controls on foreign exchange and prices. The employee stock ownership plan, unique in agribusiness, has contributed greatly to the company's growth and prosperity in some hard financial times in Jamaica.

CONTRACT FARMERS

Jamaica Broilers, the largest and oldest broiler producer in Jamaica, was founded in 1958 by three men who were involved in importing iced broilers into Jamaica. When the weekly level of importation reached 100 cases of 27 kilos each, they decided to produce the chickens locally.

From the outset, they decided to adopt the 'contract farmer system' which had been developed in the United States. Under this system, each farmer was responsible for building the broiler house to company specifications, purchasing the equipment and caring for the chickens during the eight to nine weeks required to bring them to marketable size. The company, on the other hand, would supply day-old chicks, feed, medication and technical services at no cost to the farmers. The chickens throughout their stay on the farm would remain the property of the company.

The first reaction of many Jamaicans, including the Minister of Agriculture, was to think that the contract system would not work. Many voiced the opinion that the farmers would just steal the chickens and the feed.

Nevertheless, the company put up its first chicken house with a capacity of 6,000 chickens. The contract system was initiated and proved that Jamaican farmers were reliable. During these early years, the company flourished as demand increased with the change in the retail market from the local grocery store to the more modern supermarket-type operation.

Although at first it was satisfactory to import day-old chicks from Miami, this eventually became a major problem. The chicks were actually hatched in Georgia (some 1,500 kilometers away), trucked to Miami and finally flown to Jamaica. All this stress produced a high mortality rate. When the volume reached approximately 12,000 day-old chicks per week, a decision was taken to set up a hatchery and import fertile eggs.

This decision and another to build a modern broiler processing plant marked the point at which the business exploded. Since 1965, Jamaican broiler production has grown at around 15 percent annually.

With this sort of growth, it became increasingly difficult for Jamaica Broilers to import sacked feed. Not only did it have to be ordered three months in advance, but shrinkage during transport to the farmers had also become a major problem.

DESIGNING A POULTRY FEED PROGRAM

Since feed costs amount to 80 percent of cash costs in a poultry enterprise, a proper feed program is the poultry manager's most pressing concern. Three basic types of feed programs are available:

1. In most commercially developed poultry producing areas of the world, in poultry operations with a housing capacity of 200,000 birds or more, a self contained feed mill is recommended. Under this system, all raw materials are purchased and a balanced feed is produced on the ranch.

2. In poultry operations with a housing capacity of from 100,000 to 200,000 birds, a mixing operation is recommended. In this case pre-mixed concentrates and grain are purchased and mixed on the ranch to produce a balanced feed.

3. In poultry operations with a housing capacity of 100,000 birds or less, the purchase of pre-mixed, balanced feed is recommended. Under this type of feeding program, feed may be purchased in two ways:

a. In unsacked bulk quantities whereby the feed is pumped directly from bulk tanker trucks into storage hoppers. From these hoppers, it is moved automatically to the smaller mechanical feed hoppers.

b. In sacked quantities. Until such a time as unsacked bulk quantities are available locally, sacked quantities must be used. In order to take advantage of discounts offered by feed companies, entire truckloads of sacked feed should be bought. Careful management is required to insure that feed is never stored for more than thirty days.

Broiler feed is a high protein feed that assures maximum growth rate and weight gain. Carefully controlled experiments using different strains of fryers and different commercial feeds should be conducted in order to guarantee highest possible profits. However, it should be noted that once a flock has been started on one type of feed, it should not be switched to another.

Two feeds are generally used in broiler production: starter feed which is used for the first thirty-five days; and finisher feed which is used from thirty-five days to market time.

Generally speaking, poor feed conversion ratios are caused by one or more of the following management problems:

1. Low temperatures and/or high winds. Proper ventilation control is essential to the well-being of all flocks.

2. A high number of condemnations at the processing plant.

3. Poor body weights caused by disease and lack of feeder space. Minimum requirements are five centimeters per bird of feeder space and 2.5 centimeters per bird of water space.

4. Feed wastage from poorly constructed feeders or excess shaking of the tubular feeders, causing feed spillage.

While the tubular feeders need to be filled only once or twice a week, as opposed to once or twice a day for manual linear feeders, they must be shaken from four to six times a day. It is virtually impossible to avoid some spillage during this shaking process. Mechanical feeders are recommended because they will eliminate feed spillage. They supply a low, uniform level of feed throughout the house which can be easily maintained. Moreover, hopper loading is a single operation which reduces the probability of spillage.

In 1968, Jamaica Broilers and Central Soya, Inc., its feed supplier, entered into a joint venture to build a feed mill in Jamaica. Equity was divided 55 percent for Central Soya and 45 percent for Jamaica Broilers.

Initially, the company used Bank of Nova Scotia and Barclays Bank for working capital. The major investment in the feed mill, however, outpaced the ability of the local offices to handle Jamaica Broilers financing. Accordingly, a five-year term loan from Barclays Overseas Development Corporation in London was obtained to finance the feed mill.

Named Central Soya of Jamaica, Ltd., the feed mill was completed in 1970. From that time until 1978, feed sales increased rapidly, not only to Jamaica Broilers but also to other livestock farmers throughout Jamaica.

The relationship between the partner companies was at times a difficult one. With the change of government in 1972, Central Soya became unwilling to make any major investments in the plant, as they opposed certain actions the government was taking. Finally in 1978 with the assistance of a US$1.5 million loan from Citibank N.A., Jamaica Broilers bought out Central Soya. The company was renamed Master Blend Feeds Ltd., a wholly owned subsidiary of Jamaica Broilers.

GOVERNMENT CONTROLS

During 1978 to 1980, the availability of foreign exchange in Jamaica became a severe problem. While exchange to purchase major feed ingredients such as maize and soybeans was assured through the budget of Jamaica Nutrition Holdings, the government purchasing organization, US dollar allocations for premixes, phosphates and other micro-ingredients were not being fully arranged. Packaging materials and medications were also not being funded.

An agreement with the government was reached whereby allocations for maize and soya were balanced by an equivalent allocation of foreign exchange to purchase the other inputs required by Jamaican feed mills.

The basis of the allocations was the average foreign exchange required monthly during the last six months of 1979;

however, this was insufficient to cover expanded demand in 1980 for animal feed and for broiler meat. The situation was exacerbated by signficant world inflation which had increased the base cost of the items to be imported.

This meant that the feed mill and Jamaica Broilers would have to either cut back volume or innovate. By reformulating the feeds and reallocating the funds, feed tonnage produced in 1980 exceeded that of 1979. Similarly, to make packaging dollars go further, Jamaica Broilers began to use onion bags at one-tenth the cost of the wire bound freezer crates which had previously been imported from the USA.

Table 9.1
Broiler Production in Jamaica

	Jamaica Broilers (million kilos)	Total National Production (million kilos)	Jamaica Broilers Market Share (percent)
1960	0.6	2.6	23
1965	1.7	4.3	40
1970	4.8	12.1	40
1975	8.3	27.5	30
1980	16.7	29.7	56

As early as 1969, broiler meat was brought under specific government price control. Between 1973 and the present, the number of broiler companies operating in Jamaica has been reduced from six to two. This reduction has to a great extent been caused by rigid price controls. According to Managing Director Wildish:

> When price controls are fixed at the level of the producer of average efficiency, it is almost inevitable that you will eliminate those who are less efficient. If this process is repeated each time the price of chickens is increased, there is a real danger of creating a monopoly by driving too many producers out of the marketplace.

EMPLOYEE OWNERSHIP

In 1973, Larry Udell, one of the three original partners, wished to capitalize on his initial investment. By this time,

Jamaica Broilers was owned 70 percent by Sydney Levy, one of the original Jamaican partners; 25 percent by Udell; and five percent by other local directors. The other original Jamaican partner had earlier sold his shares to Levy.

The Jamaica Broilers Employees Trust was set up to purchase Udell's shares with money loaned by the company. Although under Jamaican law it is illegal for a company to purchase its own shares, this arrangement was approved by the Central Bank and by 1977 the Employees Trust owned 25 percent of the shares of the company.

Under the terms of the trust deed, only the approximately 250 employees of the company were eligible to purchase shares from the trust. The directors of the company, however, were anxious that the approximately 180 contract farmers and owner/operators of the trucks that were contracted to Jamaica Broilers not be excluded from the share offer. The Levy family made the decision to part with 30 percent of the equity which would be offered to the contractors.

In April, 1977, shares were offered to all employees and contractors as the company continued to grow. Over 90 percent of the people eligible participated in the share offer.

Shares were paid for over a period of five years by deductions from earnings. If employees or contractors left the company, the shares were to be sold back to the trust.

In 1979, the employees of Master Blend Feeds were offered shares in the parent company, Jamaica Broilers, and all eligible employees participated in the purchase.

PRESENT CONTRACT SYSTEM

In mid-1981, Jamaica Broilers had 260 contract growers with an average of 14,000 birds on the farm. The feeding cycle for all broilers averaged just under three months.

It is the responsibility of the contract growers to provide the labor, utilities and management and to construct all buildings to the specifications of Jamaica Broilers. The company, for its part, provides the feed, chickens and medications, as well as making available the services of its staff which includes two veterinarians, a poultry nutritionist and an eight person field team.

The farmers receive three types of payments: rental, performance, and government payments. The rental payment is based on the cost of building and equipping the broiler house. There are five categories based on when the house was built and the materials used. The rental agreement guarantees a weekly payment to the contract grower whether or not birds are in the house.

The performance payment is based on the average liveweight

and feed conversion recorded for the flock. Paid when the birds are ready for slaughter, this payment reflects how efficiently the farmer used the raw materials of day-old chicks and feed supplied him.

The third type of payment is related to the pricing policies of the government. When the government increases the consumer price of frozen broilers, a certain percentage of this increase is returned to the contract grower. This payment can be as much as US$0.90 per bird.

FUTURE EXPANSION

Jamaica Broilers feels that the market for broilers in Jamaica has stablized at 15 to 16 kilograms per capital per annum and that Jamaica will never be competitive in export markets as long as it has to import feed ingredients.

For these reasons, the feed mill is expected to be the center of the company's growth as the total livestock industry in Jamaica expands. A two year capital expansion program costing US$10 million is underway to increase the capacity of the feed mill from the current 112,000 MT per year to 170,000 MT with a fully computerized batch system. The processing plant is planned to remain at 7,200 birds per hour and the hatchery at 460,000 eggs per week.

Dr. Wildish, the Managing Director, considers Jamaica Broilers' greatest success to be the development of the contract farming system. He would like to extend it to production of freshwater shrimp, fish and dairy cattle.

Jamaica Broilers currently employs 450 people, with an additional 260 contract growers and 36 truckers. The entire staff is Jamaican. Dr. Wildish attributes the continuing success of the company to the fact that so much of the profits has been reinvested, and to the employee ownership plan which has mitigated labor animosity toward management, sometimes a problem with Jamaica's extremely strong labor unions.

10 Trinidad's poultry and feed industries

JOHN FREIVALDS

'The agricultural sector in Trinidad and Tobago is in disarray,' the US Counselor for Agricultural Affairs reported recently.

Like many other oil-rich countries, Trinidad has suffered declines in agricultural production in recent years. People have left the land to seek employment in the expanding petroleum and import sectors. Production of sugar, cocoa, coffee, grapefruit, copra, and tobacco have all fallen to new lows. As a result, the food import bill is now around US$400 million per annum.

That's the bad news. The good news is that over the past decade the country has developed a modern livestock sector, especially in broiler production, by importing all the breeding stock and feeds. This development has occurred in spite of a complicated, expensive and inefficient logistics system for imported feedstuffs.

A LONG PIPELINE

Trinidad is far from everywhere. While still a Caribbean country, it is over 1,600 kilometers from Jamaica. And unlike any other Caribbean island country, oil has been discovered there.

As oil revenues and per capital incomes increased, a huge demand for meat developed. Frozen imported broilers could not keep up, and local egg and broiler production began in the early 1960s based on hatching eggs brought in from the USA.

Fifteen years ago, most feed was imported in bags, and Ralston Purina had the major share of the animal feed market. By 1973, bagged feed ingredients were being imported, and feed was mixed locally. As feed and poultry prices rose, the government tried a three-pronged strategy to control costs: price control; more local ownership of feed firms; and bulk purchasing of ingredients.

When the government tried to reduce allowable prices for mixed feed, the feed manufacturers protested. During 1973, feed manufacturers withheld supplies of feed from farmers as a protest against the government's unwillingness to raise prices for animal feeds in the face of increasing prices for imported feed ingredients. The manufacturers won that dispute. An observer at the University of the West Indies has noted, 'It can be concluded that the price increases awarded were sufficient to allow even the least efficient firm to remain in operation.'

In order to reduce feed ingredient prices, a group of Trinidadian and Canadian businessmen built a terminal to import soybean meal and maize in bulk for distribution to the seven animal feed mixers, most of whom had integrated into broiler and egg production. The elevator was built and began operations in 1973. The Ralston distributor did not participate in the scheme.

The bulk grain elevator was built through the efforts of Intercontinental Grain of Canada and Alston's, a local financial services firm. The purpose of this facility, which can store approximately 20,000 MT, was to reduce the huge logistics costs of importing bagged feed ingredients. In 1974, J. Cropper of the University of the West Indies in Trinidad noted, 'The bulk handling facilities should have a positive effect.' Bulk vessels could not only bring feed ingredients to Trinidad, but could also supply wheat for the flour mill, then privately owned.

The new company, Trinidad Grain Mill Elevator, became a very profitable operation, charging high prices for the ingredients that it imported and 'exorbitant' storage and handling charges, according to one local merchant. 'Everyone was getting rich from this scheme,' noted an executive with another large feed company. Intercontinental Grain became a target of some concern, for not only did it have a major share in the grain terminal, it was also the main shareholder in the nearby flour mill and in one of the larger feed manufacturing companies.

Prices were so high that the government eventually decided to give a subsidy to the feed mixers that used the elevator. To earn the subsidy, a feed mixer had to present to the government an invoice from the elevator showing that it had purchased ingredients from the bulk facility. 'What this meant was that the government was subsidizing inefficiency, if not pure waste,' commented a feed company official.

The subsidy was close to US$200/MT. In fact, one foreign trading firm found that it could offer bagged soymeal at a lower price than local mixers could get it through the bulk elevator. The problem was that the elevator had a monopoly. Moreover, some shippers felt that there was collusion between the harbor authority and the elevator company. One local mixer commented that if you brought in your own feed to Port-of-Spain, the harbor authority would run up your costs by making you shift your vessel several times before you could unload.

The port situation is so notorious that one Japanese firm with a construction contract negotiated an agreement with the local stevedores whereby it would unload equipment itself. The Japanese reasoned it would be less expensive to pay the stevedores to do nothing than to have them handle the cargoes.

For lack of a better means of supply, the mixers continued to buy from the bulk elevator. Ralston Purina left the feed business altogether. The company had been using Central Soya's facilities to custom mix and bag feeds. Since it did not use the bulk elevator, it did not get the subsidy, and was therefore unable to stay competitive in the large volume poultry, dairy and pork feeds. Ralston Purina, through its distributor, pursued the specialty feeds, like dog food and calf mix replacers. Central Soya, now the largest feed mixer, has about 25 percent of the business, even though the plant it operates has very little storage. Although the company uses the grain elevator extensively, it still manages to stay profitable.

THE STRATEGY OF SUPERMIX

With the retreat of Ralston Purina in the mixed feed marketplace, Supermix, another feedmixer, has experienced accelerated growth. A remarkable firm, Supermix several years ago bolted from the Trinidad Grain Elevator system to set up its own independent importing operation. The company is owned by the Ramkissoon family, which also controls Supermix Hatchery Ltd., Superagro Supplies, Supermix Breeder Farms, Calypso Chicken Fast Foods, and Calypso Service Stations. The

Supermix feed plant is one of the largest on the island, using some 10,000 MT of ingredients per month, including 3,400 MT of soymeal.

Reggie Antoni, Managing Director, says it was quite a big risk to move away from the grain elevator, but they felt they were being taken advantage of. The firm uses an old US Navy base at Chagaramas to bring in vessels of around 3,000 DWT. An FMC link crane unloads the commodities from the vessel, and a small Caterpillar D3 tractor works inside. The commodities are then put into a small holding tank where trucks come underneath and carry away the grain. Supermix recently bought five new Mack trucks with Dorsey trailers.

Supermix has had to become very mechanized because labor is difficult to attract away from the petroleum industry. Because the roads in Port-of-Spain are very congested, the trucks are loaded at night and the soymeal and maize transported the 32 kilometers to the Supermix feed mill on the outskirts of Port-of-Spain. Managing Director Antoni says that the firm has a competitive advantage in that all the competitors are located within Port-of-Spain where traffic is extremely difficult.

Supplies for Supermix are purchased from Mid-South Feeds in Nashville, Tennessee (USA). Mid-South has chartered two 3,000 DWT vessels, the Carib Dawn and the Carib Eve, for four years. The maize and soybeans, according to Antoni, come from Brunswick, Georgia.

Supermix has a current capacity of 200,000 day-old chicks per week, with plans to expand to 600,000 chicks per week. The company currently has two 100 hp pellet machines for the feed operation, but plans to double this also.

Supermix is a most innovative feed manufacturer, currently receiving stacks of proposed ventures in a number of different areas. For example, to complement the four Calypso Chicken fast-food outlets, there are proposals to develop a potato processing plant and to try to develop potato production.

MARKET GROWTH

The volumes grew: in 1980, Trinidad imported 90,000 MT of maize, 30,000 MT of soybean meal, 10,000 MT of poultry feeds, and 19,000 MT of other feeds. In 1981 these imports cost US$50 million.

The subsidies also grew. Not only did the government subsidize animal feed, it also subsidized the price of broilers. According to one local businessman, the subsidized price of broilers is so low that he could make money by exporting broilers back to the United States. One visiting US businessman commented, 'The economics in this country are as upside down as the local Hilton hotel,' referring to the main hotel in Port-of-Spain which has its floors numbered from the top down.

Production costs are high also due to continued power outages. Production is constantly disrupted by the power surges. 'We burn up a lot of motors,' commented one feed mixer.

Seventy percent of all feeds produced by the seven mixers are for poultry, including broiler starter, broiler finishers, and laying rations. For pigs, feeds produced include pig grower, pig finisher and lactation ration. Carnation Company has recently begun increasing its sales of specialty feeds, as well as premixes, in this market.

Among cattle feeds, dairy rations are the most important; the majority of the country's beef requirement is imported because of the shortage of adequate grazing land for beef cattle. There are an estimated 10,000 to 12,000 cattle in the country, of which approximately 3,500 are being milked.

The only local ingredients used for any of these feeds are coconut meal, citrus meal, and molasses, and they amount to only five percent of total ingredient usage.

FUTURE GOALS

The feed mixers are generally unhappy that the government subsidy, although generous many years ago, has not been reviewed for eight years. The subsidy is based on four factors: labor and overhead per 45 kilo bag; pretax profit; shrink; and the prices of non-maize and soya ingredients. The feed manufacturers contend that labor costs alone have gone up 60 percent in only the last three years. Some mixers are threatening to shut down if the subsidies are not raised.

The oil and gas reserves assure the continued demand for livestock, yet due to Trinidad's limited land resources and lack of desire to develop domestic agriculture, imports will continue.

To deal with the growth, new facilities are being planned. CLEPLAN, a Brazilian group, has proposed a soybean crushing plant. 'Brazilian interests want not only to sell the equipment, but eventually to supply the soybeans. All the soymeal used by Trinidad now comes from the USA.

The flour mill in Trinidad, now entirely government owned, has also recently entered into the animal feed business. It had booked a large quantity of ocean freight, and when it could not load the ships with wheat, it booked feed grains. While the flour mill does not really have any storage or logistics capability for feed grains, new storage tanks are going up. According to one source, the government sought to buy out the grain elevator, but the price was absurdly high. At the same time, the costs of running feed grains through the elevator remain inflated. One feed trade executive called the new government facility 'revenge' against the grain elevator's high cost monopoly.

Other ambitious plans to deal with the high cost feed and poultry industries which the government has recently announced include:

1. An arrest in both the absolute levels and rate of growth of imports;
2. The ordered and integrated development of domestic agriculture;
3. The provision of valuable experience in producing new crops without serious disruption to total food supplies; and
4. The orientation over time of consumer taste and preference towards more commodities of domestic origin.

Specific projects to implement these broad goals include production of hatching eggs and increased local production of maize and other feed ingredients.

'I doubt that any of these goals will be reached,' commented one Trinidadian businessman. 'We shall keep on importing, as oil and agriculture simply don't mix.'

11 The pride of the African beef industry: Botswana Meat Commission

JOHN FREIVALDS

The Botswana Meat Commission (BMC) has developed into this country's most powerful industrial undertaking, affecting in some manner the life of everyone in the country. Over the past 20 years, the Commission has developed a sophisticated beef slaughtering and marketing operation, with gross sales of US$95 million in 1982. During that time it has confronted perhaps a unique marketing challenge: maintaining consumer interest in beef while the cattle herds were constantly being wracked by foot-and-mouth disease. Botswana has met this challenge by developing its own methods of disease control and, in the process, developing its veterinary medicine industry.

The BMC has grown from a single abattoir in 1934 to a major beef slaughtering and marketing operation which is solely owned by the government of Botswana. In 1981 the BMC slaughtered 202,000 head of cattle for sale as boneless beef, whole and quartered carcasses, byproducts, corned beef, beef extract, wet salted hides, pet food, and wet blue hides. In addition to the abattoir and related facilities in Lobatse (cannery, pet food plant and tannery), the BMC owns Botswana Meat Commission (UK) Holdings Ltd., which operates the ECCO Cold Stores near London.

The ECCO Cold Stores were purchased by the BMC in 1977 for the twofold purpose of handling and storing BMC's own ECCO brand meat and arranging for its efficient distribution in the UK and Europe, and also to operate as a public cold store.

The Botswana Meat Commission came into being in 1965 when the Government of Botswana became the sole owner of the company which was then operating the abattoir in Lobatse. The Board of Commissioners is composed of representatives of both the government and the producers. The BMC is the sole buyer of cattle for export slaughtering and establishes prices for the producer. Any surpluses earned by the Commission are returned to producers as bonuses at the end of the financial year.

DEVELOPMENT OF THE CATTLE HERDS

Botswana is a huge country with extensive pastures and a cattle herd currently numbering three million head. While the plains are extensive, water resources are limited. However, the beef herd is the chief source of livelihood for 60 percent of the population.

In an effort to improve the quality of the herds, the BMC adopted a grazier scheme, lending money to small herdsmen for breeding animals and general herd improvement. The results have not been gratifying. The 1981 Annual Report states:

> We have now reached the position where court action might have to be taken against some graziers who have made no effort whatsoever to clear their outstanding debts. It is a pity that serious-minded graziers who wish to improve their herds are handicapped by the continuous suspension of the schemes as the BMC seeks to clear its accounts.

The goal of the grazier scheme was to make it possible for Botswana farmers and would-be farmers who have water, grazing space, and management skills to acquire breeding stock. The scheme also aimed at providing a market for heifers which would otherwise be delivered to the abattoir for slaughter. When started in 1977, it was hoped that '...it will enable some Botswanans to take part actively in our livestock industry with a reasonable herd size purchased with money borrowed at fairly reasonable terms.'

Initially, an applicant was given a loan to buy between 25 and 100 heifers. For every 25 heifers, a bull had to be purchased as well, or the buyer had to give evidence that he had sufficient bulls. The loans, provided by commercial banks, were made to approved applicants and guaranteed 100 percent by the BMC.

The grazier scheme was dealt a severe blow when drought struck twice during the past three years. The 1982 drought was the worst since the early 1960s when 500,000 cattle died. During times of drought, the BMC gives priority in cattle

77

purchases to areas worst affected by dry grazing conditions. Special sales are often organized and free botulism medication and Vitamin A are provided to help save cattle which cannot be purchased at that time.

ANOTHER SETBACK

BMC plans to improve herds received another setback when foot-and-mouth disease was diagnosed in Botswana in 1977. Since that time the BMC has embarked upon a number of schemes to limit the impact of the disease.

In 1982 a US$8 million vaccine unit, designed to produce 21 million doses of foot-and-mouth vaccine annually, was built in Gaborone. It was a joint venture between the Government of Botswana and the Merieux Institute of France.

Long in the planning, the unit was needed because doubts had been raised over the efficacy of vaccines produced in Europe. As one source stated, 'Either the strain had mutated, or the vaccine had lost its strength.' The unit had to be constructed in Botswana because work on vaccines is prohibited in Europe. To speed development, the Institute constructed a pilot plant and then flew it to Botswana by Hercules aircraft.

The unit now produces the SAT-1, 2, and 3 types of foot-and-mouth vaccine. The vaccine is used primarily in the northern part of the country where there is the risk of infected cattle crossing the border from Zimbabwe.

In the southern part of the country, cordon fences have been considered the best form of control. The cordon system is complicated, but it has allowed Botswana to keep shipping beef to the EEC, since the EEC will not accept cattle slaughtered within 12 months of vaccination. Figure 11.1 shows the control fence system as of April, 1982.

Only cattle from disease-free areas can be slaughtered, and the logistics have become elaborate. The 1979 annual report states:

> Only cattle from areas south of Dibete, and east of the line or rail, were slaughtered for EEC markets. Cattle from west of the railway line were being received and slaughtered separately at the abattoir for non-European markets. Ghanzi animals were also being sent to the abattoir, but only by trucks. It was, however, not until May that Ghanzi farmers were allowed to trek cattle to Lobatse, in addition to trucking them.

The program seems to have worked, for the whole of Botswana was free of foot-and-mouth disease by the end of 1980.

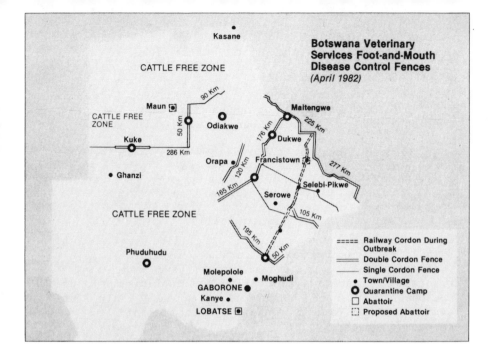

Figure 11.1 Botswana Veterinary Services Foot-and-Mouth
Disease Control Fences (April 1982)

PROCESSING

All cattlemen want to sell their beef to the BMC as it is a
ready market, and quotas have had to be set. During 1981,
prices for sound cattle per 100 kilos of cold dressed mass
ranged from US$67.50 to US$117. In 1981, the average producer
price per head was US$207.65, up from US$176.70 in 1980. In
addition, a bonus averaging US$15.78 per animal was paid. In
1981, the average cold dressed mass per head was 217
kilograms.

Producers have still to learn how to handle their cattle
properly to get better prices. Bruising is a significant
problem, and the quality of the animal has to be downgraded.
According to BMC, the main causes of bruising are:

1. Beating animals with large sticks and stones at loading.
The BMC is trying to get electric cattle prods into the
countryside to put an end to this practice.

2. Loading cattle of different sizes and sexes into the same
truck.

3. The condition of road transport. Botswana's roads are in

79

bad condition, but it is poor driving and the failure to keep a constant watch on the cattle which lead to the worst bruising. Cattle which lose their balance fall down and are often badly trampled by the time they reach Lobatse.

4. Leaving the horns on the animal. The BMC has offered a bonus of US$0.45 per head for dehorned animals, and encourages producers to dehorn animals when they are still young.

The BMC can slaughter 1,800 cattle a day, the majority of which are deboned. The deboning room, at a controlled temperature, operates with a line for frozen and chilled products using both Multi-Vac and Cry-O-Vac systems. Up to 170 tons of boneless beef is produced daily. Frozen product is blast frozen and then stored in holding rooms of 2,000 ton capacity. After reduction to 1°C, chilled meat is shipped daily in refrigerated railway cars.

Carcasses have six grades: super (excellent finish and conformation); prime (good finish and conformation); grade 1 (reasonable finish and conformation); grade 2 (fair finish of cows over five years); grade 3 (fair finish); and grade 4 (carcasses which do not comply with requirements of other grades).

All product is graded by skilled government appointed grades with red, blue and black cartons signifying the grades produced. All cartons are polyethylene lined, staple-free, and plastic strapped. Cartons of chilled boneless beef have corner strengtheners for maximum protection.

Thirty-four different products are produced by the processing line, excluding corned beef and hides. Nothing is wasted as the tendons, spleens, lungs and tails are all marketed. Given the nature of the industrial, catering, and fast food markets, BMC places particular attention on silverside, topside, thick flank and forequarters processing.

In 1978 a cannery was added to produce corned beef. Daily production comes to 45,000 cans of 340 grams each.

To increase the value added in the tannery, a major expansion which further processes the hides was made in 1980. Originally, the BMC tanning factory could only process 600 hides a day through the wet blue stage. The tannery now has a capacity to process 1,200 hides or 30,000 kg/day. Studies are currently being made on further processing the hides to crust stage and to finished leather. If feasible, outside investors will be sought.

The BMC is near completion of facilities for treatment of lime water and its recycling for use within the factory. The commission is also working to recover chrome salts from the wet blue operation.

Another adjunct to the overall processing operation was the completion of a pet food plant which daily produces 30,000

cans of 400 grams each. The plant has the capacity of increasing production to 50,000 cans/day.

Rainfall is scarce in Botswana and consequently water is expensive. To cut costs, the BMC embarked on a major water recovery scheme in 1980. Another objective has been to recover fats and proteins from factory effluent and to use them to increase output of tallow and carcass meal.

MARKETING

The BMC's success is in large measure tied to increased exports to the EEC, and particularly to the UK. The BMC purchased its cold store waterhouse in Britain in 1977 to gain some marketing flexibility. It has a total storage capacity of 6,000 tons, composed of nine chambers which can be run at temperatures ranging from -30°C to +7°C. The store has a modern blast freezer capable of freezing 50 tons in 24 hours.

The world beef market is tempered by very large quantities of heavily subsidized beef from the EEC. This beef is being sold in markets traditionally supplied from South America and Australia, causing these countries to sell in turn at low prices and to penetrate deeply into many African markets.

The ban on Botswana exports due to the foot-and-mouth disease outbreak destroyed any effort at consistent marketing from 1977 to 1980. For example, while the BMC had a quota of 21,000 tons under the Lome Convention in 1980, it could only sell 1,000 tons to the EEC. South Africa has also been a major market for the BMC, taking 11,000 tons of boneless beef and 2,000 tons of carcasses in 1981. In fact, South Africa was Botswana's largest market in 1981.

Angola and Mozambique also received sizeable shipments, but the BMC has been faced with increasing competition from South Africa and the EEC for these markets. Small quantities of boneless beef and offal are also shipped to Hong Kong, Mauritius, and Zaire, but generally these markets rely lower-priced product from South America.

Hides are marketed in Europe, while meats and tallow go Zimbabwe and Zambia. Horns, ox gall, tail and gall stones to established buyers in Japan, France, England, Germany a Hong Kong.

Overall, the BMC abattoir is generally acknowledged to one of the largest and most technically sophisticated Africa, and is managed by the BMC on a consistently compet basis.

12 Marketing commodities: new types of export contracts

JOHN FREIVALDS

'What's our sales plan to be?' asked the grain elevator manager of Eduardo Tura, the head of a grain and oil seed cooperative located in a fertile agricultural region in the state of Sao Paulo, Brazil. A new crop year was beginning and some planning had to be done. It seemed that everything could grow in the region: soybeans, sugar cane, potatoes, tomatoes, cotton and groundnuts. Although the cooperative handled several different commodities, it had a special interest in groundnuts. Groundnuts are a minor crop in Sao Paulo: 250,000 MT annually compared to 750,000 MT of soya and 55 million MT of sugar cane. The cooperative handled about 100,000 MT of groundnuts a year, part of which eventually went to export markets.

Unprocessed groundnuts for export are a difficult commodity on which to earn much money, since the tax structure and export incentives favor the export of processed groundnut products. For example, the ICM (turnover tax) on groundnuts for export is 13 percent compared to five percent for groundnut meal and zero for groundnut oil. In addition, earnings from exports of groundnut oil are not subject to income tax.

Tura was concerned over whether the cooperative was earning enough from its sales. Farmers in Brazil have always complained that their marketing system consisted of taking a commodity to town and saying to a buyer, 'What will you give me?' It was rather ironic that with all the 'production'

alternatives in Sao Paulo, the 'marketing' opportunities were limited. This same situation faces other producers around the world.

As a result, many producers are demanding new types of marketing arrangements. Two of the most innovative that have been developed are the full disclosure and the participation contracts. In both cases, the contracts are so designed that the producer can share in the proceeds from the final sale.

FULL DISCLOSURE CONTRACT

The full disclosure contract enables the cooperative or other producer to participate in a CIF (Cost, Insurance and Freight) sale by having an experienced trading firm handle all the logistics and documentation. Each party brings its strengths to the venture, and responsibilities are set forth in a Memorandum of Agreement which itemizes the exporter's costs to be charged against the final export sale price and the marketing fee (either a certain amount per MT or a percentage of the final sales price) to be retained by the exporter. The trading firm's costs in some instances are determined and agreed to by the producer before the sale is made. Finally, all the costs and revenues of the transaction are documented for all parties to see.

The firm that pioneered this concept and has used it most extensively in international trade is the I.S. Joseph Company of Minneapolis, USA. Using this contractual technique, its Brazilian subsidiary, Josco Agricola do Brasil, was able to gain a major share of Brazil's citrus pulp exports, which approach 400,000 MT, and bring in over US$60 million in foreign exchange each year. Josco has also used this technique with sunflowers, corn gluten feed, molasses, beet pulp, coffee byproducts, brewer's grains, cassava and numerous other products. A Josco executive explains the firm's commitment to this type of agreement in the following way: 'You have to try something different to get the business away from the big commodity trading firms.'

BENEFITS AND DRAWBACKS OF FULL DISCLOSURE

Michael Willis, a marketing specialist at I.S. Joseph, believes there will be more extensive use of the full disclosure contract in the future. He points to three main benefits to producers.

First, full disclosure makes the producer an established exporter by putting his name in the export market.

Table 12.1

Who Does What Under Different Contract Terms

	The Seller Must	The Buyer Must
Ex-Works (Ex-Factory, Ex-Spout, Ex-Plantation, Ex-Warehouse, etc.)	Place the goods at the disposal of the buyer at the time provided in the contract, at the point of delivery named or which is usual for the delivery of such goods, and load them on the conveyance to be provided by the buyer.	Take delivery of the goods as soon as they are placed at his disposal at the place and at the time as provided in the contract, and pay the price as provided in the contract.
FAS (Free Alongside Ship)	Deliver the goods alongside the vessel at the loading berth named by the buyer, at the named port of shipment, in the manner customary at the port, at the date or within the period stipulated, and notify the buyer, without delay, that the goods have been delivered alongside the vessel.	Bear all the charges and risks of the goods from the time when they shall have been effectively delivered alongside the vessel at the named port of shipment, at the date or within the period stipulated, and pay the price as provided in the contract.
FOB (Free on Board)	Deliver the goods on board the vessel named by the buyer, at the named port of shipment, in the manner customary at the port, at the date or within the period stipulated, and notify the buyer, without delay, that the goods have been delivered on board.	Bear all costs and risks of the goods from the time when they shall have effectively passed the ship's rail at the named port of shipment, and pay the price as provided in the contract.
C&F (Cost and Freight)	Contract on usual terms at his own expense for the carriage of the goods to the agreed port of destination by the usual route and pay freight charges and any charges for unloading at the port of discharges which may be levied by shipping lines at the time and port of shipment.	Receive the goods at the agreed port of destination and bear, with the exception of the freight, all costs and charges incurred in the course of their transit by sea until their arrival at the port of destination, as well as unloading costs, unless such costs and charges shall have been included in the freight.
CIF (Cost, Insurance, Freight)	Same as C&F with the following exception: Procure at his own cost and in a transferable form, a policy of marine insurance against the risks of the carriage involved in the contract.	Same as C&F

84

Second, the producer is aware of, understands, and controls his costs all the way to destination by dialogue with the exporter and by his decisions to sell or not to sell at a given price. In addition, he can fix certain variable expenses within the full disclosure framework.

Finally, any buyer of product short of the foreign buyer will then become a reseller and can only pay a price which will allow delivery at a profit. Thus, full disclosure provides the producer the opportunity to maximize the net return, since it is based on the foreign price.

The full disclosure contract will not be advantageous to the producer if final pricing does not correctly reflect marketing conditions; the trading firm's costs for ocean freight or other logistics are too high; or if the marketing fees paid the trading firm are too high.

According to Willis, there are four factors holding back more extensive use of full disclosure at present: (1) product originators are hesitant to step over the bounds of tradition, which heretofore have been domestic sales; (2) product originators wrongly believe that to sell close to the point of origination is both easier and less risky; (3) very few export firms have the capability to put together a total sales and logistics package on a competitive basis; and (4) very few export firms establish themselves in the export market with the objective of helping others.

SAMPLE AGREEMENT

An example of a full disclosure export agreement is as follows:

Whereas, it is in the special interest of Cooperative (Coop) to improve its return for Brazilian groundnuts and to provide itself with a continuing source of information and knowledge as to international markets and to secure for itself a premium market for its groundnuts and

Whereas, it is in the interest of the trading firm to represent Coop in international marketing efforts which representation will permit the Coop to add to its general volume and market knowledge, and,

Whereas, it is in the special interest of the Brazilian Government to improve its balance of payments and increase its exports, and,

Whereas, it is in the general interest of Coop and trading firm to cooperate to expand the trade and commercial activities of both organizations,

Therefore, it is now mutually agreed that:

A. Subject to the terms of this agreement, Coop will make available to trading firm for export into the world markets approximately (+ or - 10 percent) 20,000 metric tons of groundnuts to be shipped at frequencies and intervals agreed to between the two parties over each twelve-month period.

B. The origin of these groundnuts shall be from selected elevators in accordance with agreed schedule to be worked out between the two parties with the understanding that there can be flexibility in the schedule of shipments, both as to origin and to volume from any specific origin, over any twelve-month shipping period.

C. The pricing of such groundnuts on a per metric ton basis will be agreed to periodically in accordance with an example schedule of pricing (see Table 12.2) which provides for a Full Disclosure Concept as a relationship between Coop and trading firm.

D. Trading firm shall on a regular and periodic basis bring to Coop sales opportunities at given prices, tonnages and shipping schedules to destinations within selected world markets. If Coop accepts such a sales opportunity, then the terms of this acceptance are immediately confirmed in a written subagreement between the two parties and such tonnage at the agreed price and schedule will be shipped by Coop to trading firm in accordance with the terms of the specific transaction. Further, to document the transaction, trading firm will submit to Coop copies of trading firm's sale to trading firm's customer on a Full Disclosure Basis in accordance with the example price formula as outlined in the full disclosure example.

If Coop declines a sales opportunity, then it is trading firm's obligation to attempt to improve the terms of such a sales opportunity for Coop. Therefore, each sales opportunity will be considered on its own merits. Coop will invoice trading firm based on destination weights, and trading firm will pay such invoice upon receipt.

E. It is to the advantage of both parties, in order to enhance the logistics of arranging for inland and ocean transportation, rail cars, storage and handling, that as much lead time as possible on sales be arranged between the two parties. It is understood between the two parties that trading firm's advance planning will be based on the volume of approximately (+ or - 10 percent) 20,000 MT tons subject to the pricing and scheduling conditions outlined in paragraph D of this agreement.

F. Compensation - Trading firm shall receive from Coop US$3/metric ton compensation in the form of an allowance on the price of groundnuts invoiced by Coop to trading firm.

G. Each party has mutual and specific obligations to the other:

Table 12.2
Sample Full Disclosure Statement for Export Shipments

Final Sales Price
CIF Rotterdam or other destination   _____
Less Costs of:
Insurance   _____
Superintendence   _____
Ocean Freight   _____
Commissions   _____
Interest   _____
Forwarding   _____
Elevation   _____
Storage   _____
Domestic Freight   _____
Shrink   _____
Other Costs   _____
Allowance for Marketing   _____
        Total costs   _____
Net Return to Cooperative   _____
                                                   _____

Trading Firm

For its compensation, trading firm, under terms of this agreement, would be responsible to Coop for the following:

1. Marketing Coop groundnut production in world markets.
2. Providing current market information and related statistical reports.
3. Invoicing customers for all shipments.
4. Making collections and assuming all credit responsibilities.
5. Making all ocean freight and railroad arrangements.
6. Registration of Coop products in various world markets.
7. Gearing trading firm's sales program so that no storage problems occur at Coop's elevators.
8. Making trading firm's traffic department available to assist Coop in all shipments.

Cooperative

For its compensation, Coop will be responsible to trading firm for the following:

1. To provide all information concerning groundnut origin points, production at each elevator and related storage and shipping requirements to expedite shipments under this

87

agreement.

2. To share in full and open manner, all trade and commercial information which shall enable trading firm to formulate and carry out the most beneficial market program on behalf of both parties.

3. To provide groundnuts of high quality to enable trading firm to develop a brand name following for Coop's groundnuts.

4. To assist trading firm in working with Brazilian authorities in government and private transportation to secure the most advantageous transportation rates in support of trading firm's marketing efforts under this agreement.

Jointly

It is the responsibility of both parties to use the highest standard of conduct so that the performance of this agreement shall be a credit to each organization and each organization's country.

PARTICIPATION CONTRACTS

Participation contracts are a form of full disclosure contract which have widespread use in the sugar industry. While only recently initiated into use in the international sugar trade, they are used exclusively in the US sugar industry. The participation contract differs from the full disclosure contract in subtle ways regarding payment schedules and other logistics.

The origin of the participation contract was in the US sugar beet industry. Just before World War II, growers in the Western US sold their beets to the processor at what they thought was a fair price. However, immediately after they sold, the price of sugar rose and the processors made a lot of money. The next year the growers demanded a higher price and after it was set, the price of sugar fell; the processors lost a lot of money.

At this point, the growers and processors 'decided to ride this thing up and down together,' according to marketing specialist Art Stewart at Great Western Sugar. 'Everyone saw that the marketplace and not the other party was the enemy and that it was in everyone's interest to overcome the ups and downs of the sugar market,' notes Stewart.

Great Western Sugar Company was one of the first firms to put this type of contract to work internationally. To diversify its sources of sugar, Great Western (primarily dependent on sugar beets for its sugar) several years ago purchased the Godchaux-Henderson refinery in Louisiana to refine imported raw cane sugar. The plant, representing a sizable fixed investment, needed a constant supply of sugar to keep it operating profitably.

At the time, the standard way of buying sugar was to go to a broker and tell him what you needed; he would then seek out the sugar for you. More often than not, the broker would take ownership of the sugar he found and would resell it, adding on his commission.

Great Western found that working through brokers did not assure long term supplies and, moreover, added on an unnecessary layer of cost, the brokerage commission. To avoid the brokers, the company offered participation contracts to the Philippines, Panama and later to several other Central American countries. The developing countries liked the opportunity to reach the final consumer and it enabled them also to sidestep the brokers. The contracts provided for an initial payment as well as a final payment, thus generating the cash flow these countries required.

The international contracts met with opposition. The brokers were unhappy because they were being cut out, and government bureaucrats in sugar marketing agencies were opposed since marketing responsibility now rested with the refiners. 'The worse thing you can do to a bureaucracy,' commented one sugar industry official, 'is to tell it that it is redundant.'

Finally, government controlled marketing boards, being essentially conservative, did not want the extra risk. They wanted to have all their money in hand before the loaded ships left the port.

The participation contract has survived its initial test and others have begun using it. The participation contract between Revere Sugar in the US and the Philippines government illustrates how such a contract works.

MARKETING MECHANICS

The Revere contract runs for five years and requires the refiner to acquire 80 percent of its raw sugar requirements (estimated between 550,000 and 650,000 MT) from the supplier. According to a Revere official, participation contracts only work when the refiner has one chief source: the accounting headaches in having a number of participation contracts would make any advantages illusory.

The participation contract can become rather complex and requires precise definition of several cost items. The 'Average Selling Price' is the aggregate invoice price (per refiner's invoice) of refined sugar delivered from refiner's plants during a monthly period. 'Unit Cost' is all costs and expenses allocable to refined deliveries, including costs attributable to the loss of sugar in refining. The 'Shipping and Financing Cost' includes duty, freight, insurance and any financing costs applicable to supplier's sugar.

One initial objection to the contract was overcome when a clause was added so that the supplier could get out of the contract if the price was too low. Without that clause, the refiner could sell the refined sugar at any price whatsoever just to be rid of it. To overcome this caveat, the Revere agreement allows for a number of modifications if the average net price for a three month period is less than US$12/hundredweight (US$264/MT). If the price goes below this level, the supplier may renegotiate the agreement; receive additional payments from refiner based on a complex formula; or terminate the agreement with termination taking place five months after the giving of notice.

Clarence Davan, in charge of Great Western participation contracts, notes that a forthright attitude is essential to the operation of this contract. 'Our books are constantly open for inspection by our supplier.'

MARKETING ALTERNATIVES

Creative contract arrangements are not the only marketing alternatives available to producers in developing countries. A wide variety of strategies exist for marketing almost any commodity. For example, the US Department of Agriculture has identified nine marketing alternatives for wheat:

1. selling cash wheat at harvest.
2. storing cash wheat at harvest for later sale.
3. contracting cash wheat before harvest.
4. contracting cash wheat at harvest for deferred payment.
5. forward pricing wheat by the use of futures and selling cash.
6. forward pricing wheat by the use of futures and then storing wheat at harvest.
7. tranferring speculation from cash grain to futures.
8. hedging wheat on a short term basis in transit to a higher market.
9. marketing wheat as feed.

Although some of these options are unique to US agriculture, others could work in developing countries. In the case of Brazil, for instance, the use of commodity futures markets by Brazilian firms was unheard of ten years ago, but when the Central Bank changed the law to provide foreign exchange to cover margin requirements at US commodity exchanges, many firms began using futures markets. Now Brazil spends around US$20 million in commissions annually to conduct its hedging operations.

Although more and more Brazilian commodities are going for export, cooperatives are not getting into export. At present, they account for around 25 percent of Brazil's storage capacity and close to 40 percent of its soybean crushing capacity, but only nine percent of total agricultural exports.

Eduardo Tura of the grain and oil seed cooperative in the State of Sao Paulo, Brazil, like most other cooperative marketing directors, had generally sold his crops on a spot basis to the highest bidders. There were always many bidders to choose from, including Yokana-Bozzo, Nidera, Sanbra, Cargill, several Japanese trading firms and many smaller firms. In recent years as the cooperative had improved its logistics capability, it had begun to make FOB port offerings, thereby earning a small margin on freight.

Although some members of the cooperative had urged that a plan be developed to make CIF sales to the end customer, Tura knew that this would require an overseas sales office, a market intelligence network, shipping and financial facilities and, finally, more capital, so there would be more risk.

Because of the increased risk, most members of the cooperative were happy with the present arrangements. Selling for cash at harvest avoided storage problems and provided quick income, but it eliminated the opportunity to wait for higher prices. Tura recalled the skeptical comment of one commodity broker when he heard the cooperative was interested in marketing alternatives: 'If you think you can shorten the marketing pipeline, you are stupid. Don't get so mad that the trading firms make a profit on your commodities. They take all the risks and should have all the profit.'

The Brazilian government has set up a state trading firm, Interbras, to help small producers market their commodities. In trying to break into the international commodities export business, Interbras has been trying to make more C&F (Cost and Freight) and CIF transactions. In 1978, no less than 60 percent of its trades were closed under those terms, up from 55 percent in 1977 and 33 percent in 1976.

Tura studied all the alternatives available and recommended entering into a full disclosure contract with an international trading firm. The cooperative's conservative Board of Directors, believing their role was to provide stability, turned down his idea. They felt selling their commodities on a spot cash basis with few variations was still preferable because a definite cash price was established and because the quantity along with discounts for quality were set at the time of sale.

Farmers are cash oriented and would dislike having to wait for their money until after an export sale has been made. Perhaps more to the point was Tura's suspicion that one member of the Board had an interest in a grain brokerage firm that the cooperative had used. One of the problems with cooperatives in Brazil is that not everyone has the real cooperative idea; members too easily break rank and buy and sell outside the organization. Any new marketing arrangement would have changed the status quo.

Despite the Brazilian example, alternative contractual arrangements may well be the wave of the future. One commodities executive has noted 'only the creative survive in this business. Besides,' he continued, 'the full disclosure contract enables a greater degree of integration without the capital investment.'

13 Organizing commodity trading groups

JOHN FREIVALDS

'Buy low and sell high,' the senior trader implored the young recruit. 'That's the essence of the commodity business, yet a lot of people never understand this simple point.'

He may be right, because for each new agricultural commodity trading firm or organization that is created, another seems to fail. They falter because of mistakes in choosing personnel, in establishing a sound organizational structure, and in implementing appropriate risk management techniques.

In recent years, private companies as well as producer groups and governmental organizations have set up their own agricultural commodity trading firms.

For private multinational firms, commodity trading offers an opportunity to take advantage of logistics capabilities or overseas offices they may already possess. This was the motivation for Leo Raphaely and Sons, a South African trading firm, and Philipp Brothers, a New York based firm, to enter commodity trading. Both had large fleets of vessels and overseas contracts. They handled other goods and they were aware of commodity price movements and the risks and opportunities these represented. To get going, they hired away experienced traders from established firms.

The Japanese trading houses have also expanded their commodity trading. Originally their function was to buy commodities for shipment to Japan, but they have become more involved in 'off-shore' trades, that is, selling in areas other than Japan.

Producer groups have entered into commodity trading to avoid selling through a middleman. In the international grain trade, a very few firms dominate trading. According to one report, only five firms (Cargill, Continental, Garnac, Dreyfus and Bunge) handle 90 percent of US grain exports. The trading firms justify their existence by maintaining, correctly in most cases, that they bring buyer and seller together, provide logistics and assume risks.

'That may be so,' noted one US farmer, 'but they charge too much to do that.' Accordingly, farmers through their cooperatives have formed commodity trading firms. FARMARCO in the United States, Zen-Noh in Japan, and Cotia in Brazil are examples of producer groups that have set up trading operations to 'avoid the middleman.'

Interesting reactions have met some of the new producer group commodity firms. Gold Kist, a large cooperative in the southeastern United States, discovered when calling on Eastern European buyers that the Eastern Europeans thought their central trading organizations were the same as producer cooperatives. Says a Gold Kist Executive Vice President: 'It may be that they want to eliminate the middleman, or it may be that they have a complete misunderstanding of what a cooperative is. The cooperative is the epitome of the capitalistic system working with large and small growers.'

Finally, governments have established their own commodity trading operations, either for exporting (like Interbras in Brazil) or importing (like Bulog in Indonesia).

The rationale for establishing governmental trading firms is similar in most cases to that expressed by an official of the Nigerian Cocoa Board: to secure the most favorable arrangements for the purchase for export of products; to maintain stable producer prices; and to promote the economic development of the producers and the areas of production.

Interbras, the Brazilian state trading firm, began commodity trading operations 'to provide a solid support base for the private sector. By such means as the organization of export pools...highly positive opportunities were opened up to large, medium, and small domestic concerns.'

Still another reason for exporting countries to establish state trading firms is to enable state-to-state trading and to facilitate long term agreements which would be difficult between private exporting companies.

There is also the argument that given the growing number of state trading systems, a centralized trading partner would be best able to prevent what happened to the US in 1972. In that year, Exportkhleb, the Soviet grain importing agency, made individual purchases from several private US firms. Each kept its individual trades quiet, and as a result, prices rose after all the trades had been completed. Proponents of centralized trading argue that had the US negotiated on a state-to-state basis, the sales could have been made at a higher price.

CAN STATE SYSTEMS WORK?

Not everyone is convinced that state commodity trading can work. Whatever gains a government controlled trading operation can provide have to be weighed against certain losses. Marketing costs under a state system may exceed those under a competitive system. In addition, adjustments to changing markets may be more cumbersome in a state system.

Another criticism of state-run commodity trading firms comes from an executive of a large commodity futures firm:

> When a government assumes the functions of a commercial organization in its efforts to improve the well-being of its citizens, it must arm itself with the same business techniques used by commercial companies from whom it may be buying or to whom it may be selling. While this may seem to be self-evident, it is actually in conflict with the nature of a government bureaucracy. That conflict arises out of the necessity for risk taking in a commercial company, and the abhorrence of risk by governmental employees. The officers of a commercial company may be encouraged to assume certain business risks and are well rewarded when their judgment is correct. The government functionary, on the other hand, gains nothing if he is right, but may lose his job if he is wrong.

ORGANIZATION MUST BE RESPONSIVE

Since trading is essentially an 'opportunistic' business, the trading departments must be structured so as to allow the traders to respond to opportunities as they present themselves. At the same time, however, the organizational structure must provide control and definition of responsibility.

A very tightly structured organization may create an environment in which traders do not have the authority to react to market forces as needed. The system must respond quickly when circumstances dictate. Too little organization, however, encourages reckless trading and overcommitment. Cook Industries, one of the major US grain trading firms until a few years ago, overcommitted itself to speculative market positions and was forced out of the grain business.

Most trading firms organize themselves along product profit center lines. For example, one trading department deals with wheat, another with maize and so forth. The head of each department is then responsible for the profit and loss of that department. Each department is assessed a percentage of the administrative costs of the overall trading operation. Administration must provide a constant accounting of where each trader stands - whether is he 'long', 'short' or even - as well as the status of all receivables.

Since logistics is a crucial part of any trading operation, a separate shipping group must also exist. It is often a separate profit center as well. One large New York commodity trading firm's shipping group provides a daily chart of shipping rates for various commodities and destinations to each trading group.

THE PERFECT TRADER

Regardless of the type of commodity trading operation, good flexible people are required. Experts agree that trading is an art which defies simple description. But successful traders do share certain characteristics. When Cargill employees interview a young applicant for a trading position, they often inquire if he traded baseball cards or toys as a child. They want someone who is accustomed to taking risks and weighing relative values.

According to one international trading executive, a successful trader is not a conventional corporate or bureaucratic person. He must be an independent thinker - even slightly neurotic. The perfect trader, says this executive, should be arrogant enough to make a statement about the future and take a market position, but tough skinned enough to be wrong and take criticism. The ability to work on a number of projects simultaneously is important. So is a certain philosophical acceptance of frequent dead ends. Of course, the perfect trader has infinite patience and is able to thrive in an unstructured environment.

Every good trader asks himself, 'How much can I lose?' He weighs probable profit against possible loss. Success in commodity trading calls for 'charm, good instincts, luck and audacity - the qualities of a gambler, salesman and entrepreneur rolled into one,' commented another observer.

The commodity trade attracts a lot of dealers, since anyone can make representations of non-trademarked commodities. All you have to do is pick up a phone and convince a commodity firm or a government that you are 'for real' and can actually be of some use. Bombarded with dealers, many governments have tried to establish credibility by demanding a US$50,000 refundable deposit for any offer submitted and a bond equal to ten percent of the transaction if the offer is accepted.

The dealer's chief goal is to make you believe he can help you get your deal through. Part of the trick is reaching this goal is the use - and misuse - of certain key words. Table 13.1 provides a 'Dealer's Dictionary,' a tongue-in-cheek look at dealer semantics and their reality, as experienced by commodity traders.

EXPERIENCE CRITICAL

While conceptual understanding of the commodity is very important, concrete experience with the traded product is more valuable. Grain traders who once labored in the fields are likely to have a sense of the product - an understanding not gained elsewhere. This kind of experience is important in anticipating the impact of various market forces, or in determining the validity of a buyer's quality claims.

Unfortunately in the case of many state trading firms, managers have had no commodity experience at all. In one South American country, the commodity purchasing agency always had a lawyer as its head. 'That's great for making contracts, but of little use in analyzing markets,' commented one observer.

Understanding of logistics is critical in trading. Freight variations are where profit is made or lost. Most profitable trades require 85 percent logistical effort with only 15 percent concentration on marketing and sourcing. Usually the costs of a product are essentially the same at the source, and the market has little deviation. Cargill, perhaps the world's largest commodity firm, considers freight its chief commodity.

One South American firm new to commodity trading made what it thought was a profitable trade, but the trader had chartered a vessel which was too large to enter the harbor of delivery. The profits evaporated when the ship had to be unloaded in another location and the product trucked to the buyer.

BANKS AS ALLIES

Similarly, money management requires special attention. When trading in international commodities, available margins can easily be lost through insensitivity to the cost of money and the timing of its transfer. Extreme efficiency in money management, in tax considerations and in customer relations is essential. One of the most important allies an international

Table 13.1
Dealer's Dictionary

Dealer's choice of words	How they are explained to you	What they really mean
I have contacts	Dealer knows someone to put deal through.	Knows another dealer.
I'm 'in' with a 'high' government official.	Knows 'touchable' bureaucrat who makes purchase decisions.	Friend of his partner's cousin who works on 27th floor.
I would like your cooperation.	10% of sale price for dealer.	20%.
Inside information.	Information that will help you outbid competition.	Information supplied by competition.
100% financing available.	Amount other party will make available to put deal together.	Amount you have to put up to close deal.
My partner is ruler's cousin.	Family members get best deal.	Youngest of ruler's 75 cousins; eldest works for competition.
Make my staff available to you.	Professionals who will work night and day to put deal through.	His driver will take you to bank to cash checks.
If you had more time, we could go to my country place to relax.	Successful deals have enabled me to buy country home.	His mother's house where he goes when money runs out.
Petrodollars.	Dollars that oil producers have to buy your goods.	Money you supply to buy gas for dealer's car.

Source: Grain Trade, by John Freivalds (Stein and Day Publishers, 1976.)

trading firm can have is a sophisticated international bank to arrange credit lines, assure collections, convert currencies and expedite completion of transactions.

The more exclusive an agreement between buyer and seller, the better. As a middleman, even though a contracting principal, it is possible to be undercut by the competition. So exclusivity is important in protecting the trade and in guaranteeing continuity to both buyers and suppliers. However, poorly conceived and drafted agreements of exclusivity can become straitjackets rather than positive marketing tools.

Signed contracts must always be honored. The temptation to back out of unprofitable deals is strong, especially when the original contract was left vague and open to different interpretations. However, one of the most important assets any trader has is the trust and esteem that his supplier and buyers hold for him.

'The commodity trading world is small,' noted one London merchant. 'If someone breaks the rules looking for a quick gain or to get out of a bad position, the trade will hear about it and he will be finished.'

Many trades are made verbally and then confirmed by telex or letter. These verbal agreements have been held up in courts of law. Formal rules and contracts, such as those promulgated by GAFTA (Grain and Feed Trade Association) in London, do exist.

INGENUITY NEEDED

Up-to-date information is critical in trading. One commodity trader stated, 'I don't sell commodities, but rather information. The commodity just happens to be the medium.' Commodity traders are tireless in their quest for that one extra piece of information the competitor or customer does not have.

Traders use a variety of information systems including news services and direct phone and telex lines. One innovative firm obtained some Russian wheat varieties and planted them in North Dakota. It then had infra-red high altitude photos made of their progress and correlated them with on-ground sampling. These results were then compared with photos of the Soviet grain crop to better predict the upcoming harvest.

One US firm which recently entered into international rice trading immediately realized that it lacked good market information. Its first step was to establish a relationship with a rice broker, in this case Jackson Brothers in London. Brokers are often the best source of information since they act as intermediaries between buyers and sellers. Because the broker wanted to get the new firm's business, it was willing to share information. At the same time, the trading firm established agents in all major rice exporting countries. 'This is the only way to know what's going on. By the time any information appears in newsletters or journals, it's old news that's already been acted on,' commented the executive in charge of rice trading.

Commodity trading companies in various stages of growth seem to face quite different problems. The new trading company struggles to gain the 'critical mass' necessary for supporting overhead - telex, travel, and salary. The established group, having survived the initial hard times, faces other pressing problems - exclusive tariffs or quality claim litigation. The very difficulty of long distance business, however, is the reason trading firms exist. For those firms that have personnel with the experience and the personality, that have access to timely and exclusive information, it can be an exciting and profitable challenge.

If marketing commodities requires skill, so does buying them. Cereal deficits in developing countries may leap to 94 million metric tons by the mid-1980s, which at current values represents US$17 billion.

To help these countries do a better job in importing grain, the United Nations Development Program (UNDP) is providing a handbook, advice and training. In a preliminary survey, government officials of grain importing countries told the UNDP directors that they needed the most assistance in securing up-to-date, reliable and comprehensive market information for major imported food commodities; understanding the functioning of world grain markets; taking full advantage of seasonal price fluctuations and patterns of supply; coordinating more efficiently the government agencies involved in importing food; learning alternative procurement methods and commercial practices; taking advantage of price differentials in varying qualities and quantities of grain; and securing the best financial arrangements on ocean transport.

14 Airfreighting high value perishables: flowers from Colombia

CAROL M. MORGAN

A tourist in New Orleans buys a bunch of chrysanthemums from a flower-laden cart. A woman in Milwaukee carefully arranges a bouquet of carnations - a birthday gift from her husband. A man in a Baltimore grocery store picks up a dozen roses for his mother.

All of these persons have something in common: they have purchased flowers grown thousands of kilometers away on the savannah surrounding Bogota, Colombia. Only 32 hours before, the flowers had been growing in the rich, black Colombian soil.

Today flowers are the third largest of Colombia's non-traditional agricultural exports. They are the fifth largest in terms of foreign exchange in the minor exports category. Revenues from their export exceeded US$100 million in 1980, almost 350 times more than the US$300,000 generated in 1968.

Colombia is now the cut flower capital of the world. It produces about 62 percent of the carnations - the mainstay of the cut flower industry - which are grown for sale; 21 percent of the pompons; eight percent of the chrysanthemums; and four percent of the roses.

In 1980, 70 percent of Colombian flower production was shipped to the United States; twenty percent was sold to European countries; and ten percent to other South American countries, Canada, Japan, and Australia.

In 1968 Colombian flowers shipped to the United States were

valued at US$73,098. By 1980 Colombian flowers shipped to the US were worth US$68.9 million, a large slice of the US$3 billion cut flower market there. Today about 50 percent of the carnations, about half the pompons, and seven to ten percent of the roses sold in the United States each year are grown on the Colombian savannah.

Flowers are grown and exported by 120 firms which use 1,000 hectares of land for their cultivation. Flower growing in Colombia is not a family type operation: it is an industrial effort dependent on hired labor, and Colombia flower cultivation has created 40,000 direct unskilled labor jobs. About 11 workers are employed per hectare of carnations produced. In this highly labor intensive industry, labor represents about 50 percent of total costs.

THE ORIGINAL INVESTORS

Colombia has reached a dominant position in flower exports in only a dozen years. Flowers were first grown commercially in Colombia in 1964, when about one-half hectare of savannah was sprinkled with carnation seeds. Given Colombia's exceedingly low per capita income, the flower growing industry there could not look forward to rapid expansion without exporting.

By 1968 there were eight producer organizations and total exports were valued at US$277,000. In 1970 there were 31 organizations and exports had grown fourfold to US$976,000. Even then 78 percent of the flowers produced in Colombia were shipped to the United States.

One influence on the 28 percent growth of the flower industry in Colombia between 1968 and 1970 came from the chance meeting of three men. They were to form one of the early flower growing organizations in Colombia and assist in the industry's new and expanded course.

One of these persons, Dave Cheever, had discovered that the savannah surrounding Bogota had an almost perfect climate for growing carnations. The temperature there is cool and constant - 18°C to 21°C year round. Its soil is loose and black, and the days are almost evenly divided between hours of light and darkness. Carnations thrive under these conditions and grow there almost like weeds. Flower growers, in fact, average 3.2 crops per year there.

Harmon Brown, another of the original investors, was a flower grower in California USA who was looking for new opportunities. In 1969 when the Colombian flower growing project was first developed, the cost of a hectare of land around San Diego was US$45,000 compared to US$5,000 in Bogota. At that time labor costs were around US$20 to US$25 per man day in the US, compared to US$1.30 per day in Bogota. The

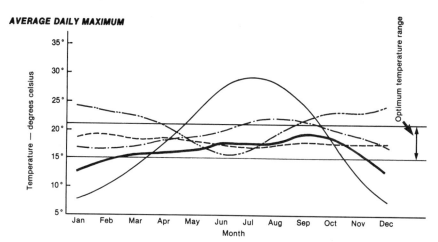

AVERAGE DAILY MAXIMUM

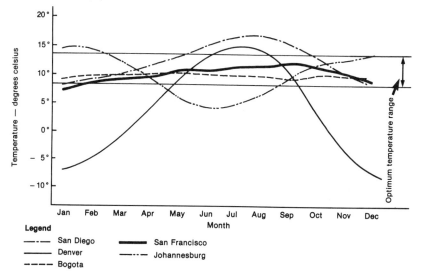

AVERAGE DAILY MINIMUM

Legend

—·— San Diego   ▬▬▬ San Francisco
——— Denver   —··— Johannesburg
- - - - Bogota

Figure 14.1 Temperature relationships in five carnation
growing areas

original investors knew that if they could produce a high
quality product at a lower cost and sell it at US prices, they
could make an excellent profit.

The third member of the original team was Bill Mott, then a
consultant for Development and Resources Corporation, an
international firm which was searching for agricultural
investments in South America.

Once they were committed to a Colombian flower venture, the original three members brought in a manager with experience in Colombian agriculture. As Harmon Brown has commented, 'More than anything, success in the flower business depends on management.'

With the management team assembled, operations began in October, 1969. The venture became Floramerica, a farm outside of Bogota, and Sunburst Farms, a cut flower marketing venture in Miami. By 1977 Floramerica was growing eight percent of all the carnations and pompons sold in the United States. Sales in that year from both operations were between US$7 and US$8 million, twice the amount which had been originally projected. In 1976, the pre-tax profit of both operations was US$800,000.

The flower growing industry in Colombia is dominated by small operations: only 23 percent of the plots are larger than five hectares. Most flower producers in Colombia grow only one flower and do not produce other crops. Floramerica is now the largest flower producer in the Colombian flower industry with approximately 24 hectares in greenhouses, six hectares in field crops, and 80 hectares in vegetables.

Besides the excellent climate and growing conditions, the key factor in the success of Floramerica farms was the availability of air transportation and the interest of major air carriers in handling exports. At that time, shipping costs from Bogota to Miami were reasonable. In 1969 it cost US$0.08 to ship a bunch of carnations from Bogota to Miami, where they sold for US$1.05. Thanks to the energy crisis, shipping costs have increased three and fourfold over the past twelve years. It now costs US$0.27 to ship the same bunch of flowers from Bogota to Miami, while the price has increased to US$1.42.

Another important influence on the success of the new project was the favorable attitude of the Colombian government.

FINANCING

When the project was undertaken in 1969, the initial capital structure for both companies consisted of US$110,000 in equity and US$200,000 in five year and short term loans. In retrospect, Harmon Brown believes that, 'Most of the financing was short term when what we should have had was long term. But you take what you can get.'

The cut flower venture in Colombia expanded rapidly. Of course, both companies suffered through the minor problems always encountered in dealing with perishable agricultural products. However, problems of a larger magnitude hit

Floramerica and Sunburst in 1971 and 1974. The earlier crisis developed when two of the partners wanted to be bought out. Development and Resources Corporation felt it had accomplished its goals. When D & R sold out in 1971, it was rewarded with a 500 percent return on its money: a US$29,000 investment paid US$150,000 after 18 months.

Dave Cheever, another original investor, also wanted to go his own way. The departure of these two partners drained away money which should have been reinvested.

During the next few years, Floramerica continued to grow and to diversify, producing crops other than flowers. Some of this experimentation was successful, some was not. The expansion, however, continued to be financed with borrowed money.

MONEY PROBLEMS

In 1974 a crisis occurred when a credit crunch developed, accompanied by high interest rates. The banks which had loaned money to Floramerica wanted their short term notes paid off. At that time Floramerica was almost US$1.5 million in debt, and its interest costs soared.

Another negative influence on Floramerica's fortunes occurred in 1974 when the Colombian government terminated its 13 percent rebate to the flower growers on exports. The rebate had been worth US$250,000 to Floramerica in 1974, tax free.

The recession in 1974 reduced discretionary incomes and the market price for cut flowers fell. The US market, which still views flowers as a 'special event' purchase, cut them out.

As the prices for flowers fell, the production of flowers tripled. In 1970 there were 31 organizations growing flowers; by 1973 there were 95. This increase in the number of flower producers was stimulated by the International Flower Exposition held in Bogota. As a result of that favorable meeting, the value of cut flowers from Bogota increased from US$3.1 million to US$8.4 million.

Faced with negative market conditions, Floramerica produced its own set of complications. In Brown's words, 'We had grown so fast that our management systems couldn't keep up.' By that time Floramerica had also bought a cargo airlines which proved to be a cash and management drain.

Losing money in 1974, Floramerica and Sunburst Farms were forced to sell a majority interest in the two companies to secure additional capital. By 1975, however, the flower market had turned around and between mid-1975 and mid-1976, Floramerica and Sunburst earned about US$750,000 net before taxes.

The last of the three original investors, Harmon Brown, sold out in the fall of 1976. At that time he reviewed the importance of the contribution to cut flower production in Colombia by Floramerica and Sunburst. 'We like to think,' he said, 'that we made a number of innovations, but the two things that stand out involve market development and personnel.'

MARKETING

Sunburst Farms placed special emphasis on developing a mass market for cut flowers. For example, it worked closely with the Stop & Shop chain of Boston to supply their 27 in-store flower shops. It developed a rack-jobbing supply operation for 200 Winn Dixie supermarkets which generated US$700,000 in sales.

In the US, the vast majority of flowers are sold around five specific times: Mother's Day, Valentine's Day, Easter, Secretary's Week, and Christmas. Floramerica and Sunburst developed a special cold storage program that allows them to store flowers 30 days before these key flower purchasing holidays. Since retail prices for flowers increase 30-40 percent during these peak times, the wholesaler as well as the retailer benefit from having cold storage available.

On the personnel side, Floramerica had 850 employees and 10 technically trained Colombian supervisors in 1977. Brown is justifiably proud of the high retention rate of these employees, 'All the other new growers wanted these people,' he says, 'but over six years we lost only two key people.' Fringe benefits which Brown's company gave its employees included: uniforms and clothing supplies; medical services for the entire family, including grandparents; a night school program; training in the USA for technical staff; and a bicycle financing program.

Brown, speaking in 1977, believed that the opportunities in Colombia were still fantastic. 'The country is unique in that it has almost any climate you want. Good quality land, water, and labor are available.' He said, however, that floraculture there would now have to be developed differently. But other crops, such as mushrooms, asparagus or strawberries, '...look attractive. Frankly, I think we can fly fresh vegetables from Colombia to Baltimore for the same cost as trucking produce from San Francisco.' It is still true that the cost of shipping flowers from Colombia to US East Coast markets is about the same as shipping there from the West Coast of the USA.

However, it cannot be denied that the favorable factors which led to the formation of Floramerica and Sunburst Farms began to dissipate in the 1970s. Unions began to organize floraculture workers, and salaries rose from US$1.30 per day to US$5.00 per day. Salaries have, in fact, increased by 30 percent over the past four years. A typical floraculture worker in Colombia earns US$150 per month in salary and a similar amount in benefits. These expenses account for half of the production costs of cut flowers in Colombia.

Profits have also been reduced by higher land prices, high interest rates, and steeper prices for petroleum products. Each year for the past five years, these factors have increased the cost of producing flowers in Colombia. In addition, overproduction of cut flowers in Colombia complicates the profit picture, while a recession casts a gloomy shadow over the ability of Colombian floraculture to expand.

Throughout its development, the flower industry in Colombia has also faced the problem of its lack of an agriculture experimentation and education service to assist its growth. 'One result,' says Brown, 'is a growing disease problem. The soil in Colombia is now over-infected.' This infestation affects both the shelf-life and the size of Colombian flowers.

The Colombians must develop a way of increasing the demand for their flowers. Price increases in cut flowers have not kept pace with rising costs, and the lackluster performance of the US flower market for the past six years has not helped producers absorb their fixed costs.

Although Colombia can deliver a superior product which is grown year-round, it is possible that increases in labor, land, and energy costs will shift cut flower production to new areas, such as the Dominican Republic, Mexico, or Venezuela.

15 Sabritas' backward integration into agricultural production

DENNIS A. JOHNSON

When Sabritas, SA, began operations in 1967, it had no intention of developing potato fields in the cool Mexican plateaus. Corporate strategy outlined a processing and marketing plan for snack foods in a country uncluttered by competition. A sharp drop in potato production, however, forced the company to launch a seed improvement program, or face the consequences of a diminishing supply of raw material.

Resembling an agricultural demonstration project, the seed program led Sabritas to invest several years and several million dollars in studying imported potato seed strains. It is clear today that the decision by Sabritas President John A. Warner and his management team in the mid 1970s to develop new sources of potatoes helped insure the firm's continued growth in the Mexican snack food industry.

The story of how Sabritas, a wholly-owned subsidiary of Pepsico, Inc., USA, introduced hybrid potato farming to Mexico is but one success for the company since it acquired a modest home based potato chip kitchen in Mexico City 14 years ago and turned it into the market leader. The company has maintained its impressive growth and 14 percent profit margins despite restrictive foreign investment laws, government censure of 'junk food' manufacturers, and increasingly competitive and less favorable market conditions.

SEIZING A MARKET

At the time Sabritas bought out Pedro Noriega's potato chip line, 'Selectos,' and the 37 bicycles used for distribution to neighborhood grocery stores, Mexico was ready for mass marketed snack foods. Coca-Cola and Pepsi-Cola soft drinks had been introduced to the Mexicans in the 1930s. The habit of sipping 'refrescos' and eating snacks, whether purchased from an independent street vendor or made at home, was not new.

Capitalizing on existing cultural habits, Sabritas offered its brand of plain potato chips and several other snacks, including Ruffle potato chips, Fritos corn chips, Adobadas, Doritos, Nachos, Cheetos, Sabritones and pork rinds. Some of these imitated snacks Mexicans made at home; others were simple variations of typical potato or corn products.

Sabritas' early success was encouraged by a favorable government policy towards multinationals, the country's fast paced industrialization, a healthy eight percent growth rate in gross national product, and snack food trends in affluent countries the Mexicans were eager to copy. Within five years – from 1967 to 1972 – the company tripled the size of its Mexico City plant and constructed a second facility in Guadalajara, northwest of the capital city. With completion of the new site, Pepsico's investment in the Latin America venture totalled US$1.2 million. Sales had also risen dramatically, climbing from US$1.8 million in 1968, one year after opening the plant in Mexico City, to over US$100 million a decade later.

Keeping pace with consumer demand meant substituting Volkswagen vans for the bicycle distribution system. The drivers became the crucial link in the company's marketing and distribution plan, crisscrossing the country in an intricate network of sales routes.

'The heart of the company rests with the route salesmen', said Rodolfo P. Jacinto, a division manager. 'We've been able to saturate the country, and today we have over 3,000 routes. By far, it's one of the best distribution systems in Mexico,' Jacinto boasted, explaining the drivers pick up the products from regional warehouses and distribute them to the family owned stores and neighborhood shops along their routes. Supermarkets represent only six percent of sales.

SABRITAS SEED PROGRAM

During the early 1970s, Sabritas found its growth constrained by an insufficient supply of frying potatoes. Production of potatoes in Mexico was lagging behind market demand. Annual per capita consumption of potatoes had increased from 9.7

109

kilos in 1964 to 11.2 kilos in 1974. Population was growing at an annual rate of 3.4 percent, yet the Ministry of Agriculture estimated that the area sown with potatoes had decreased from 43,800 hectares in 1964 to 32,200 hectares in 1974.

Potato hectarage was decreasing due to the golden nematode ('Heretodera rostochiensis'), a potato disease which causes root knots and shriveled tubers. Once introduced into the soil, it will persist indefinitely. Agronomists found that some farmers were unknowingly helping to spread the disease. An infected potato, when planted, will yield some large healthy potatoes and some shriveled diseased potatoes. Since only the large potatoes were commercially acceptable, farmers were selling the large potatoes and keeping the infected potatoes for seed. The infected seed then yielded fewer healthy potatoes and more shriveled potatoes; the cycle continued until the farmer abandoned potato production.

As the quality of available potatoes declined, and the area sown with potatoes continued to decrease, the management of Sabritas decided in 1974 to initiate a potato improvement program to help assure potato supply.

The potato improvement program presented the management of Sabritas with a difficult challenge since it involved seed research, seed multiplication, and agricultural extension, areas in which the company had no experience. Furthermore, as a private manufacturing concern, Sabritas was prohibited by Mexican law from farming or importing seed.

SEEDS FOR THE INDUSTRY

With its basic resource in jeopardy, Sabritas sought government approval to form a non-profit organization, Seeds for the Industry, S.C. (SISC), which would enable the corporation to conduct potato seed research despite laws preventing private companies from integrating agricultural production and processing.

Through SISC, Sabritas was able to lease farmland and import potato seeds. A variety of seeds were evaluated at a research center in Tinguindin, Michoacan, northwest of Mexico City. Initial tests were conducted on the Mexican potato Alpha, followed by an imported variety which later became diseased and was destroyed. In 1976 several seeds were imported from the US and Holland and tested under clonal selection, a method SISC used to discard unsuitable plants and tubers. Later tests showed the yellow-colored Dutch varieties more popular with Mexican consumers than the US white seed varieties.

To insure that the seeds remained free of contamination, the tubers were planted one meter apart, allowing the scientists enough room to move around the plants without accidentally

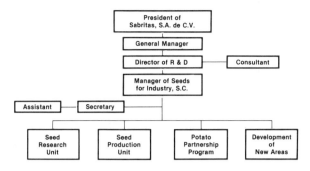

Figure 15.1 Sabritas Organizational Structure of Seeds for
the Industry, S.C.

touching the leaves and passing along germs. Only the best
seeds were selected from the initial crop - 900 out of 3,000
tubers. During the second planting the seeds were placed in
families of 20, each family containing tubers of one variety.
Again a rigid selection process insured only the best seeds
were used for the third planting.

During the last propagation, the seeds were grouped in
families of 40. Seed sanitation or rogueing was used to insure
only the highest quality seeds were selected for founding
stock.

After developing several suitable seeds, the Mexican Alpha,
Patrone and the high altitude strain Prevalent, SISC leased
450 hectares of land to multiply a base supply. High yields
were obtained using 1,200 kilos of fertilizer per hectare.
After harvesting in October and November, the seeds were
shipped to farmers for planting.

PARTNERSHIP PROGRAM

Because Sabritas could not grow the potatoes directly, a
second organization was formed, the Potato Partnership
Program, to contract farmers to produce the potatoes. SISC
provided the necessary seeds, financial and technical
assistance, and a guaranteed market. In turn, farmers agreed
to sell 60 percent of their crop to Sabritas at a prearranged
price, and to turn over 40 percent to the corporation under a
partnership provision in the contract. Sabritas purchased all
potatoes meeting its quality standard, and found buyers for
the potatoes it rejected.

Farmers using the hybrid seeds nearly doubled their
production of potatoes per hectare, increasing yields from

11.3 MT to 20 MT per hectare. Further incentives were offered to interest farmers in obtaining even higher yields: 70 percent of production about 20 MT per hectare would belong to the farmer and 30 percent to Sabritas.

Potato farming is capital intensive. A 1976 study by the Ministry of Agriculture estimated that the costs of production of large scale efficient potato farmers were US$6,000 per hectare, excluding the cost of the land. The study indicated that while the average agricultural bank loan extended in 1976 had been US$124 per hectare, the average bank loan to potato farmers had been US$1,552 per hectare, second only in annual crops to tomato farmers. Jaime Alvarez, President of SISC and the person who created the Potato Partnership Program, stated: 'We are really financiers, not farmers.'

Although the program has been quite successful, Sabritas hopes to reduce costs by matching potato production with potato chip demand, and insuring a year round potato supply in order to reduce storage and spoilage problems. Sabritas is also striving to increase the number of potatoes purchased through the partnership. In 1979, 35 percent of its potatoes cam through the program; this figure increased to 50 percent in 1980. Corporate officers are optimistic the amount can reach 70 percent in the near future.

Sabritas is also attempting to expand potato production to areas near its processing plants in Mexico City, Guadalajara and Saltillo, reducing transportation and shipping costs.

Not only has the seed program solved a major raw material supply problem, it has helped to boost potato harvests in the country. The project has also provided Sabritas with a model for maize and wheat research programs.

INVESTMENT PROBLEMS

The seed program saved Sabritas from a potentially disastrous supply problem despite a tangle of government rules that prevented the corporation from integrating production and processing. Another obstacle - limited production capability - was circumvented during negotiations with government officials for permits to construct a third potato chip factory at Saltillo, near Monterrey. The plant, which went into operation in 1980, insured that production could keep pace with rising sales.

Unlike the Mexico City and Guadalajara plants, construction of the Saltillo facility came in the wake of the Foreign Investment Act of 1973, the law bringing an end to the days of unrestricted development by foreign subsidiaries. Bargaining continued over two years, and Sabritas made a number of concessions requiring expansion into exports of both finished sporting goods through the Pepsico subsidiary Wilson Sporting Goods, and of snack foods to the United States. Such trade-offs were necessary, company officers explain, despite marginal profitability. Last year Sabritas lost US$60,000 on the sporting goods.

Still pending are two additional snack food processing plants, facilities Sabritas expects to open by 1985, according to development strategies. The fourth plant will likely be located near Mexico City, and the fifth is proposed near the US-Mexican border for export production.

Remarkably, Sabritas' sales volume and market share have continued to grow despite a business environment that has become increasingly hostile. In 1978 the privately-held Barcel Productos, SA, purchased the Kellogg Foods, Inc, USA, line of snacks and initiated a major advertising campaign. Barcel succeeded in taking over 20 percent of the market, mostly at the expense of smaller, regional brand potato chips.

'Having competition today could work to the advantage of Sabritas,' said Pepsico Foods International executive Allan Pitman. 'Barcel will strengthen the market, and keep Sabritas on its toes,' Pitman added, noting that Sabritas now controls 70 percent of the market.

LEGISLATING NUTRITION

A more serious threat to Sabritas, as well as to other snack food processors, is government control. The National Institute for Consumer Protection, a federally-funded organization, has mounted a public campaign to expose Sabritas, Barcel and others as manufacturers of nutritionally worthless 'junk' foods. In July, 1979, the Institute, publisher of 'Revista del Consumidor' (Consumer Magazine), took Sabritas to task in an article charging the company's products were nothing more than expensive potatoes treated with oil and salt. In a subsequent article, the consumer group did an expose of the entire soft drink, snack food and candy industry, condemning it as a marketer of high-priced foods that were decaying the diets of the nation's children.

The government's campaign against snack food led in 1978 to restricting the type of television advertising Sabritas and others can direct towards children. In 1980, President Jose Lopez Portillo further stressed the importance of minimum per capita daily diets with at least 80 grams of protein and 2,750 calories during his announcement of the 'Sistema Alimentario Mexicano,' a program to wean the country of grain and maize imports.

In response to these government campaigns, considered by some snack food promoters as unethical, Sabritas is gearing up its own 'fact campaign.' Warner says there is nothing harmful or unhealthy about Sabritas snacks, and stresses the products satisfy the hunger of a nation 'on the move.' Sabritas has provided the industry with high quality products that are safe to eat, compared with other lesser known brands often packaged without labels.

Sabritas quality standards demand that 75 percent of all potatoes delivered to their processing plants be greater than 45 millimeters in diameter. All potatoes must be without cuts and appear healthy. Since potatoes with deep 'eyes' do not peel well, they are also rejected. Potatoes are sampled for color, sugar content, and potato solid content. Those with a sugar content over one percent are rejected because the sugar would burn in the frying process, leaving the chip a dark brown shade which consumers dislike.

Potatoes are washed and peeled by strong hot water jets and then automatically placed on a conveyor belt where they are inspected once again. Unhealthy looking potatoes are discarded, and overly large potatoes are chopped. Large potatoes make large chips which fill the cellophane bags with too few chips. Furthermore, large potato chips tend to break in handling, leaving a bag full of broken chips which consumers do not like. The potatoes are then cut into flat or 'ruffled' patterns and fried in oil and salt at 160°C. The chips are then cooled, bagged, inspected, and placed in cartons for distribution. The entire process from washing to bagging takes less than five minutes.

Besides its own public relations campaign, Sabritas is consumer-testing a new, wheat-based snack that is vitamin and protein enriched. Sabritas officials are hopeful this product, Nutri-Snack, will help to improve its image among consumers. The company has also proposed to help establish a school lunch program. The proposal includes several fortified products – powdered drink, nutritional snack, brownie and bean dip – and is modeled after programs in the United States. However, government officials have not yet responded to the idea.

Nearly 6,000 people, primarily Mexicans, are currently employed by Sabritas, which last year tallied over US$163.2 million in sales. Projections call for sales over US$200 million in 1981.

Strong competition, confining government policy and new consumer attitudes have combined to force Sabritas into defending gains of the 1960s and 1970s at the expense of expansion in the 1980s. More and more emphasis will be placed on its role as a corporate citizen, and on its contributions to the Mexican economy.

Whether Sabritas can continue its long term growth in a country becoming increasingly nationalistic and maintain profit margins and sales records in an economy with 40 percent inflation and a declining peso are the troubling questions with no easy solutions which Sabritas faces today.

16 A lobster tale: the collective marketing of Brazilian seafood

DAVID LEVY

'I was going back and forth all the time,' lamented Leonard Parry, manager of Internor, the North American subsidiary of Interbras. During the past four years, Parry has been in perpetual motion between New York, Rio de Janeiro and Fortaleza, Brazil, in organizing 19 separate fishing boat operators and cooperatives into one international marketing organization. The success of his efforts is shown in the fact that Brazil is now the largest exporter of lobster tails to the US, earning some US$32 million in foreign exchange in 1979; in 1980, Interbras hopes to reach US$50 million.

Interbras is a state trading company organized by the Brazilian government in 1976 for the express purpose of developing exports from Brazil. Created as a direct response to OPEC oil price increases, Interbras is a subsidiary company of Petrobras, the largest company in Brazil with sales of US$10 billion. To pay for oil imports, Brazil had to generate foreign exchange earnings through increased exports. At the present time, Interbras trades in a number of commodities including wheat, coffee, maize, sugar, soybeans, soybean oil and bran, as well as manufactured goods and services.

POTENTIAL FOR PROFITS

Brazil's extensive coastline has ample supplies of fish and other seafood, and Interbras set out to examine what could be

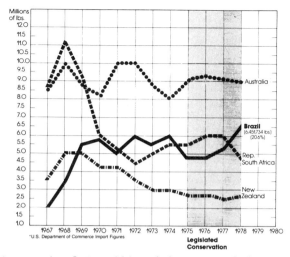

Figure 16.1 Growth of Brazilian lobster tail imports into the
United States compared with other major suppliers

done to increase the amount of foreign exchange coming from
this sector, particularly with lobsters. The size of the US
lobster tail market was large and inviting: US$124 million in
1974, by 1978 it had grown to US$180 million. Brazil's
production had remained constant at 14 million kilos, due in
part to conservation measures adopted by the various exporting
governments. Internor believed that Brazil could increase its
share of the market if it could overcome a number of problems.
Specifically, Internor needed to: convince Interbras
headquarters that a collective marketing project was feasible;
organize the fishing operators to provide a stable, dependable
supply; develop a brand identity for Brazilian lobster tails
in the United States to compete against other exporting
countries; establish a distribution network within the United
States to offer a stable on-call supply; and show a profit
while doing all of the above.

THE OLD STRUCTURE

When Parry first came to Interbras, he had an idea that
enormous opportunities existed for the fragmented Brazilian
lobster industry:

> There were 15 or 16 different US importers who would
> all go down to Brazil and buy from different people.
> So there was one level of competition among the

117

producers selling to the buyers. Then the importers came up to the US and competed among themselves to sell to the distributors and restaurants.

Only the US buyers benefited from this structure.

To remove some of the competition, Interbras short-circuited the established channels and, as Parry describes, 'stepped in on a commercial basis and paid a better return to the shippers in return for exclusivity on the product. We then pooled the lobsters and sold through US brokers who did not overlap.' The business was done directly with only one middleman, Interbras.

By bringing some marketing efficiencies into the system which did not exist before, Interbras was able to pay a premium to the shipper and thereby obtain a commanding position. According to Parry, 'The overall purpose was to ensure that as much value went back to the Brazilian economy as possible - that's our overall purpose in life.'

Typically the lobster fishing was done by a small fisherman. 'I don't know if there is such a thing as a typical one,' notes Parry. The three or four largest have fleets of 40 boats each, ranging in size from 6 meters to 15 meters long. While some of the larger boats have a freezing plant on board, the smaller ones take ice on board and ice the tails.

Parry personally had four meetings with the skippers over a period of nine months while the Rio and Fortaleza staff conducted many more. Not everyone went along with the concept of 'cooperative marketing.'

There were several objections. Some skippers were reluctant to work with a government agency, sensing it would turn out to be another form of taxation. Others had very good relationships with importers and did not want to disrupt them. Finally, several operators were concerned that Interbras might form a production cooperative and take away their jobs.

Success has muffled the objectors. When Interbras began this program in 1979 with a core of perhaps 50 percent of the skippers, it now has 85-90 percent of the lobster tail exporters under its wing.

PRICING

Interbras went in on a straight competitive basis against what other US importers were paying from Brazil. Prices during the early part of 1980 were US$15.50/kilo.

However, in setting prices, Interbras introduced some new features. Interbras bids for the product in Brazil with a firm price which it holds good for three months. On the selling end, the lobster tails are also offered at one unchanging price for the entire three-month period. Traditionally, the market price has vacillated in response to changes in the supply and demand forces as the product was sold on a 'spot' basis. Interbras, in a sense, offers a short term fixed-price contract as seller and buyer.

'What we have done,' Parry claims, 'is bring an inherent stability to the market. We've maintained the same price throughout the year. That's an advantage to the restaurant owner because he knows where he can go and what he has to pay.'

Another incentive to producers is a profit sharing scheme. If the lobsters are sold at prices above Interbras' margin goal, any excess profits are returned to the cooperative.

Although Interbras buys almost the entire local production, all but eliminating competition, this at the same time creates an enormous risk. If the market were to weaken or collapse, Interbras would face serious problems trying to honor all its contracts with local fishermen. Unlike most commodity markets, there is no institutionalized way to 'hedge' lobsters.

DEVELOPING AN IDENTITY

For years the South Africans have promoted their lobsters in the United States through the South African Seafood Association, the exclusive importer and distributor of South African lobsters. Throughout the industry, it is commonly agreed that their promotional efforts have created an enviable top-quality image for the South African lobster. Buyers have long been accustomed to seek out South African lobster tails, associating them with the superior grade competitors.

Using the South African example more or less as a model, Interbras formed Brasmar (Brazilian Seafood Marketing Associates) to give identity to Brazil's competing lobsters. The first order of business was to mold a unified image for the Brazilian imports, accomplished in part by packing the lobsters in sturdy sea-worthy cartons conspicuously marked with the 'Brasmar' label. Before the Brasmar labeling, the various producers had branded their own production individually, which confused buyers and created no uniform product identification. Now the Brazilian lobsters are all presented with a single image, an image which may erode the strong market position of the South Africans.

The marketing theme 'A Lobster Tail for All Seasons' was adopted. It has been run in the major trade publications read by seafood buyers in the US.

However, a brand name is meaningless if it does not represent a certain level of quality. To ensure that the lobsters are of the highest caliber, Interbras has instigated a rigorous quality control system. Joe Gribbon of Harrison and

Pierce, a major US seafood broker, praises the Interbras quality control effort. 'They've been forward-thinking in having quality control experts go to Brazil to show the producers what has to be done in terms of the US market. Quality problems have been held to a bare minimum.'

Specifically, lobster buyers are looking for uniformity of size (portion control), so the Interbras quality control experts have systematically graded Brazilian lobsters in 14 different size categories (instead of the usual six) from 3 to 16 ounces (84 to 448 grams). Each 4.5 kilo carton contains similar sized lobster tails with those of 5 ounces (140 grams) the most popular. With this system, restaurant owners have fewer surprises when they open a case and can feel confident they are serving consistently first-rate tails. Scrambled cartons of lobster tails in various and disproportionate sizes have been eliminated.

Interbras has eliminated some of the original participants in the collective marketing program because they failed to maintain quality.

DEVELOPING A DISTRIBUTION NETWORK

To market the amount of lobster tails that Internor was contemplating required one of two distribution methods. It was necessary either to build up an internal sales force or to use established brokers and distributors. It was quickly decided that using established brokers and distributors would be the more efficient and cheaper method.

Some of the established distributors of lobster tails did not want a new player in the market and a low-level campaign to discredit Internor began. Rumors relating to the honesty and viability of the operation circulated, but the campaign proved ineffective. Many brokers wanted to handle the Internor business. Internor eventually chose four brokers from the more than 300 in the US. They are actually more than brokers as Internor invoices them directly.

To complement the distribution network, Internor wanted to maintain an inventory of lobster tails at key locations across the US. Buyers seemed more concerned about supply than price and, as a result, relations were established with public cold storage warehouses in New York, Philadelphia, Baltimore, Los Angeles, Chicago, New Orleans and Boston. At present, the turnover for lobster tails is between three and five months. The goal is three months in storage.

Internor's interest cost is in carrying the float from the time it pays the fishing operators (by letter of credit) to the time the brokers send checks for their purchases.

Figure 16.2 Brasmar Marketing Chain

PROFITABILITY OF THE ENTERPRISE

At the present time, 15 people are involved in the collective marketing program in the US and Brazil. The revenues from the operation cover expenses and leave a nice profit margin, according to Interbras.

Of greater importance, perhaps, is the fact that the collective marketing by Brasmar is providing Brazil with US$6 million more than under the old form of marketing.

With the lobster business going nicely, Interbras managers are looking for other opportunities that might fit the well-established seafood network in the United States. Looking forward optimistically, Parry says, 'From lobsters we can move to shrimp, which is five times the size of the lobster business. The Brazilian shrimp industry is in its infancy; in fact, the whole Brazilian fishing industry is rather primitive.'

About three years ago, the Brazilians began to exercise the 320 km offshore fishing rights limit and are no longer giving permits to foreign fleets to fish for shrimp. That action may well open the door for Brazil's next success story – the development, consolidation and promotion of an international shrimp business.

17 How 'Chiquita' helped United Fruit

JOHN M. FOX

It is the dream of every commodity producer to get a premium price for his product. To get this price, of course, high quality standards are necessary, and sometimes even this is not enough. When the United Fruit Company was faced with the problems of dealing with a serious plant disease that forced it to change banana varieties and shipping techniques, an opportunity arose to brand its bananas and thus distinguish them in the marketplace to achieve the premium price.

This opportunity marked the beginning of a new era that converted a highly perishable tropical commodity into an important item of world trade. How the United Fruit Company built up this business and introduced such innovations as boxing and branding bananas offers an example of how to increase revenues to other producers of tropical commodities such as coffee, tropical fruits, cocoa and tea.

'I'M CHIQUITA BANANA AND I'M HERE TO SAY...'

Nearly everyone in the US over 25 years old remembers 'I'm Chiquita Banana and I'm here to say...' - the first line of one of the most popular commercial songs ever produced. It was heard for nearly ten years, from the mid-1940s until the mid-1950s, reminding the consumer never to put bananas in the refrigerator. Although at the time there was no such thing as a Chiquita branded banana in the grocery stores and supermarkets, it made economic sense for the United Fruit Company to spend its advertising dollars this way. It encouraged the purchase and consumption of bananas, and since United owned a very high share of the market, it enjoyed most of the benefits. It also kept the fruit out in plain sight where it was more likely to be eaten.

That was back in the mid-1950s. Profits for 'The Fruit Company' (as it was known in the trade and throughout Central America) were handsome indeed. In 1953 the company earned just less than US$45 million - a net return of approximately 15 per cent on the sales dollar! Not bad for any business, let alone the food business.

Ten years later, the picture had changed dramatically. In 1963, with a comparable sales dollar volume, the company lost US$500,000. No longer was United Fruit the major source of quality bananas. No longer was the 'Great White Fleet,' as United Fruit's ocean ships were called, the only dependable furnisher of refrigerated transport of the fruit from the tropics. No longer could the company count on a predictable US$2.00 gross profit per hundred-weight of bananas. By 1963, tropical production costs had gone up and average sales prices had dropped to the point where the returns were often less than the cost of growing and shipping the bananas to the States.

PROBLEMS DEVELOP

What had happened to bring United Fruit down? First, there was the emergence of Ecuador as a major low-cost producer of bananas. With their government's financial help and a spectacularly fertile volcanic soil, the Ecuador growers in less than ten short years had taken over the number one spot in world banana production. For example, in 1952 Ecuador was exporting only 216,000 MT of bananas, but by 1962, exports had increased to 991,000 MT. The Ecuadorian Government had built the necessary infrastructure of roads, packing houses, railroads and wharves for its growers, whose holdings ranged in size from ten to several thousand hectares. The grower, therefore, did not have to add on this infrastructural cost to his sales price as did United Fruit.

Second, Panama disease, the scourge of the Gros Michel variety of banana, was making increasing inroads on the Fruit Company's Central American plantations. Once this fusarium wilt virus became established in a Gros Michel farm - which it did in seemingly shorter and shorter time spans from the initial planting - the farm was doomed. United Fruit had spent millions of US dollars in attempts to restore and salvage the contaminated farms with their huge infrastructure investments, all to no avail. The only apparent solution was to open up new hectarages of virgin rain forest. By 1963, the company was replacing 6,000 hectares of banana lands a year just to stay even, at a capital drain of between US$25 and US$30 million annually.

Third, the US Department of Justice had moved into the picture with an antitrust action that was settled (or at least temporarily stalled) by a consent decree that curtailed the company's marketing and shipping clout considerably, and that would eventually require United to create a competitor in the US of approximately one-third its size.

United Fruit Company was a totally integrated operation, which was necessary due to the exceptionally heavy capital requirements for establishing and maintaining hectarage, the encroachment of disease, the recurrent blowdowns and floods that led to a diversity of sources of supply, and the complicated logistics of distribution.

Finally, and most important of all, the combination of the above factors turned the banana business into a commodity auction. The trade, the chain stores, and the banana ripener-distributors were in complete control of the US banana market. They could and did dictate the price, and the result was pure economic chaos for the corporate producers. The Ecuadorean grower, with his lower costs and no need to build houses and roads for his workers, was thriving. The trade was doing fine. The banana companies, chiefly United and Standard Fruit, were in deep trouble.

NEW APPROACHES CALLED FOR

A new management team was brought in which quickly grasped the need for a major rethinking of the company's operating policies and organizational structure. Up to this point, United had been run as three nearly separate and autonomous entities: production, shipping and sales. Tropical production was managed from Panama; the fleet operated from New Orleans; sales was masterminded in New York. Theoretically, this was all coordinated by the corporate headquarters group in Boston. It may have worked in the 1940s, but it wasn't working in the 1960s.

The new managers moved the key people responsible for tropical production, shipping and marketing to new quarters in Boston to attack the two most urgent problems that had to be solved if the company was to stay afloat: the high cost of replacing Panama disease riddled farms and the growing marketing problems facing the company.

The banana belongs to the genus 'Musa,' in reality a large herb. The Gros Michel variety was the favorite of the United Fruit agronomists for four main reasons: It produced large bananas, ripened uniformly, withstood the hazards of handling, and possessed a longer retail shelf life. But this variety, nicknamed 'Big Mike' by the company agronomists, was susceptible to Panama disease.

There was resistance on the part of some agronomists to finding a replacement. Apart from the fear of an adverse consumer reaction to anything but the Gros Michel variety, there was a reluctance to abandon the huge investment the company had made in the existing varieties. The assembly of a modern banana producing unit of 8,000 hectares in the mid 1950s cost between US$20 and US$25 million. But regardless of the cost, the new management saw no future with 'Big Mike.'

Agronomy teams were sent all over the world to collect banana varieties that might be better than the Gros Michel. Among the 400 specimens that were shipped to a quarantined research facility in Honduras was a variety that seemed to be the answer to United Fruit's problems. It was a variety named Valery that had been discovered in Vietnam.

Resistant to Panama disease, the Valery could be planted in areas that had been abandoned but were already served by roads, housing, and irrigation systems, which were, in fact, ready for production at a minimum cost. As a further bonus, the Valery was a much lower growing plant (about 2.5 meters), and it could withstand higher winds than the Gros Michel, which could stand as high as six meters. Being shorter, the Valery was easier to harvest. In addition, a banana-laden stem of Valery could weigh as much as 45 kilos, compared to 34 kilos for the Gros Michel.

However, there were some severe problems with the shipping and marketing of the Valery: the fruit was more tender and much more easily bruised, and the stems were easily broken when transported from farm to the US ripeners who were United's customers; it was more difficult to ripen than the Gros Michel; and the sales department was solidly against it, viewing it an inferior banana.

OVERCOMING THE HANDLING PROBLEM

Four characteristics of the banana heavily affect and influence its handling requirements: the fruit bruises easily; it has a lifespan of 21 days from the time of cutting to the retail shelf; significant variations in either temperature or humidity can cause extensive damage; and it gives off carbon

Table 17.1
The US Banana Marketing Chain

Duration	Location	Activities
1 day	Farms and Plantations	Cutting Assembling Selection Packing Transporting
5 days Total	Receiving Station	Selection Purchase Grading Packaging Transportation
	Docks	Selection Grading Packaging Loading
	Banana Ships	Refrigerated Ships
3-6 days	Ripener	Ripening Handling Store delivery
6 days	Retail Stores	Retail handling Selling

dioxide, making proper storage and ventilation essential.

To solve the problems of handling the tender Valery, United decided to dehand the fruit in the tropics and to ship it in 18 kilogram containers. Easily said - not so easily done. Hundreds of boxing stations had to be erected on the farms, thousands of workers trained to dehand, wash and pack carefully the clusters of bananas. Since eventually over 100 million boxes of bananas were shipped, this was a program that took tremendous effort and not inconsiderable cost. The mistakes, the box design changes, and the production trials that took place during the three year conversion to Valery plantings were costly.

The change to boxing clusters of bananas at the plantation offered better protection during transport and also eliminated shipping the stem, which had no value. According to one trade authority, this packaging innovation resulted in a 50 percent increase in bulk density compared to the old method of shipping the bananas intact on the stems.

MARKETING THE NEW VARIETY

The next problem was to convince the sales staff and the banana distributors that the Valery would sell. This was tackled on two fronts. First, a consulting firm was retained to use its taste expertise to ascertain if the Valery would score as well as the Gros Michel on its taste panel's palates. The Valery proved as acceptable as the Gros Michel.

With these results in hand, United's own salesmen and jobber customers had to be convinced that the consumer would not shun this new banana. With this in mind, United ran a series of controlled store placements in selected markets in the US Midwest. First, Gros Michel were put on display, then the produce bins were switched to Valery, then back to Gros Michel. Careful sales records were kept and house-to-house calls were made on the consumers. The results were as expected: no complaints, no drop-off in sales when Valery were on display; actually very few buyers knew there was any difference.

BRANDING BANANAS

With consumer acceptance of the new variety assured, United was then set for the next major banana marketing innovation, branding. The new United management had been raised and schooled in the value of a trademark and the importance of a consumer franchise.

However, no one had tried branding a perishable at the source and then shipping the product by sea and land thousands of kilometers to the retail outlets. True, Sunkist, a citrus cooperative, had succeeded with lemons and oranges in California, but a lemon or an orange is not a banana. The former can take a beating and hold up for weeks while the latter turns speckled and brown in a few short days after ripening and cannot withstand any rough handling whatsoever.

United Fruit faced the problems of quality assurance and identification which led to several questions:

How would the specifications be established for first-class fruit?
How could the disciplines needed to assure adherence to these specifications be imparted to tropical workers?
What name would be put on this carefully selected fruit?
How would it be marked?

To get the quality control answers, United brought in a quality control expert, whose first job was to determine the standards the branded fruit should live up to. To do this intelligently, teams of interviewers were sent into the homes of hundreds of US families, armed with plastic samples demonstrating a variety of sizes and colors that covered the spectrum of banana appearance. From the consumer preference data gathered this way, the specifications were written.

With the specifications developed, United Fruit then hired and trained Spanish speaking quality assurance inspectors who were installed in each of the company's tropical divisions. A training film was produced in full color and in Spanish to be used in the instruction of the workers in the boxing stations. Again, this all sounds simple and straightforward, but it wasn't. Every tropical division manager had his own ideas on boxing station design and management. Not many were alike.

United Fruit's management eventually asked each division to develop its own boxing station design and management. As a result, some 12 different designs were developed; one finally was accepted to serve as the standard for the company.

On the name selection, there was no problem. 'Chiquita Banana' was still a household word, but the application of the name to the fruit proved difficult. First, the clusters were wrapped in decorated shrink film. It didn't work in the tropics, and it failed in the Denver test market. An attempt was then made to bag the fruit in polyethylene bags. It ripened the bananas unevenly and often too fast.

United even looked into electrostatic printing, but the machinery probably would never have held up in the humidity of Central America.

Finally, and somewhat reluctantly, United settled on the little blue sticker. A special adhesive that would adhere to wet banana skins had to be developed, dispensers for the fruit packers had to be invented, and disciplines for packing and handling had to be established and policed. Nearly a billion stickers were initially required for this effort.

The rest is history. After testing the concept in 30 markets with a clever advertising campaign that extolled the protective virtues of boxing fruit in the tropics, they were convinced the concept was sound and would make money for the company.

RESULTS

The branding effort yielded measurable results for United Fruit.

On the financial front, the early objective was to get the full cost of branding and advertising, about US$0.20 a box,

128

back in premium price. The first six month bite was a target of US$0.10 a box. It was then raised to US$0.20. Over the years it has varied, but recently it has been running between US$0.30 and US$0.50 a box. With the US market calling for 35 to 45 million boxes of United Fruit bananas, of which 85 percent on the average were Chiquitas, every US$0.10 of incremental profit brought US$2.9 to US$3.8 million to the net earnings of the company.

Eventually, United Fruit shipped Chiquita bananas to Europe and to Japan, so the total incremental profit from branding was two to three times the US segment.

But that was only the beginning of the financial improvement. As the consumer became aware of the brand and its consistent quality, the control of the market slipped away from the trade and towards United Fruit. Prices still fluctuated as oversupplies and shortages occurred in the industry, but Chiquita did not need to respond erratically. United's prices lagged on the declines and recovered earlier on the upswings.

An equally important benefit from the brand, however, was the effective job it did on converting the chain stores and jobbers, United's basic customers, to the Valery variety, and to convince them it was as good as, and eventually better than, Gros Michel.

There is no question that the major improvement in the Fruit Company's earnings and cash flow came from the successful conversion from Gros Michel to Valery. By 1969, United's net earnings had climbed back to nearly US$30 million and the company had accumulated nearly US$100 million in the bank with no debt outstanding.

The brand had a salutary effect on company morale. Everyone from farm worker to key executive became proud of the company and its product. There is no doubt that this renewed pride played a major role in the improved corporate performance.

Finally, the boxing and branding of Valery created a major social upheaval in the tropics. For the first time the company could employ thousands of women, women who never before had been able to earn a salary. The workers' incomes were enhanced, their job satisfaction improved, and the labor relations aspect of the tropical operations was greatly stabilized.

Part II
Agricultural and
livestock production

18 Farming failures: the fate of large scale agribusiness in Iran

RICHARD J. STROHL

'With enough water for irrigation, enough power for processing plants, and enough insecticides and fertilizers from the petrochemical plants nearby, success is almost guaranteed...Anyone who cannot make it in Khuzestan has no business being a farmer.'

FORTUNE, November, 1970

'After the failure of three large scale farming ventures in the last year and the nearby failure of a fourth, many experts in Iran believe that big farms are not the answer.'

MIDEAST MARKETS, September 12, 1977

Both of these statements concern the recent large scale, highly mechanized attempt at the agricultural development of 100,000 hectares in the province of Khuzestan, southwestern Iran. It resulted in an enormous gap between the expectations which agribusinessmen had for development in Khuzestan in the late 1960s and early 1970s and the results obtained after ten years of large scale, modern, diversified farming there.

The promise that large scale farming holds was tarnished by what happened, or rather what failed to happen. According to one spokesman, the World Bank, which lent US$40 million to the Dez Irrigation Project, admits it 'should have done more' to effect changes in the way agribusiness was handled there.

Why did all the agribusinesses end up with losses? Unreasonable expectations and the inability to change these

133

expectations when they proved themselves unsound resulted in some formidable obstacles to success. Among the most significant were: neglected field improvement; no contingency planning; undercapitalization; too little staff and equipment; management inflexibility; poor labor relations; governmental noncooperation; and machinery mismanagement.

THE PROMISE OF KHUZESTAN

Agricultural development is not new to Khuzestan. Men and women have tilled the fertile flood plain soils in this area along the banks of the Dez and Karkheh rivers for millennia. Darius the Great built extensive irrigation works there that Shush (Susa or Susiana) and the Achaemenids might prosper in the fifth century BC. The Parthians and Sassanians rebuilt the canals and dams six centuries later and grew sugar cane. (Khuzestan means 'land of sugar' in Farsi.)

The canals and irrigation works had been in disrepair for centuries. Then in the 1950s, with a rapidly growing population and a source of capital in their oil, the leaders of Iran naturally looked to Khuzestan where there was more productive land and good water than anywhere in Iran. They reflected on the glory that had been Iran's centuries ago and the role Khuzestan's fertile soils had played, and they decided to reclaim Khuzestan and make it more productive than it had ever been.

The first step in this reclamation and development scheme was a dam. Before the Dez was caught and caged with a towering sculpture of cement and steel, it wreaked havoc every spring on the small dams and diversions that the men on its banks erected to gain the benefit of its waters. Its sister streams and rivers washed out the irrigation canals so laboriously dug. Every year these works were renewed in time for the summer crops of rice, sesame, eggplant and tomatoes, and for the orchards and vineyards. But every year the flood waters passed, met the waters of the Karun, flowed by Ahwaz, and flanked by pipelines filled with the oil of Masjed-e-Suleiman, made their way to Abadan and the Persian Gulf.

After the flood there was only a trickle, sometimes more, sometimes less, unpredictable and unreliable. The Dez Dam stopped these floods, held a reservoir of water for irrigation, and provided power and light from its generators. A reregulation dam was built and the Dez was harnessed for the Dez Irrigation Project.

Land reform, begun in 1962, broke up the estates around Dezful and distributed these lands among the farmers who had been farming them. Farmers who had had to ask their landlords for permission to go to town were suddenly on their own.

Table 18.1
Actual and Projected Yields for Dez Irrigation Project
(metric tons per hectare)

	1970 Actual	Projected	Trial Farm 1967-68[a]
Alfalfa	14.0	18.0	16.0
Berseem	40-45[b]	65.0[b]	80.0
Wheat	1.5	3.5	4.0
Milo	–	4.5	5.0
Barley	1.5	3.0	3.0
Beet, Sugar	–	60.0	70.0
Blackeye Pea	0.9-1.0	1.0	2.2
Broad Bean	1.5	2.0	1.2
Sunflower	0.9	1.9	2.3
Tomato	15.0	20.0	24.0
Cucumber	8-9	18.0	11.0
Eggplant	17.0	12.0	14.0
Melon	10.0	15.0	18.0
Onion	22-24	30.0	50.0
Carrot	15.0	20.0	25.0
Lettuce	20.0	25.0	20.0
Grape	2.5	7.0	5.0

a. Safiabad Trial Farm, DIP-1969; b. Green chop

Tremendous energies were released but production did not rise as fast as Iran's Ministry of Agriculture had hoped. They thought that farmers supplied with their own land, more water, and technical assistance would produce more per unit of land. But the Ministry based its expectations on figures which its experiment station at Safiabad, in the middle of the Dez Irrigation Project, had recorded from experimental and trial plots and extrapolated from yields recorded in California's Imperial Valley, which has a similar climate.

These figures proved to be unrealistic for the farmers in the 1960s as well as the agribusinesses in the 1970s. Safiabad Experiment Station recorded alfalfa yields as high as 25 tons per hectare from eight to ten cuttings, wheat yields of six tons per hectare, cotton yields of five tons, and sugar beet yields of 60 tons per hectare. Throughout the six years from the start of land reform until the arrival of the agribusinesses, the Ministry kept pushing the Dez Project farmers to obtain these high yields by urging them to use fertilizer and better farming methods as a way of increasing total production and making money. Subsidizing prices as a means of pulling higher production from the land was not used even though price incentives or the profit motive are always successful in getting higher production. After all, Iran never suffers from want of onions for long after the price reaches US$1 per kilogram, which it occasionally does.

AGRIBUSINESS THE ANSWER

At this point, the Ministry of Agriculture wanted something more in the way of development and production than the first small farmers were able to provide. Therefore, under the leadership of a new Minister of Agriculture, land was made available in 1968 to foreign agribusinesses. The Ministry wanted the highly productive agriculture of California transferred to Iran. The way they chose to do this was to bring Californian entrepreneurs to Khuzestan, to have them coax superior yields on a par with those of California's Imperial Valley from the soils of the Dez Irrigation Project.

Of course, California's Imperial Valley had gone through 50 years of modern agricultural development to reach its excellent yields, but the Ministry expected the Californians and the Englishmen, who were apparently asked in to guarantee a good performance from the Californians, to duplicate these yields from crop season number one.

Interestingly, no one tried very hard to disabuse the Ministry of its misconception about the efficiencies of technological transfers in agriculture, not even old-timers who had gone through the development of the Imperial Valley. In fact, experts sent from the USA and England to research the agricultural potential of Khuzestan put their wetted forefingers to the wind and then affirmed the Ministry's assumptions by using 25 ton alfalfa yields, four ton cotton yields and 40 ton sugar beet yields for their income and cash flow projections. So the agribusinesses came to replace the small farmers in the Dez Irrigation Project.

The terms under which the land was leased to the agribusinesses were good. The leases were for thirty years for 10,000 to 20,000 hectares at US$21 per hectare annual rent. The land varied from sandy to clay, thus satisfying the cultural demands of all the temperate and subtropical crops growable in the area. The Ministry required that one-tenth of the leased land be leveled and brought into production every year, but payment on each block of land was to begin only after Khuzestan's Water and Power Authority had delivered water to that block. The water was good with less than 500 parts per million of dissolved solids, cheap at US$0.03 per cubic meter, and abundant.

The five agribusinesses which were attracted to the project

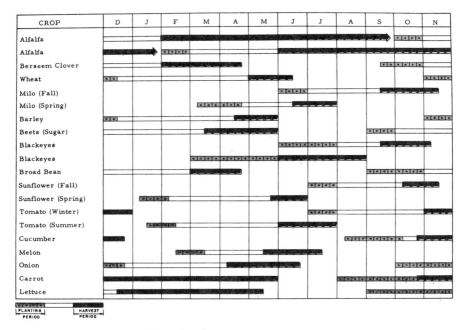

CROP	D	J	F	M	A	M	J	J	A	S	O	N
Alfalfa												
Alfalfa												
Berseem Clover												
Wheat												
Milo (Fall)												
Milo (Spring)												
Barley												
Beets (Sugar)												
Blackeyes												
Blackeyes												
Broad Bean												
Sunflower (Fall)												
Sunflower (Spring)												
Tomato (Winter)												
Tomato (Summer)												
Cucumber												
Melon												
Onion												
Carrot												
Lettuce												

| PLANTING PERIOD | HARVEST PERIOD |

Figure 18.1 Crop schedule for the Dez Irrigation Project

differed in their backgrounds, goals and methods.

IRAN-AMERICA

The first agribusiness to come to Khuzestan was Iran-America Agro Industrial Company, which started in 1968 with 20,000 hectares of land in three different areas. To emphasize the promise of agribusiness, Iran-America paraded all its agricultural machinery by highway from the Port of Khorramshahr to the Dez Irrigation Project.

The US organizers of Iran-America were basically tree and vine growers who thought in terms of perennials, with the notable exception of cotton. Consequently, they established nurseries and several hundred hectares of trees and vines as well as 200 hectares of asparagus. Twenty thousand head of sheep were also purchased, and Iran-America built a modern cotton gin in Andimeshk to process the cotton from all the agribusinesses and farm corporations in the area.

As the 1970s progressed, the wisdom of the organizers of Iran-America became evident. The imported farm equipment depreciated each year and eventually wore out and was abandoned or cannibalized, but the trees and vines grew more productive and the asparagus crop became more and more valuable. The profits from these sources, however, were not large enough to offset the losses incurred while growing vegetables and field crops.

Iran-America's vineyards were particularly successful because the grapes were trellised (a practice previously unknown in the area) which improved yields, made irrigation and harvesting more efficient, and reduced disease problems. Furthermore, when the managers of Iran-America sold the grapes and fruit on the vines and on the trees, that is, in the field, and left the problems of harvest management and protection from theft to the buyers, the vine and fruit enterprises became very successful.

The sheep enterprise, however, was unsuccessful. After eight years the herd had dropped to 15,000 head due to theft and poor husbandry. Cotton was almost totally abandoned and only 4,000 hectares of the original 20,000 were leveled to grade.

But Iran-America's superior method of growing vines and fruit trees has been a great contribution to the development of the Dez Project. Iran-America took tried and true crops of the area and applied modern growing methods. Therefore, they did not have to acquire the experience and go through the adaptation process which all of the agribusinesses went through with sugar beets, cotton and alfalfa.

IRAN-CALIFORNIA

The second of the agribusinesses, Iran-California Company (ICC), began in 1970 with 10,000 hectares in two areas: light soil in the Sagvan area and heavy soil in the Deylam area. The organizers of Iran-California were crop farmers, vegetable farmers in particular. They had made money growing vegetables and looked upon field crops as filler crops to occupy the land when the more profitable vegetable crops were not being grown. Their attitude was that while anyone could grow field crops, only the best could grow vegetables profitably. This attitude resulted in very little time being spent lowering the production costs and increasing the yields of field crops in ICC's first few years, with the exception of cotton. A lot of time and effort was put into growing cotton at Iran-California, but by not allocating enough money for the salary of a topnotch entomologist, much cotton was lost to insects.

Nevertheless, Iran-California did make some management contributions to the agriculture of the area through persistence and innovation. Through persistence, the managers of Iran-California achieved meticulous field preparation, precision planting, efficient irrigation, and orderly harvesting. Realizing what men and machines could do, for example, they would not accept anything but straight rows. ICC was the only agribusiness which leveled its land properly, but it had only enough money to level about 4,000 of its 10,000 hectares.

On the innovative side, ICC introduced joint venture production of melons to the agribusinesses. Management reasoned that since Iran-California did not have the wherewithal to farm much of its land which had already received water but was not yet leveled to grade, why not let farmers who had the capital and labor farm this land in the interim. Of course, to the Iranian government this looked like a return to landlordism, but after many months of argument, the Ministry agreed to let Iran-California enter into a joint venture on 40 hectares of land. Iran-California provided the land and water and the melon farmers (who were from Esfahan, 650 kms. away) provided capital, labor and marketing services. The melon farmers guaranteed a fixed return per hectare plus a percentage of sales above a certain figure.

The scheme was so successful that within three years, several thousand hectares of unleveled land in the agribusinesses were farmed in this way. In fact, there was such a demand for melon land that melons were planted on the same fields for three years. As a result, wilt wiped out virtually the whole Dez Irrigation Project melon crop in 1978.

ICC also introduced the practice of company financing of field vehicles rather than company ownership. Under this plan, ICC financed the purchase of a vehicle for each field foreman with ownership, maintenance and repair of the vehicle resting with the foreman. This not only got ICC out of the transportation business, but also gave the foreman a stake in his vehicle which resulted in better care.

IRAN-SHELLCOTT

The third agribusiness, Iran-Shellcott, started in 1971 with 15,000 hectares in the west Dez area. It was the only one of four foreign agribusinesses in which more than 50 percent of the shares were foreign owned, in this case by Shell Oil Company. It was also the only agribusiness which used a plane for sowing wheat and spreading fertilizer as well as spraying. In addition, Iran-Shellcott had the one sprinkler irrigation system among agribusinesses with 800 hectares under sprinklers.

Mitchell Cott, Ltd., which had the management contract, was experienced in African plantation agriculture, and assembled a group of agriculturists to grow cotton. Although well financed, Mitchell Cott failed to spend the US$20,000 to US$100,000 needed to keep an experienced entomologist in the cotton fields. As a consequence, Iran-Shellcott loss 1,500 hectares of cotton to spider mites in its first full year of production - a setback from which it never fully recovered. Added to the financial problems from this loss were the depreciation on the equipment which had been purchased for cotton but was not being used, and repayment of the debt incurred to build a large living compound for staff members. In short, a company which had planned to pay its debts and turn a profit by raising four ton cotton had a lot of money problems when it switched to raising two ton wheat.

On the other hand, Iran-Shellcott had the best administration of any of the agribusinesses and its accounting department knew where the money was going on a field-by-field basis as well as on a crop-by-crop basis. In comparison, accounting in the other agribusinesses was sloppy, to say the least. Of course, good accounting procedures thoroughly performed do not solve management problems nor rectify poor plans, but because Iran-Shellcott insisted on proper accounting, it did have accurate figures on which to base decisions.

INTERNATIONAL AGRO-BUSINESS AND GALLEH

The fourth foreign agribusiness, International Agro-business Corporation of Iran (IACI), started in 1973 with 16,000 hectares in one area of the West Dez near the town of Shush. Part of the ownership and all of the management of IACI was in the hands of Hawaiian Agronomics Company, a Hawaiian sugar company. IACI's manager had successfully managed Hawaiian Agronomic's other development project in the area, the 10,000 hectare Haft Tappeh sugar cane plantation and sugar mill.

IACI believed that sugar production was the best place to make money and with world prices sky high in 1973 when IACI was getting started, no one could well dispute this. Therefore, IACI concentrated on sugar beets, with a flock of sheep and a herd of imported beef cattle as sidelines.

Sugar beets, however, are not a reclamation crop and that was what was needed on the newly leveled land around Shush. However, IACI persisted in planting sugar beets until they had planted more than they could harvest. They also planted sugar beets in the same fields until they had serious insect problems. Like all of the agribusinesses, IACI's sugar beets yielded around 25 tons/hectare.

In 1976, not having made any money raising sugar beets, IACI began concentrating on alfalfa. Hay cubes found a ready market in Tehran's milkshed and alfalfa kept fields in crop year round, reducing the need for tillage equipment. Alfalfa was also a good reclamation crop; however, the US varieties of non-dormant alfalfa like Mesa Sirsa did not yield well under Khuzestani conditions, nor did any other varieties tried. Alfalfa yields in all areas of the Dez Irrigation Project averaged six to seven tons per hectare, which was two or three tons short of profitability.

All in all, IACI neither learned from the mistakes of the other agribusinesses in raising sugar beets nor benefited from their successes, but simply went along making the same mistakes and incurring the same costs.

The fifth agribusiness, Galleh, was started in the West Dez by the Shah's twin sister Princess Ashraf. 'Galleh' means flock or herd in Farsi, but there were neither flocks nor herds on Galleh's 4,000 hectares from the time it started in 1975 until late 1978 when everything in the project area had come to a standstill.

Some citrus was planted by Galleh and several fields of sugar beets, maize, wheat and alfalfa were planted and harvested. A consultant supervised the ensiling of sugar beet tops and maize in the summer of 1977 in preparation for a dairy herd, but the herd never materialized.

THE FARM CORPORATION

While the strategy in the Dez Irrigation Project favored large scale farming over traditional small farm agriculture, a third alternative for agricultural development was also tried. The Farm Corporation was created as a means to combine the traditional village structure with modern farm management by consolidating individual farm plots into larger units.

The Farm Corporation was formally part of Iran's fourth economic plan (1968-1972). On January 16, 1978, The Bill for the Formation of Farm Corporations was passed. Article I of the law summarized the goals of the Farm Corporation: to increase the per capital income of the farmers; to create widespread facilities for farm mechanization; to acquaint farmers with modern methods of agriculture; and to utilize maximum manpower in the villages.

The Farm Corporation combined many of the cohesive characteristics of the traditional village while introducing heretofore alien concepts of large scale farming and consolidated management.

Shareholders who contributed land to the Farm Corporation lost the right to make the management decisions they had as farmers; the professional manager, with the consent of the Board of Directors, determined what would be planted and where. The manager determined the most efficient field plot sizes, and assigned shareholders to specific work tasks such as irrigating, maintenance or pest control. Since the quality of the shareholder's work, similar to that of an employee of any large farm, would be reflected in his overall dividend at the end of the year, he had a direct stake in doing a good job.

Were Farm Corporations successful? 'The concept was a good one,' commented a World Bank official, 'but in practice they tried to be too mechanized and modern. The heavy use of machinery eliminated rather than created jobs.'

According to this official, of the 85 Farm Corporations operating or in formation in 1977, only one was financially successful – and it raised opium. Not only was opium profitable, but it required a great deal of hand labor: to collect raw opium from 25 hectares, 150 people are necessary.

Farm Corporations did not succeed in producing more jobs or income and consequently were not able to stop the rural to urban flow which has contributed to Iran's unrest.

REASONS FOR FAILURE

With large scale farming replacing traditional farmers on more and more hectares of land worldwide, the failures of the agribusinesses in the Dez must be examined so as to avoid, if possible, similar dissappointments.

The agribusinesses in the Dez, although varying in size and organization, shared the following obstacles to success.

1. Neglected field improvement. Expectations of success (which can also be read 'get rich quick') were so high that reason and critical opinion went unheeded. Plans were not subjected to scrutiny. For example, foreign investors and Iranian technocrats had convinced themselves that the development phase of fields would not extend beyond the first crop or could be dispensed with altogether.

This was one of the biggest mistakes that all of the agribusinesses made. They did not plan for an extended soil improvement phase. Properly leveled fields for diversified crop production with border and row crop irrigation in the Dez Irrigation Project soils needed .2 to .4 of a percent slope from head to tail and about the same side slope. After fields were cut and filled to level them to grade, soil structure changed for the worse. Infiltration rates were poorer and the capacity of the soil to hold water was reduced.

Furthermore, micronutrient deficiencies showed up in crops grown on the cut areas of the fields. reclamation crops, requiring comparatively little mechanization, could have corrected these problems by improving the soil structure and concentrating micronutrients. Instead of pausing to improve the soils with a rotation of berseem clover, milo and wheat, all of which could have been planted with a minimum of tillage, the agribusinesses charged ahead with sugar beets or cotton on the newly leveled land. Although the returns from the soil improvement rotation would have been low, so too would have been the cost.

2. No contingency planning. The alternative which the agribusinesses chose resulted in low returns, high costs and unimproved soil. They never recovered from this because they were bound by their poor financial and agronomic planning. The psychological states of the directors of the companies and the socio-political designs of the Iranian government were all postulated on the agribusinesses and the Dez Irrigation Project being romping successes from the very first day.

When the costs of equipment nearly doubled in 1973-74, no one was prepared or willing to deal with this problem. There were no contingency plans because everyone had believed there was no chance of failure. There were no reserves to muster, on the one hand, and no willingness to retreat, on the other.

3. Undercapitalization. Poor financial planning resulted in undercapitalization which prevented the agribusinesses from learning from their mistakes. By 1972, Iran-California had realized the wisdom of establishing trees, but since they did not have the money to do so, they continued to plant sugar beets and wheat on land which could not return a profitable yield. Iran-Shellcott also wanted to plant trees in 1975, but due to undercapitalization, they continued to wear out their machinery on 4,000 hectares of wheat, of which only 500 hectares were profitable.

Everyone tried to raise cotton without an experienced entomologist even though cotton growing had been abandoned in Khuzestan 20 years before because of insect problems.

Galleh leveled land without engineering their programs: They were trying to save money but this omission resulted in having the field drain at the head of the field.

4. Too little staff and equipment. Saddled with poor plans and fired with great expectations, the agribusinesses tried to do the impossible. Iran-California, for example, had contracted with the Iranian government, as part of its lease, to level and put into production 1,000 hectares every year for ten years. It simply was not staffed, financed or equipped to do this.

From 600 to 1,000 cubic meters of soil per hectare had to be moved to level the land and ICC had four motorized scrapers and two pull-type scrapers pulled by John Deere 5020 tractors with which to do this work. While the 5020's were helping level 1,000 hectares per year, they also had to do the primary tillage on the 1,000 hectares leveled in the previous year. This schedule wore them out long before all the land was leveled.

Men, equipment and money were stretched over too many hectares. This did not mean that production costs were lowered all that much, since seed, fertilizer, insecticide and water costs were the same. But the yields were low because operations were not timely and were rushed and many of the fields were not level. A lesser amount well-done would have been a great improvement.

5. Management inflexibility. Rather than admit to poor planning, the directors of the companies frequently looked for scapegoats in the field. When the cost of leveling land for surface irrigation proved to be US$1,000 per hectare instead of the US$500 per hectare budgeted for the job, the directors accused the agribusiness managers and engineers of being incompetent and these directors then began making more and more decisions. But from their distance, they were unable to imagine the conditions which existed in the Dez Irrigation Project and they continued to make decisions that were divorced from reality.

Inflexibility combined with stubborness and blindness among the directors meant that they could not change their initial direction. They were determined to stay with their original concept of fully mechanized agribusinesses using only the most modern techniques, despite experiences in the field showing superior results, in some instances, using traditional cultural practices.

In the spring of 1976 ICC proved that it was cheaper to harvest beets by hand with hired crews paid by the ton of loaded beets rather than with mechanical beet harvesters and loaders. But the next year Iran-America and IACI bought new beet harvesters.

When the Agricultural Development Bank of Iran (ADBI) representatives took over the day-to-day operations of ICC, wheat was being bagged by a crew which specialized in this type of harvesting. This crew was fast, efficient and cheaper on a per-ton basis than day labor. But the ADBI representatives fired the bagging crew because, they felt, its members were making five times as much money per day as common labor was supposed to make.

None of the agribusinesses could accept local agricultural methods. For instance, the local method of controlling winter weeds in preparation for the winter vegetable crops was to work the fields lightly in the summer when the air temperature was 50°C and the soil temperature in the first few centimeters of soil was approximately 65°C. They would then level the fields exactly the way they wanted them for vegetable planting and flood them. The combination of water and heat germinated the winter weeds or rotted their seeds. Those seeds that did germinate could not live under the intense heat and so died.

As long as the soil was not stirred thus bringing up more winter weed seeds, there would be almost complete control of winter weeds. But the agribusinesses could not accept this. It was too traditional, too old fashioned, not mechanical enough.

6. Poor labor relations. Labor management was also an area of blindness for the agribusinesses. Labor was not paid regularly nor frequently enough. People who are being paid only US$1-2 per day need their pay every day to buy daily necessities. If they are not so paid, they have to borrow the money or buy on credit and then their loyalties go to their creditors, not to their employers. If they can get a job where they are paid daily, they will take it, even for less money.

Furthermore, if pay day is Friday and you are not paid until the following Wednesday, you begin to doubt that you will ever be paid, so you don't work very hard on Monday, Tuesday and Wednesday. The directors of the companies, some of whom were exlandlords, could not seem to understand this. They were used to dividing up the crops two or three times a year and providing credit the rest of the time.

7. Governmental noncooperation. Nor did the Iranian government organizations with which the agribusinesses had to work give their wholehearted cooperation. Agreements arrived at between high government officials and the agribusiness managers and owners were not implemented by the bureaucracy.

For example, an agreement had been made to allow direct shipments of spare parts from the manufacturers to the agribusinesses without going through the local distributors and with priority customs clearance. This agreement was never implemented. Parts could not be obtained directly and frequently parts and machinery were tied up in customs for months.

On one occasion, a manager for Iran-California went to the port with what he thought was the proper paperwork to get a shipment of seeds and spare parts out of customs. He spent several days there getting the papers stamped and signed by no less than 27 people. However, customs would still not release the shipment.

Frustrated, he called a General on ICC's Board of Directors who sent six policemen to the port. With guns drawn on the customs officials, they finally succeeded in getting the shipment out of customs.

Importing certified seeds was also very difficult because the Plant Protection Department of the Ministry of Agriculture would not clear seeds even though they arrived with phytosanitary certificates. Advance approval of importation was necessary but nearly impossible to get. Consequently, seeds frequently arrived too late for the planting season.

145

The Director of the Iran American Chamber of Commerce wrote in June, 1975:

> We see opportunities for agribusiness in Iran as outstanding. We see performance falling far short. The difference between potentials and actualities is due, in large measure, to the complete lack of procedures for processing valid proposals in the field and inability to assure the flow of the tremendous subsidies promised. Each venture is treated as though there never had been any other processed here.

8. Machinery mismanagement. The biggest technical failure of the agribusinesses was in machinery management, again caused by the unrealistic expectations of instant success and the poor planning that resulted from these expectations. The first mistake made in machinery management was not limiting acquisitions to two tractor sizes - one for primary tillage and one for planting, cultivating, etc. - with all tractors of each size being of the same model and manufacture. The agribusinesses failed to standardize probably because they were not considering the long haul, but also because the men who rejected standardization were not the men who were being asked to keep the tractors in the field.

What the agribusinesses needed was a tractor of the Caterpillar D-7 type for primary tillage and another of 90-100 hp for listing, planting, etc. In actual fact, by 1977 the agribusinesses had twenty-one models of tractors from eight different manufacturers. There was no way that they could maintain a parts inventory for twenty-one different tractors located as they were 15,000 kilometers from the parts factories and with raw recruits for mechanics. For example, during the summer of 1977, IACI could keep only 25 of its 100 tractors running and the other agribusinesses were in similar straits.

Nor did this madness, this propensity to differentiate and avoid standardization stop with tractors. It was repeated with tillage tools, listers, planters, swathers, balers, beet harvesters, and cotton pickers. Neither the agribusinesses nor the Dez Irrigation Project benefited from this random acquisition of machinery and it was a major factor contributing to the poor showing.

Naturally, with tractors and machinery down and abandoned for want of parts, the agribusiness managers needed to rent equipment from local contractors which was available at reasonable rates. But the directors of the companies prohibited this, for the most part, because they could not justify renting tractors when their own companies had tractors sitting idle for lack of a US$10 part.

19 The Moldavia Tomato Project

JOHN FREIVALDS

The Russian official was skeptical: 'Guaranteed yields?' The
US negotiators confirmed what appeared in the draft contract.
If the California-based FMC corporation supplied all the
inputs for a tomato processing project in the Soviet Republic
of Moldavia, it would guarantee the yields.

The Soviet Union wanted to increase its supply of consumer
goods, including tomato paste. It had already used California
tomato varieties, but yields did not approach those attained
in California. While the country had purchased several FMC
tomato harvesters, it did not have a total system. According
to FMC spokesperson Germaine Cummings, the Soviet goals were
to reduce the amount of labor needed to produce tomatoes and
to improve yields and quality.

The Soviet Union, with its centrally planned economy,
understands large integrated projects. The one FMC proposed
included agricultural machinery, seeds, chemicals, packing
house, processing facilities, and on-going technology.

The proposed FMC project was based on the California system
in which the tomato growing, trucking to plant, processing,
and retail distribution were done primarily by separate
groups, each of which hoped to make a profit in the
transaction. The traditional Soviet system, in contrast, was
based on having the necessary materials on hand, irrespective
of cost, with little economic incentive involved. The Soviets
thought the California system could be adapted on a piecemeal
basis, but FMC disagreed.

147

Two key questions remained. Could an integrated system from a capitalist country be successfully introduced into a socialist environment? Perhaps more importantly, would the Soviets agree to purchase inputs, such as agrochemicals and tractors, for the complex after its construction?

The most difficult aspect of the project for the Soviets to accept was the requirement that they import inputs which were already being produced domestically. However, the FMC negotiators stated, 'The whole project is a package. We can't break it up and still guarantee performance.'

Intensive negotiations between FMC and the Soviets began in January 1975. This was the second attempt, an earlier proposal having been submitted in 1973. Most of the Soviet negotiations were conducted with the foreign trade organization Traktoro Export.

After months of negotiations, a contract was drawn. Germaine Cummings said:

> The original contract was the standard Soviet contract with some nonstandard performance guarantees. The usual letter of credit against late deliveries was required, but additionally there was a nonstandard letter of credit against performance based partly on the output of the agricultural operations and the processing facility.

The contract was finally signed in April 1975, and since that time the project has gone through several contract extensions. The project site is the Dnester State Farm near Tiraspol in Moldavia SSR, with the Moldavia Institute for Vegetable Growing and Irrigation as the local host organization. The initial project had three parts: demonstration farm, tomato production, and tomato processing.

THREE PHASES

First of all, soil and climate conditions were studied to determine the feasibility of expanding and improving existing mechanized production of a variety of vegetables for both fresh market and processing.

As a result of their findings, US specialists established a 350 hectare demonstration farm in the Soviet Union to produce cucumbers, onions, and carrots, as well as tomatoes. Existing and potential diseases and weed problems were considered; agrochemicals were selected; and seed varieties best suited for quality production and highest yields were introduced. Expatriates selected, purchased, and shipped farm equipment, seed, chemicals, fertilizers and other miscellaneous supplies as required for the operation of the farm. In addition, small sorting and grading lines for cucumbers, onions and carrots were installed.

The specialists trained supervisory and support personnel for all phases of production, including operation and maintenance of equipment, soil preparation, planting, irrigation, weed control, and cultural practices. An additional experimental plot was established to test and determine the ideal crops to supply the existing market.

In periodical progress reports developed for the Soviet Union, FMC detailed project activities and results. On the demonstration farm, yields were three times the previous Soviet averages and 40 percent above the stated objectives. Some plots exceeded 100 tons per hectare, 30 percent above the California state average.

Results of the Phase I project determined the feasibility of a fully integrated agro-industrial complex with emphasis on tomato production and processing. Phase II was contracted, and utilized experience gained on the 350 hectare demonstration farm. It involved development of a 650 hectare mechanized tomato production system that included a central color sorting station for the first production season.

Phase II furthered the mechanized technology in the production of tomatoes - 200 hectares for fresh market and 450 for processing. The specialists again selected, purchased, and shipped farm equipment, seeds, agrochemicals, and other miscellaneous supplies for the production of tomatoes. The contractor also provided for the supervisory personnel necessary to carry out the contract objectives.

FMC is currently studying how its tomato production system might be expanded through use of Soviet-produced equipment, seeds and chemicals, so as to minimize imported materials.

In order to process the tomatoes produced on the 650 hectare farm, FMC designed a tomato processing plant that included tomato paste production, aseptic tomato paste bulk storage and transport, and a whole-peeled tomato line. To implement plant construction, the contractor selected, tested, and shipped all plant machinery to the site, and FMC specialists managed plant installation and start-up. FMC's process technology was made available to the Soviet Union through manuals, plant layout drawings, and equipment drawings. Local personnel were trained to operate the system, and FMC remained available for servicing the equipment and ordering replacement parts.

COMPONENTS OF THE SYSTEM

Tomato processing is an involved system, and all parts had to function cooperatively to make the Moldavia project work. The major components are:

1. Tomato harvester. This machine, which has four-wheel drive and four-wheel steering, also has an electronic color sorter which reduces the percentage of green tomatoes.

2. Tomato chopper. After tomatoes are washed and inspected, they are conveyed into the feed hopper. A rotating feed screw forces the tomatoes through the stationary sheer plate into a rotary cutter. The results are tomato particles specially sized for maximum heat penetration during processing.

3. Hot break tank. Within seconds, chopped tomatoes are heated to temperatures of 85°C or more in a hot break tank. This rapid heating destroys enzymes that degrade pectin. As a result, maximum flavor, color, aroma and taste of the product are preserved.

4. Pulper/finisher. This operation reduces tomato pulp to a liquid state by eliminating seeds, skins and any extraneous materials.

5. Evaporator. A continuous evaporator ensures product flavor and color by using short-time heating, high velocity flow and forced flow circulation. Through the quick absorption of transferred heat, the tomato juice downstream boils and begins to concentrate.

6. Heat exchanger. The heat exchanger is designed for a wide range of pasteurization, heating and cooling processes. The processed tomato juice and the service liquids flow between alternate plates and create extremely high heat transfers.

7. Unifiller. This filler is designed for accurate high speed filling of light liquids and semi-viscous and viscous products, and performs with minimal product waste. Fill volume can also be adjusted during operation.

8. Can closer. Fully automatic units are used to close light weight tin plate, deep drawn aluminim and composite containers. A special 'no-can-no-cover' proximity sensor prevents a cover from being applied when there is no container present.

9. Draper cooler. The draper cooler's motor driven wire belt can convey most any size or shape container through the pasteurization, cooling and drying processes. After cans are pasteurized with hot water or steam, the belt moves under a water spray manifold for cooling. A final blow dryer section removes excess water from the container surfaces.

10. Sterilmatic cooker/cooler. Utilizing induced convection, this pressure cooker's three phase rotation system permits fast and even heat penetration at temperatures up to 146°C. Pressure cooling techniques use overriding air pressure to compensate internal can pressure while counter flow water cools can contents. Often referred to as the 'one man cook room,' this equipment requires only one operator for several

continuous lines.

11. Caser. The caser is engineered to assemble and load cans into top loading shipping cases in single or multiple tier patterns. Upright handling decreases the amount of product damage and contributes to operating speeds in excess of 20 cases per minute.

12. Case sealer. The case sealer glues and seals case openings. Adaptable to different case sizes, it will operate with enclosed pressurized cold glue or a hot melt gluing system.

13. Filled case palletizer. Readily adjustable to any case size or pattern, it automatically palletizes cartons and cases.

14. Automatic pallet strapper. The pallet strapper is designed for high production speeds with a minimum of labor. Its push-button operation can apply tension, heat, seal, and cut a plastic strap for up to 30 average size pallets per hour. Adjustments for the strapping of various load sizes can be made during work flow.

OUTLOOK

While this project was successful, it was expensive for FMC to develop and for the Soviets to purchase. While FMC still sells food processing equipment, it has discontinued trying to sell these large integrated complexes. Sales were not large enough to justify the specialized staff needed to market these hugh complexes.

The Soviet officials who promoted this project were rewarded within their system as the project became a showcase, albeit an expensive one. Total contract costs have been estimated at more than US$5 million. While FMC has not sold any more vegetable complexes in the USSR, it did install in 1980 a plant to make meat baby food.

According to one trade expert, 'Countries like to buy these systems because they are "instant agriculture", but it's hard to pay for them.' Many of the complexes currently being built have a 'compensation' feature in which the seller takes part of the production as payment.

20 Amazonia agro-forestry: Projeto do Jari

RICHARD J. STROHL

Endeavor to grow your own pulp trees in the tropics in response to a rapidly growing demand for paper and board, and you can end up with 1.5 million hectares of land on the Rio Jari in Brazil's developing Amazon region, as well as a floating pulp mill, a kaolin mine, 3,500 hectares of continuously cropped rice land, several thousand head of cattle and water buffalo, a city of 10,000 people, thousands of hectares of 'Gmelina arborea' trees which grow 30 meters tall in ten years, and a great contribution to the science of tropical agro-forestry - not to mention administrative, financial, and public relations headaches. At least that is the present result of shipping magnate D.K. Ludwig's US$1 billion, quarter-century quest to establish a forest products complex in the tropics. The future of this enterprise stands to be even more exciting and impressive, since only a fraction of the land has been developed to date, and only a few ideas have had time to flower and bear fruit.

Although technically successful beyond expectations, the project's financial success will require the cooperation of the Brazilian government and a few more years at full production. To facilitate this, the 85-year-old Ludwig has transferred controlling stock and most assets of Projeto do Jari to a new Brazilian holding company, Companhia do Jari, composed of 23 Brazilian entrepreneurs and the Banco do Brasil.

Projeto do Jari now has 100,000 hectares planted to three introduced species - gmelina, Caribbean pine and eucalyptus.

The average annual growth of these trees is expected to be 25 cubic meters per hectare, which amounts to at least five tons of pulp per hectare per year. Since one ton of hardwood pulp sells for around US$400 in Europe and North America (northern softwood pulp is US$500 to US$550 per MT), the possible gross income per hectare is near US$2,000 annually.

The Projeto do Jari pulp mill has an annual capacity of more than 200,000 tons, or about 750 tons per day. During 1981, the mill regularly exceeded design capacity, producing as much as 900 tons of pulp per day. At 200,000 tons of pulp annually and US$400/ton, gross revenues from the mill would be US$80 million. Add to that 10,000 to 14,000 tons of rice at US$500/ton and lumber sales, etc., and the gross annual income of Projeto do Jari approaches US$100 million, without the kaolin mine. With full development of all land, US$1 billion gross annual income will be possible.

THE BEGINNINGS

The road to this juncture has not been short, but it has been direct. In the 1950s Ludwig foresaw the possibility of profiting from the rising demand for wood products, particularly paper, if he could find and cultivate a very rapidly growing tropical tree with good pulping qualities. Traditional temperate zone sources of pulpwood could not keep up with the rising demand, or so it seemed, and there were no substitutes for wood pulp looming on the horizon. (World production of paper and board was around 50 million tons annually at that time; today it is over 170 million tons.)

The obvious place to go for trees was the hardwood rainforests of the tropics, but most of these tropical hardwoods were poor quality pulpwood even with the best of pulping processes. Furthermore, tropical hardwood species do not grow in dense, single species stands, but rather are scattered individually throughout the forest, thus making cutting and hauling very expensive. Pulpwood could not and cannot stand those costs of collection. Therefore, if tropical climates were to be used for the production of pulpwood, the pulpwood trees had to be grown in dense stands – in plantations. So Ludwig began the search for a tree which could make tropical pulpwood growing profitable.

He found that tree, Gmelina arborea, in Nigeria where it was being grown for mining timbers. Gmelina is actually native to Burma and east India where it occurs occasionally in the forest. It is not, however, an outstanding wood producer in its native habitat. But under Nigerian conditions it produced very good mine pit props very quickly.

Ludwig's foresters tried gmelina in Honduras and it grew

well (ten meters in ten years), and produced up to 50 cubic meters of pulpwood per hectare annually. Lumber, pulp and veneer qualities were good. At that point Ludwig decided to plan his tropical forest products complex around gmelina in the belief that concentrating attention on one species would get positive results faster than would diffusing attention to several species.

The next task was to find an accessible place in the tropics on which to grow gmelina on a scale large enough to make an investment in pulp mills, transportation, and marketing feasible. The location was found in 1967 along the Rio Jari - a tributary of the Amazon - in the Brazilian State of Para and the Federal Territory of Amapa. A group of Brazilian businessmen owned approximately 1.5 million hectares of land there and they were willing to sell it for US$1 million.

AMAZONIA

Amazonia is a term used to describe a physical region of the Amazon River drainage which has a similar complex of tropical vegetation. The most common plant genus in Amazonia is 'Hevea,' which includes the Para rubber tree, the major source of natural rubber.

Amazonia is not the name of a state or administrative unit. It is an enormous tropical rainforest region of over three million square kilometers centered in northwestern Brazil and extending from 50°W longitude to 75°W longitude and from 3°N latitude to near 10°S latitude. In addition to Brazil, parts of Bolivia, Peru, Colombia and Venezuela are also included.

Amazonia has a small population of approximately five million people and is currently quite underdeveloped. Rainfall is high, ranging from 2,000 to 3,000 millimeters annually, but it varies considerably from season to season and from year to year in the same area. Furthermore, onset and duration of rainy and dry seasons are irregular. No doubt this will lead to widespread irrigation of the upland soils as Amazonia is developed agriculturally.

This irregularity in weather is due in part to the fact that very little of Amazonia is more than 250 meters above sea level. (The northernmost part of Projeto do Jari has some elevations of 600 meters.) Consequently, there is little variation in temperature, which stays within a few degrees of 28°C. The Amazon River itself falls only ten meters in its final 3,000 kilometer course to the Atlantic Ocean. There are three common classifications of land in Amazonia:

1. 'Igopos,' which is permanently covered with water and supports a heavy growth of aquatic plants, has little

agricultural value but can provide adequate graze for water buffalo.

2. 'Varzeas,' flood plain land consisting of heavy textured silts and silty clays, is covered with water only during the rainy season. Trees and other plants which can withstand several weeks of flooding make up the natural vegetation of varzeas. It is potentially very productive rice land.

3. Upland areas of hills, valleys, and plateaus have soils ranging from very heavy textured clay to quite sandy loams. It is on these acid soils (pH 4 to 5) that hundreds of species of trees (over 400 species have been identified to date) and more hundreds of species of shrubs, plants and vines grow. This is the tropical rainforest - the Brazilian selva. The gross timber volume of the natural forest on the upland soils is from 70 cubic meters per hectare on the sandy soils to over 300 cubic meters per hectare on the heavy clays.

PHYSICAL CHARACTERISTICS

A survey at the time of the Jari purchase found the dominant tree species in the area was the Brazil nut tree ('Bertolletia excelsa') which towered majestically over the forest. The primary economic activity of the 2,000 to 3,000 people who lived in the area was the collection and selling of Brazil nuts. (Servicos Agrorios e Silviculturas Ltda, part of Projecto do Jari, further encouraged Brazil nut harvesting by providing a ready market for all the Brazil nuts brought in.)

Surveyors also found that there are two distinct soil types on Jari lands, a heavy clay - predominant in the northern part - and a sandy soil in the south. The sandy soil was recognized as being unsuitable for achieving maximum genetic potential from Gmelina arborea, but it has proven to be an excellent soil for Caribbean pine ('Pinus caribaea'). These two soil types have provided Projecto do Jari with both softwood and hardwood potential and the opportunity for wider market penetration with its product 'Jaripulp.'

Trees do very well on Jari soils. There are hundreds of species growing in the region, from very large to very small, and they grow so thickly that they form a canopy over the soil. But Jari soils are not repositories for plant nutrients; in fact, they appear to be incapable of storing nutrients for long periods. Instead, the trees which are growing and decaying on the Jari soils hold most of the nutrients available for tree growth in this eco-system. Very soon after these nutrients are released by decaying plants, they filter into the soil and are taken up by roots and again stored in the plants. Under this cycle of continuous tree growth and decay, the Jari soils are able to maintain a structure which is conducive to root growth.

There are sufficient air spaces for water to filter through, and nutrients are available to the roots as they are leached into the root zone from the decaying trees on the soil surface. However, if this cycle is stopped by cutting and burning the trees and suppressing all subsequent plant growth, then the cycle becomes difficult to start again because many nutrients are lost in runoff once the soil is no longer protected from rainfall by a canopy of leaves. Moreover, nutrients in the soil will be leached below the root zone if there are not active roots to take them up. In addition, there are large areas of the Jari Project which have fine-textured clay soils (Belterra Clay-Kaolinitic Yellow Latosol) which lose their structure when exposed to the impact of rainfall, sunlight, and traffic by heavy equipment. Without structure these soils become hard and neither roots nor water can penetrate them. Consequently, regeneration of a cycle of vegetation is very difficult and takes years to accomplish.

In managing the Jari soils for maximum tree growth, the rule that must be followed is: Do not break the nutrient cycle. Land can be lost to production for many years if this rule is not observed.

Jari soils are classified as Plinthitic soils. The main types are Kaolinitic Yellow Latosols, Red Yellow Podzolic soils, Red Yellow Latosols, and Kaolinitic Latosolic sand in the upland forest areas and Humic Gley soils in the flood plains. The pH of these soils is between four and five. Potential cation exchange capacity varies from near zero to about 20 m.e./100g of soil. The gross timber volume of natural forest on Kaolinitic Yellow Latosols, Red Yellow Latosols, and Red Yellow Podzolic soils is 200 to 250 m^3/hectare. Gross timber volume on Kaolinitic Latosolic sand is 130 m^3/hectare.

Other finds of great economic importance to the project included an area suitable for the cultivation of rice at the confluence of the Rio Jari and the Amazon, and a major deposit of high quality kaolin on the eastern bank of the Rio Jari. (Kaolin or china clay is a pure form of clay that is used to make ceramics and as a filler in paper making.)

To make the most of all the opportunities which presented themselves at Jari, Ludwig added the development of the rice land and the kaolin deposit to his plans for growing pulpwood trees, making pulp and paper, sawing and selling the valuable hardwood lumber cut from the areas being planted to gmelina and raising cattle and water buffalo. Then, to gain management efficiency and maximize the possibility of profit, he established five companies for the five major operations of the project: Caulim do Amazonia Ltda. for mining kaolin; Jari Florestal e Agropecuaria Ltda. for pulp and paper making;

Madeiras do Jari Ltda. for lumber; Servicos Agrorios e Silviculturas Ltda. for agricultural and forest products; and Navegacao Sion Ltda. for shipping on the Amazon and Rio Jari.

A SELF-SUFFICIENT UNIT

Although Projeto do Jari is accessible via the Rio Jari by ships of up to 30,000 tons, it is still hundreds of kilometers and many hours from Belem, the closest major city. Consequently, from the outset the project was planned and built with self-sufficiency in mind.

There are no roads or railroads connecting the project to the developed parts of Brazil, only the Rio Jari and the Amazon. But it has modern equipment to maintain and up to 10,000 people - many with families - on the payroll. In all it has attracted more than 30,000 people to the area. This means there has to be housing, food, water, transportation, sanitation, medical care, schools, and recreation facilities.

Long-range goals coupled with complete resource utilization and economies of scale have by necessity dominated the planning and organization of Jari. Moreover, the Brazilian government recognized Jari as a step toward its goals of permanent settlement and development in Amazonia and gave its qualified support. Government loan guarantees were given; export agreements were made so that Jari could export products and thereby gain hard currencies with which to service its debt; most imported equipment was not taxed. Now that Jari ownership is in primarily Brazilian hands, more assistance can be given by the government to maintain the costly infrastructure built by Projeto do Jari and for the social services now provided.

Self-sufficiency is important because any requirements that can be met at Jari, that can be grown, recovered, mined or made there, cut transportation and input costs and save time. Furthermore, efforts toward self-sufficiency sharpen the skills of management and labor and lead to higher productivity. Of course, Jari is not self-sufficient by any means; much has to be imported. It does, however, produce a large share of its food needs, and will produce nearly all in the future.

Both livestock and poultry are raised. Approximately 5,000 head of cattle graze in upland areas, including some areas which are planted to pine and then interplanted to palatable grasses. This intergrazing makes good use of the land while the pine trees are small, eliminates for the most part the need to weed the pine plantations, and the grass cover also protects the soil from the adverse effects of rainfall and sunlight. Herd vigor and quality are built and maintained by a systematic breeding program using the best tropically-adapted breeds – mainly of Indian origin.

Five thousand water buffalo are raised along the Amazon where they can graze on aquatic plants as well as upland grasses. Platforms have been constructed in the water for the water buffalo to rest on and for corrals. The water buffalo have proven easier to maintain and handle than the cattle, and both calving and growth rates have been better for the water buffalo than for the cattle. Selective breeding is also used to promote vigor, growth and carcass quality.

Neither species has been used to any extent for milk production at Jari, although water buffalo are particularly well-suited for this purpose. The water buffalo's ability to produce meat and milk in unimproved marshy areas makes it valuable in many parts of Amazonia, which is the reason that one goal of Brazilian livestock policy is to double the number of water buffalo within five years. (There are presently around 500,000 water buffalo in Brazil.)

Hogs are also raised and fed rice millings, garbage, and offal from the slaughterhouse. Thousands of chickens are fattened at Jari, and some thought has also been given to raising ducks and geese.

RICE PRODUCTION

Rice is one commodity that Jari does not have to import. In fact, thousands of tons are sold each year to other parts of Brazil and to other countries from the 3,500 hectares which have been brought under cultivation since the early 1970s. This rice land along the Amazon has proven very productive and quite cheap to develop at only about US$600 per hectare.

The main land improvement required was an extensive canal and dike system so that land can be flooded quickly to a uniform depth, protected from river flood waters, and drained quickly. The many kilometers of canals that have been built through and around this rice development have been dug with backhoes mounted on pontoon rafts. With this system, flotation and mobility for the backhoes never vary. The changing soil conditions would cause land-bound backhoes to become frequently mired. Furthermore, servicing backhoes by water is much easier and cheaper than servicing them by land. Another problem peculiar to Jari rice lands is muck and peat-filled streambeds that meander through the fields. This organic matter will not support tractors and combines, so it must be removed and replaced with mineral soils.

Tillage and leveling are done with wide-track D-5 Caterpillar tractors with plank extensions on the tracks for added flotation. The rice is planted, fertilized, and sprayed for pest control by airplane. An airstrip has been built next to the rice fields, along with storage facilities and handling equipment for all inputs. Track-equipped Sperry-New Holland combines harvest the rice, which is then dried and milled on site.

The present practice of year-round planting and harvesting is keeping costs per unit of output for machinery ownership and labor very low. Originally, agronomists thought rice would grow well only during certain seasons of the year. However, Doug Thompson, manager of Projeto do Jari in the late 1970s, noticed that rice planted after the 'ideal' time yielded as well as rice planted at any other time. Henceforth, an equal amount of land has been planted and harvested each month.

Year-round planting combined with the four to five month growing period of the semi-dwarf varieties (some have as little as a 115-day growing period) means that two crops of rice per year on all land is the norm. Yields produced have been exceptionally high: four to five tons of rough rice per hectare per crop means yields of eight to ten tons per hectare annually.

Of course, yields of this magnitude have been achieved and maintained only by applying adequate amounts of fertilizers, providing good plant protection against diseases and insects, and weed control. An experimental farm has been maintained at Jari from the outset to test rice varieties. Many other crops are also tested at the farm, including vegetables, cassava, soybeans, maize and tree crops that can be profitably grown on the highlands or in rotation with rice.

JARIPULP

While growing rice is nothing unusual, growing trees in the Amazon basin to supply a pulp mill built in Japan and towed across the ocean to a site on the banks of the Jari river is, to say the least, out of the ordinary. Nevertheless, now, a mere fifteen years after the land was purchased, there are 100,000 hectares of gmelina, Caribbean pine, and eucalyptus planted and growing on Projeto do Jari, and bales of 'Jaripulp' are rolling out of the pulp mill.

There have been some hard lessons learned on the way to this success. First, clearing the land with bulldozers and pushing the trees into a pile to burn them did not work. The heavy equipment ruined the soil structure, making it very hard. Furthermore, many US$10,000 tractor engines were burned up when the radiator hoses were knocked off by branches. Other such accidents ruined a lot of equipment. Thus all trees were felled with chain saws and those which were not valuable for lumber, pilings, or culverts were burned in place.

159

With the demand for electricity at the town of Monte Duardo and for the pulp mill, all of the logs being cut currently are utilized either for lumber or for boiler fuel. Burning wood is a temporary solution to energy needs at Projeto do Jari: plans call for a dam on the Jari river to supply all energy needs. Tops and branches are still burned, and are estimated to release over US$100/hectare in fertilizer equivalent.

The main planting season begins in January when the heavy rains begin. Where a thorough burn has been accomplished, gmelina seeds are sown directly in the field by hand. Results have been good with this direct seeding and establishment costs have been reduced as a result. Elsewhere, four to six-month old gmelina seedlings are pulled from the nursery and pruned to four-centimeter tops and ten-centimeter roots, and planted three meters x two meters. Eucalyptus and Caribbean pine are raised in plastic bags and also planted 3 m x 2 m, except where pasture grasses are planted in the pine for cattle grazing. In those cases, the spacing is 4 m x 2.25 m. Pine is planted on the sandiest soils, gmelina on clay, and eucalyptus on the sandy clay loam soils. Planting requires five to six man-days per hectare.

Planting grass in the pine plantations controls other competing vegetation and eliminates one or two hand-weedings, each of which takes six to eight man-days per hectare. After the pine are 18 months old, cattle can be grazed on the grass until the pine shades it out. Beans, maize, and cassava have also been raised successfully between the tree rows to offset weeding cost with some short-term crop production. Herbicides are used to suppress competing vegetation, but hand-weeding and grazing sown grasses are currently cheaper methods of keeping the crowns of the trees in full sunlight. Gmelina and eucalyptus quickly outgrow competing vegetation - gmelina will grow three meters the first year and eucalyptus over five meters - but the other major pest, leaf-cutting ants, continues to plague all three species and can even kill pine and eucalyptus. These ants are controlled during the dry season by applying Mirex bait to their nests at the rate of 15 grams per square meter. During the wet season, Arbinex is spread in the nests with engine exhaust fumes to keep the population low.

Gmelina and eucalyptus grow to pulpwood size in six years and to timber size in ten years. Once cut, both species will regrow from the stump. Jari foresters expect to be able to regrow trees from the stumps twice before replanting will be needed. Pine reaches pulpwood size in about 12 years.

The current maximum annual production of wood per hectare of the three species is as follows: 42 m^3/ha/year for eucalyptus; 38 m^3/ha/year for gmelina; and 25 m^3/ha/year for pine. These are astronomical yields in comparison to temperate zone yields

(3 m^3/ha/year around 45°N latitude to 15 m^3/ha/year around 35°N latitude, for example), but Jari foresters believe that even these yields can be increased substantially through selection. In tests at Jari, Caribbean pine from different sources show a 40 percent differential in growth rates and 'Eucalyptus deglupta' from different sources show a 30 percent differential. Selection and propagation of superior trees now underway in seed orchards at Jari will lead to a 15 percent gain in yield.

The goal at Jari is to achieve yields of 50 m^3/ha/year from both gmelina and eucalyptus, and 35 m^3/ha/year from Caribbean pine. With yields like that, some experts foresee the time when much of temperate zone pulpwood production may not be able to compete with Amazonia production, and the bulk of the world's pulpwood production will then shift to Brazil.

The present objective at Projeto do Jari, however, is to get the highest return from each tree, regardless of species. Every species of the forest is being identified and analyzed. Over 230 species have been studied and catalogued, with another 200 species identified. Many make good lumber, and others can be mixed with the introduced species for pulp. Dozens of these trees also produce edible fruit and nuts which promise to give the tropics even more tree crops to exploit for food. No doubt many other species will yield valuable pharmaceuticals, not to mention oils, waxes, fibers and flowers.

Projeto do Jari is succeeding not only in the production of rice, water buffalo, cattle, China clay and trees, it is also, and more importantly, introducing a permanent and integrated agro-forestry economy into Amazonia and, by extension, into other tropical rainforest regions. It is, in addition, initiating the development of hundreds of plant species, any one of which may pay for the start-up costs of Projeto do Jari over the next few decades.

21 Tapping Alaska's agricultural potential: the Delta Project

J. MICHAEL HARKER

Just 320 kilometers south of the Arctic Circle, near the community of Delta Junction, Alaska, 6,400 hectares of barley are benefiting from the twenty hours of daylight available during summer months. This land, plus 13,600 additional hectares which will be ready for planting by the 1982 cropping season, is all part of the Delta Agricultural Project: a state supported effort which is viewed as the first step in creating a viable agricultural sector within Alaska's economy.

In the agricultural development of Alaska, government is acting as the catalyst while private enterprise is expected to be the actual agent of development. State government envisions itself as having a role of developmental stimulus that will gradually lessen and, with the exception of land conveyance, be terminated within approximately ten years.

It is Alaska's goal by the end of the 1980s to have established a commercial agricultural industry capable of making a significant contribution to the State's economy. Beyond the 1980s, further expansion of the industry is expected to occur unaided in response to economic opportunity. Specific goals for this decade include: 200,000 hectares in agricultural production; self sufficiency in milk production; establishment of a viable grain export industry; local production of 75 percent of the red meat consumed in the state; development of a red meat slaughter/processing and marketing system; and phased conversion from state to private sector capital sources.

Alaska's agricultural development efforts have suffered misfortunes that surely befall such development anywhere in the world: unexpected problems in weather, conflicts with other potential resource uses, difficulty in precise coordination of farm and infrastructure development, marketing, agronomics, and world market economics. It has, however, progressed despite these problems. This year's grain production, when it is harvested, stored, transported, and finally exported, will mark completion of the test/demonstration envisioned when the Delta Agricultural Project was begun.

THE ALASKAN CHALLENGE

Although agricultural production has existed in Alaska since the arrival of the first Russian settlers in the 18th century, significant development of a commercial industry has not occurred. Several factors have contributed to this condition, but the preeminent factor is that until recently no systematic effort had been undertaken to develop agriculture as a major industry within the state.

At Alaska's Second Annual Agricultural Symposium, the comments of Jay Hammond, Governor of the State of Alaska, reflected new intentions for the industry:

> With our current agricultural development efforts, we have, for the first time in the history of Alaskan agriculture, paused and made a conscious and systematic assessment of the uniqueness of our agriculture development challenge. Consequently, we have begun to undertake the challenge of building not only agricultural production, but also the complete set of components essential to an agricultural support system.

In concert with private enterprise, it is the state goal to bring 200,000 hectares under production by the end of the decade. Concurrent with this goal is recognition of the necessity to create an effective marketing, processing and transportation system, a network of businesses providing agricultural supplies and also to create a livestock production, slaughter/processing and distribution sector to parallel feed grain development.

Although the growing strength of export markets for US grains has stimulated interest in expanding Alaskan agricultural production, it is activity within the Alaskan economy that provides the prime impetus for development. The major oil discovery made near Prudhoe Bay on Alaska's north coast is the basis for that activity. The oil revenues received by the state in fiscal 1980, more than US$2 billion, are expected to increase annually in accord with OPEC inspired price increases.

Recognizing the finite life of this wealth, Governor Hammond went on to state:

> Alaskans must take advantage of our current opportunity to use the earnings from our one time only, nonrenewable resources to develop our renewable resource industries; to develop them in such a way (that they will) generate sufficient new income to offset the costs of services required.

Agricultural development, achieved in part by the use of short term oil revenues, is a unique opportunity to provide sustainable social and economic benefit for the citizens of Alaska.

The president of one of Alaska's leading financial institutions states that his organization '...feels agriculture can and should evolve into a major force in our Alaskan economy providing not only industrial diversification, but greater independence from external economic pressure.' Expanded agriculture will mitigate Alaska's near total dependence on imported food; a concern not only for economic reasons, but also because disruption of supplies would leave the state with only a four day food supply.

Employment opportunity in agriculture is also significant. The long term stability of agriculture can offset the 'boom or bust' cycles of the current economic base of extractive industries. Though oil revenues put the economy on a firm footing today, sustaining economic well being in the future requires renewable resource based development.

THE DELTA AGRICULTURAL PROJECT

The US Department of Agriculture's Soil Conservation Service has identified in excess of six million hectares of potential agricultural lands in Alaska, of which almost 3.6 million hectares have soils particularly well suited to agricultural development. In 1976, several studies were completed that suggested that a development project involving at least 20,000 hectares and based on feed grain production and export marketing would provide a good test/demonstration of the probable success of commercial production agriculture. After considerable public input and with support from the Governor, the 1978 legislature approved plans and funding for what would come to be known as the Delta Agricultural Project.

Twenty-two parcels ranging in size from 800 to 1,440 hectares were sold by lottery on August 5, 1978. Determination of tract size was based on a study which suggested that at least 800 hectares would be necessary to realize the economies of size offered by current equipment technology. Also, size determination attempted to create family farm units intended to provide a family income which would not have to be supplemented by off-farm employment.

Lottery sale, as opposed to auction sale, was deemed necessary so that speculative value would not be capitalized into land prices. To avoid speculative pressure on the value of agricultural lands, Alaska Land Statutes specify that land classified as agricultural land must be sold with restricted, fee-simple title stating that the land must be used only for agricultural purposes. Eligibility requirements for the lottery included Alaska residency, agricultural experience, and availability of US$35,000 unencumbered investment capital.

Purchase price was set by the state at US$126 per hectare. A five percent down payment was required and the balance of the purchase price was financed by the state at six percent for forty years. The land was sold in an uncleared state. Individual owners were allowed to borrow up to US$408 per hectare for clearing the land. Again, terms were six percent interest and a forty year repayment period. In order to allow crop production to begin prior to incurring the burden of loan payments, initial payments and interest accrual were deferred until 1982.

THE FIRST YEAR

Clearing work began in the winter of 1978–1979. By November of 1979, the trees had been knocked down on 80 percent of the project land and one enterprising farmer had produced more than 2.5 tons per hectare of barley on the only 100 hectares seeded on the project that year. Also in 1979, state loan funds were made available to a locally formed cooperative to construct a 10,000 ton capacity grain elevator and handling facility.

The project encouraged many of the already established, small farms in the area to concentrate on barley production. A total of 3,000 tons of US #2 or better quality barley was produced on 1,400 hectares. With the exception of minor on-farm storage, the entire crop was stored and handled by the new elevator.

After the successes of the previous year, cropping on the project expanded to 3,200 hectares in 1980. Ample rains during the growing season produced what looked like a bumper crop with field samples indicating yields in excess of three and one-half tons per hectare. The spring and summer rains so essential to good crop development continued into the harvest period and became an enemy rather than a friend to farmers. A great deal of the grain lodged and was unable to be harvested. Grain that was harvested required drying. When harvest was finally completed in early October, what had earlier looked like a bumper crop averaged a yield of only a little over one and three-quarters tons per hectare. Drying time exceeded the capacity of the elevator, causing serious delays.

The marginal nature of the northern climate was demonstrated and an important lesson was learned. Farmers who had been effective in seeding their crops as early as possible were able to harvest much earlier and avoided much of the damage caused by the rain. In fact, one such farmer had an average yield of 3.7 tons per hectare. The less timely the planting, the more serious was the delay in harvest.

The impact of the results of 1980 was apparent as the 1981 cropping season arrived. Project land in barley increased to approximately 5,200 hectares and early seeding was of prime concern to most farmers. Loans had been received by the cooperative from the state and work began to renovate the elevator system to increase drying, storage and handling capacity. Problems of the previous year in supplying fertilizer had prompted construction of a fertilizer blending and bulk distribution plant which was operational for the spring of 1981.

By September, harvest was under way and the local extension agent estimated average yields to be between 2.5 and three tons per hectare for the 1981 crop. Virtually all trees on the project lands have been knocked down and piled into berms ready to be burned. About three-fourths, or 17,200 hectares, of the land has been broken and will be ready for planting in 1982. According to the terms of the purchase contracts, all farms are to be fully cleared and ready for planting by the end of 1982.

MARKETS AND MARKETING

Prior to the Delta Agricultural Project, Alaska was an importer of barley. Thus, local price for grain established itself as the US West Coast price plus cost of freight to Alaska (approximately US$50 to US$70 greater than US West Coast price). Knowing this pricing scenario could not continue as Project production pushed supply above local demand levels, the state created an interim 'test marketing' program. During 1979 and 1980 the state essentially set barley prices by committing itself to buy and sell barley at a fixed price. In 1979 the price was set at US$120 per ton and in 1980 at US$130. State owned barley stocks still unsold at the end of the 1980-81 marketing season were approximately 2,000 tons.

The test marketing program has now been terminated with the

intention of allowing free market forces and private enterprise to fulfill the marketing function. To aid the private sector, however, the state made US$8.2 million available for loans for the construction of a tidewater export facility and for improvements to the inland transportation and handling system. Because the project is 126 kilometers from the nearest railhead, export bound grain will move this distance by truck.

A private businessman, now in the process of building a feed mill, was awarded a state loan (part of the US$8.2 million) to construct a transfer facility at railhead to off-load grain from trucks and onto railcars. A fleet of twenty hopper bottom rail cars has been ordered and will be used to move the grain from the transfer facility in Fairbanks to a tidewater export facility being built in the town of Seward. Cost to the farmer of grain movement from the project to the export facility is expected to be approximately US$30 per ton.

Japan has been identified as a prime potential market because it is a major feed importer (particularly feed barley) and because of its proximity to Alaska. Taiwan and South Korea are also seen as prospective markets. In 1977 and 1978, trade missions were sent by the State of Alaska to these three countries to acquaint potential buyers with the Delta Agricultural Project and with the potential for future feed grain sales.

A small but growing local livestock industry also provides an important market. As a result of the lower price of Alaska produced barley relative to earlier costs of imported barley, feed grain consumption in-state has more than doubled in the past two years. To further encourage expansion of Alaskan agriculture generally and particularly to encourage in-state barley use, the legislature has appropriated US$2.45 million to be loaned to private enterprise for construction of a multi-species slaughter/processing facility. Construction is expected to be underway within one year and completion is anticipated within three years.

While several well recognized economists have identified development of a livestock industry as the means of creating the highest value market for Alaskan produced feed grains, grain production potential far exceeds the levels that could be consumed locally. Stability of local markets will be dependent on an effective export system to market excess production.

Essentially, grain production for use by a local livestock industry would alone not be of sufficient scale to support development of an efficient grain production industry.

The 2,000 ton carry-over from 1980 plus surpluses in 1981 will be offered for sale on the world market in early 1982. Since the volume will be less than 20,000 tons, it will be very small by world grain trade standards. For Alaska, though, it will be a very important step in opening the door for expanded grain sales and thus to development of the state's agricultural potential.

GOVERNMENT'S ROLE

Capitalizing on agricultural potential in Alaska is as much a social as an economic challenge. Dr. Charles Logsdon, an agricultural consultant with more than 20 years experience in Alaskan agriculture, points out the most crucial factor facing agricultural development. 'Where (twentieth century man) has been successful in moving northward with agriculture, he seems to have been dependent on a government policy which recognizes the desirability for development of agriculture in the north.'
There is not a Department of Agriculture within Alaska's state government. Administration of agricultural development has involved various departments and divisions within the state. To provide for cohesive administration across several departments, the legislature created the Alaska Agricultural Action Council in 1979 to plan and manage agricultural development projects. The five-member council, appointed by the governor, is responsible for proposing specific farm and infrastructure development projects, for cooperating in land selections for projects, for conducting pilot marketing programs, and for identifying financial requirements related to agricultural development.
The philosophy of the council has been to pursue development of projects and units within projects each of which is of sufficient size to perform as a viable economic unit. Its approach has been to encourage state assistance in development of infrastructure that, while ultimately expected to be self-sufficient, is not immediately so because of the development stage of agriculture. Current construction of an export facility and an improved transportation system are good examples. Hectarages are currently insufficient to support economical operations of these facilities. However, both are critical to the success of agriculture development, and with increased agricultural hectarages in production, they will become self supporting.
The Delta Agricultural Project is just a first step in the agricultural development of Alaska. In the longer term, industry growth is required if agriculture is to become a viable contributor to the state's economy. The Project has demonstrated what can be done. The need for renewable resource development should provide the sustained initiative to insure that progress continue.

22 Rice production at Big Falls Ranch

RICHARD J. STROHL

Intent on quickly transforming several thousand hectares of cheap land covered with tropical trees and vegetation into a productive rice farm in order to take advantage of a strong and growing demand for rice in the Caribbean region, the Big Falls Ranch Corporation of Belmopan, Belize, transferred many of the components of California's mechanized, high yield rice production system to the Belize River valley during the late 1960s and early 1970s.

Big Falls Ranch's challenge in its pioneering venture was to shape these components of agricultural systems from disparate parts of the world into a large scale, efficient, rice producing operation. But the components – rice, management, labor, soil, and equipment – had very different rates at which they could achieve an efficient level of production. Equipment, labor, and management made the necessary adjustments to the conditions of the Belize River valley and forged ahead clearing land, preparing rice paddies, sowing rice, and applying fertilizer, herbicides, and insecticides.

However, rice, the essential component which paid the bills, was left behind in this race toward productive efficiency, because it could only be modified to fit the new environment at its own rate of reproductive cycles. Neither could the soil regenerate and adjust as fast as the land was cleared and leveled.

As a result, income fell far short of costs in the early years. The costs of a high yielding and highly mechanized rice growing system were incurred each and every year and added to the cost of land clearing and paddy construction. But the available rice varieties and the soil which supported them could not produce high yields. Consequently, this potentially profitable agricultural venture is now weighed down with a burden of debt which it may not be able to carry.

Modern agricultural technology combined with good and cheap land, abundant water, a tropical climate, and a strong market had not given Big Falls Ranch quick profits - quite the opposite. This failure to generate profits in its first few years of operation stems from the fact that all agricultural systems develop around the peculiarities of an area's environment, its soil and climate. No area has exactly the same growing conditions as another; therefore, no efficient agricultural system is exactly like another. For the utmost in efficiency (the highest yield), each system must consist of components - crop varieties, cultural practices, soil amendments, equipment - which conform as closely as possible to the dictates of its environment.

Unfortunately, high yielding crop varieties able to fit an area's growing conditions must be found through a time consuming process of trial and error, selection and breeding. Nor will a soil subjected to a new regime of clearing, tilling, and flooding be immediately ready to support high crop yields. Only over time will it become stable, reveal some of its mysteries, and respond in a predictable manner to soil amendments and cultivation.

THE ORIGINAL PLAN

Prospects were bright for Big Falls Ranch (BFR) on August 5, 1963, when it was incorporated by US citizens Elizabeth, Calbert, Charles and James Bevis with share capital of US$700,000. Kern County Land Company of California joined the Bevis family as one of the early shareholders in BFR, and together they acquired a concession of 14,575 hectares of rich alluvial soil on the banks of the Belize River.

Certainly no mistake was made in selecting this land for rice production. Although it held little valuable timber in 1963, great quantities of mahogany, rosewood and logwood had been cut from the land. The old axiom that 'Wherever mahogany will grow, there every tropical product will flourish; and wherever logwood grows, there you can produce the finest rice,' has always proven true. Moreover, modern methods of soil and site analysis applied by Agricultural Consultants, Inc., in 1965 verified the conclusion that rice would do well in the Belize River Valley.

Rice was in great demand not only in Belize, which was

importing several thousand tons each year during the 1960s, but also in many other Caribbean nations. These nations have long sought to reduce their imports of rice, which now exceed US$1 billion annually, by gaining self-sufficiency in this staple. Jamaica alone imports over 50,000 tons each year and its rice production has been dropping.

So any efforts to grow rice in the region were officially welcomed and encouraged. Belize had long been viewed as the potential rice bowl of the Caribbean because of its many thousands of hectares of uncultivated land suitable for rice production. Thus BFR's investment in the establishment of a large scale, mechanized rice growing venture was looked upon with great favor by the Belize government, which hoped to reduce or eliminate its imports of rice in short order and later gain export earnings from rice as the project expanded.

So with great optimism, bulldozers cleared the land. Engineers surveyed it, laid out rice paddies, and precision leveled them. Irrigation pumps were installed to draw water from the Belize River and levees built to contain it. Tractors and disc harrows prepared the seedbed, and airplanes sowed rice seed and applied fertilizers, herbicides, and insecticides. Track-equipped combines harvested the rice which was then dried, milled, bagged, sold and shipped by Big Falls Ranch.

But financial success did not follow these technology transfers. In fact, by 1976 the lack of profits forced a cessation of land clearing and new paddy preparation. Since then the area under cultivation has been reduced to cut losses and the premise on which the original development plan was based has been re-evaluated.

THE PROBLEMS

Equipment can be quickly adjusted and modified to work efficiently under new conditions. After all, it is designed to work well over a wide range of conditions to gain as large a market as possible. Similarly, managers can learn in a short time to compensate for the distance between their sources of equipment, parts and other inputs required by a high yield, mechanized agricultural system. Compensating for the lack of agronomic information that only time can yield is not so easy and, in the case of Big Falls Ranch, turned out to be very costly.

Money, men and steel were put to work in an area with little or no infrastructure to support the technology which was imported. Nor was there any data on what to expect when the land was cleared and rice sowed. There were no agricultural experiment stations which had been conducting experiments and gathering information for many years on land clearing techniques, land leveling, paddy size, irrigation schedules, fertilization, weed control, rice varieties and all the other factors involved in high yield, mechanized rice growing. Therefore, there was little scientific data on which to base projections. BFR had to collect information gained from its own experience - a process of large scale trial and error that proved very costly.

Land clearing cost several hundred US dollars per hectare, and land leveling, levee building, and irrigation facilities added several hundred more US dollars per hectare to the cost of land development. Added to this was the cost of building and maintaining an infrastructure of roads, houses, and other support facilities. Consequently, before a kernel of rice was sowed, over US$1,000 per hectare had been invested.

Neither was growing the rice cheap. Imported equipment needed modification to work efficiently in Belize and the modifications took time and money. Paddies had to be leveled and re-leveled to assure even water depths. An old network of drainage ditches on BFR land which was built by the Mayas thousands of years ago had to be filled and leveled repeatedly at considerable expense - an unexpected additional cost.

Furthermore, the soil responded to clearing and tillage in unforeseen ways. 'The soil in the Belize River valley looks like temperate zone clay, but doesn't act like it,' says Laurence G. Harris of Mechanized Agriculture, Inc., who was involved in land leveling and paddy construction for BFR. His statement indicated that it not only took time for the soil to adjust to supporting rice, but it also took time for the rice growers to learn how to handle the soil. Similarly, new cultural practices for growing rice had to be learned on the job to make the most of the available rice varieties, many of which did not respond with superlative yields in BFR's environment. In fact, many varieties succumbed to the local plant diseases.

Initially BFR had intended to clear 1,600 hectares yearly for nine years. Paddy construction and farming were to be carried on apace. Of course, the cash flow and income projections based on these plans had the investors smiling, but those who were in charge of turning BFR's land into rice paddies were skeptical.

The project got underway in 1968 when 250 hectares of rice were planted. Harvested yields of this crop and subsequent crops hovered around 1,000 kgs. of rough rice per hectare, which did not cover operating expenses let alone land development costs. Nor did yields overall improve much over the next nine years. Land clearing and paddy construction continued, however, and by 1973, 2,852 hectares were put into rice, with yields of 1,449 kgs. of rough rice per hectare.

Table 22.1

Average Yields of Dry Paddy per Hectare, 1973-1980

	Hectares Cropped	Total Production (Metric Ton)	Yield (Kg/ha)
1973	2,582	4,132	1,449
1974	3,245	5,202	1,603
1975	1,456	2,326	1,598
1976	2,653	3,530	1,331
1977	2,007	3,661	1,824
1978	970	2,994	3,087
1979	1,031	3,174	3,079
1980	1,284	4,643	3,616

Cropped hectarage reached a peak in 1974 at 3,245 hectares and the yield increased somewhat to 1,603 kgs. of rough rice per hectare.

BOOKER'S STRATEGY

Obviously, something had to be done to get the yields up, and in 1977, BFR signed a management contract with Booker Agriculture International, Ltd. Booker's strategy to solve the problems that were holding down yields was to do applied research in the traditional manner. The amount of land cultivated was cut back to those fields which had proven their capacity to produce high yields, and experiments with different methods of cultivation were untaken on these fields.

Of course, losses were immediately cut because less land was being cultivated. Furthermore, Booker managers began using less fertilizer and changing the irrigation regime to several flushings of a paddy instead of a single flooding. Yields did increase although on fewer hectares. In 1978 only 970 hectares of rice were planted with an average yield of 3,087 kgs. per hectare. By 1980 more land had been re-leveled and the average yield from 1,284 hectares was 3,616 kgs. per hectare, mainly from two varieties (CICA-8 from Colombia and CR11-13 from Costa Rica).

Big Falls Ranch remains a highly mechanized rice growing operation with two crops of rice per year planted and harvested, one in the late fall and the other in the spring. Approximately 90 kgs. of pre-germinated rice seed are sowed per hectare, with Propanel, Molinate, 2,4-D, Paraquat and Dalapon used to control weeds. Although research continues on the timing and amount of fertilizer use to maximize yields, diammonium phosphate and urea are the principal fertilizers used. Similarly, disease and insect control awaits more knowledge of the local pests.

Land development and paddy construction are carried out with Caterpillar tractors. Land preparation is done with wheel tractors and Cessna planes are used to sow the rice, spray herbicides and insecticides, and spread fertilizer. Tracked combines harvest the rice.

Booker Agriculture International remains confident that its trials and experiments will eventually lead to cultural methods of rice varieties which will push yields to 6,000 kgs. of rough rice per hectare. That will definitely be a profitable level of production at the present price of US$0.13 for rough rice and would give BFR's investors hope of recovering the over US$12 million invested to date. Unfortunately, at a time when BFR could use more capital to expand production at a profitable yield level, one of its major investors, ADELA Investment Company S.A., has been liquidated (ADELA was dissolved in January, 1982.)

Rice production goes on elsewhere in Belize. Attracted by the yields of 3,000 to 4,000 kgs. of rough rice per hectare proven possible by BFR, other rice growing ventures have begun. BFR's pioneering effort has paid off for others, if not for itself. Rio Dorado Estate now has 200 hectares under fully mechanized cultivation in the Golden Stream area of Toledo district. A Jamaican investor, Donald Hoe, has 80 hectares producing in Stann Creek District and is expanding to 400 hectares. In Orange Walk District, Mennonite farmers from the USA have 80 hectares in mechanized rice production.

For Belize this means that annual production is now near nine million kgs. With only 5.5 million kgs. needed domestically, several thousands tons are available for export. Furthermore, success in more than meeting the national demand for rice gives impetus to the other agricultural development projects which have been undertaken in grains, oilseeds and dairy products. No doubt self-sufficiency in beans and maize will be achieved soon and Belize will go on to become a major source of agricultural commodities for the Caribbean.

Big Falls Ranch now has the experience on which to base an efficient agricultural system. With a little more time and some more capital, the Belize River valley could be made to flourish like it has not flourished since the days of the Mayan Civilization.

23 Hummingbird Farm: Hershey's hope for more abundant and improved cocoa

CURT HARLER

Although production from its 728 hectare Hummingbird Farm will make hardly a dent in world cocoa output levels, Hershey Foods Corporation has launched a program it hopes will have great impact on both the yields and quality of world cocoa production.

The Chinese have an oft quoted saying: give a man a fish and he will eat for a day; teach him to fish and he can eat forever. The program begun at Hummingbird-Hershey, Ltd. in Belize (formerly British Honduras) has a bit of that philosophy behind it. Even more important to a profits-oriented industry, Hershey Foods foresees the day when its efforts will pay off not only from its own farming operations but also from other cocoa growers who will have learned from Hershey's experience.

Glenn A. Trout, Hershey's director of agribusiness, maintains that there is no other major crop in the world for which actual farm practices lag so far behind scientific and agronomic experimentation as they do in cocoa. So Hershey, as part of an on-going program, decided to do something about it.

CORPORATE STRATEGY

The firm did not enter the field with the idea of being a 'big brother' who could give all the answers to the world's growers. In fact, Trout warns against US and Canadian businessmen falling prey to such an idea. 'The glamour leads them astray,' Trout says of businessmen who seek to expand into overseas projects.

'Remember how hard it was making a success of the business in your own country. Now you are facing other governments, other cultures, and are often in a field of business you never were in before,' he says.

Hershey Foods did not wander into Belize quite as blindly as Trout's stereotyped manager. The cocoa project was the third phase of Hershey's continuing program to improve and control the inputs which go into its chocolate manufacturing business located in Hershey, Pennsylvania, USA.

Back in the late 1960s, Hershey made a corporate decision to institute improved control standards for the raw materials going into its plants. Trout was hired at that time and brought to the corporation as a manager with technical training as a chemist. His first two projects at Hershey were to address and refine the milk and peanut procurement systems.

Another, perhaps more crucial project for Trout involved cocoa beans. In 1973-74, a shortage of cocoa caused the price on the US market to skyrocket from US$0.66 per kilo to over US$4.40. The shortage resulted not only from increased world demand, but also from dwindling, uncertain production and a high rate of crop failure.

Bean quality has always been important to Hershey, and decreased supply, coupled with the trend of producing nations to ship semi-processed beans, indicated potential quality assurance problems.

Hershey did not believe the solution to cocoa's quantity/quality dilemma was in vertical integration, or owning and operating its own plantations. Instead, Hershey believed the long term solution was for cocoa users somehow to show growers that cocoa could compete economically with other crop choices and that good farming could also improve quality. This belief eventually took the shape of a demonstration farm where modern management and scientific techniques would hopefully keep an ancient crop viable.

CHOOSING A SITE

Very little data was available to Hershey for its project. Between 65 and 75 percent of the cocoa grown in the world is grown in Africa under primitive conditions on farms of one to three hectares in size. The farmers use a minimum of fertilizer and chemicals for pest and disease control. Underplanting using forest trees as high shade is common. Under this sytem, it is not surprising that yields are only 325 to 350 kilograms per hectare.

Hershey saw little reason to doubt it could triple or quadruple those yields if scientific agricultural principles were applied to the growing of cocoa.

Africa was the natural first place a cocoa producer would consider for such a growing program. But Africa was rejected in favor of the Western Hemisphere for a number of reasons. 'The African nations' production system, entire culture and the way they do business are significantly different from ours. A whole nation could decide to stop growing cocoa, and we would be in a poor position to have adequate raw materials,' Trout says.

As a member of the American Cocoa Research Institute, which works primarily in the Western Hemisphere, Hershey turned its emphasis to that area of the world. Business considerations, such as shipping costs to the US, also favored a site in Central or South America.

When Trout looked for the site for the project, though, he was not looking for any particular location - rather, he was concerned about putting together a practical management team. Hershey started its first cocoa-growing operation in Costa Rica with an expatriate manager from the USA who shared its management and production philosophies.

At about the same time, Trout became aware of Hummingbird Farm, which had been started by some Jamaicans in the late 1950s, but had been abandoned in 1961. This was the time when the extra shade should have been removed from the young cocoa trees, but the operator died, the bottom fell out of the cocoa market, and the farm was left to the jungle. No care was given the farm for the next 15 years. The Jamaicans sold their interest to a US company in 1964, which in turn sold it to a Canadian real estate man in 1970.

The Hummingbird-Hershey cocoa growing operation was started as a joint venture on a portion of the land owned by the Canadian, but in 1978 Hershey purchased the Canadian's share to obtain sole ownership.

There were several factors in favor of the farm's location. The Commonwealth Development Corporation (formerly the Colonial Development Company) had identified the Hummingbird-Hershey farm area as a reasonably good site for cocoa.

The farm is located in the Hummingbird Valley along the Hummingbird Highway, an all-weather, hardtopped road which leads to Belize City. The road is excellent by Central American standards, a definite advantage for shipping the cocoa to market. The only potential bottleneck between farm and dockside was the Western Highway, which floods on occasion. Still, the farm's location was excellent for a project like Hershey's.

The Belizean government agreed to grant Hershey permission

to bring into the country duty-free, for a certain time, machinery and other farm equipment which were not locally available. Trout, while emphasizing the development concessions were worthwhile, noted the time period allowed was short compared to the length of time it takes to get a tree crop established. Nevertheless, being able to import farm equipment without paying duty resulted in a major savings in time. Taxes on sales and profits also were adjusted to allow a land developer to get off to a reasonably good start.

In turn, Hershey agreed to spend a certain sum of money in development and to create a certain number of jobs. Today about 100 Belizean nationals, from top management to labor, are working on the farm. All on-site management is in the hands of Belizean nationals.

DESIGNING THE OPERATION

Hershey was hard-pressed to find any expert help for its newly acquired farm. 'Our expertise came from reading the literature,' Trout says. Hershey put together a team with combined experience in agribusiness, chemistry, and botany, who visited some working farms and set out to unravel the mysteries of growing a unique tree crop. None of the Belize-based management had a true background in cocoa, either.

'That way we didn't need to beat the poor ideas out of our heads,' quips B.K. Matlick, Hershey's Manager of Agribusiness.

The resident farmer on the Hummingbird plantation is Norris Wade, a Belizean national who received his training at Arizona State University in the USA. Wade had worked with the Belize Ministry of Agriculture, and had experience on a citrus operation.

Hershey's feasibility study projected land clearing would take four to five years, starting in March 1977. In 1978, a nursery was established. Hershey began thinning out the old trees, a somewhat questionable venture because it was unknown what varieties were planted, how old they were, what past fertility conditions were - in short, hardly a good base for a scientific program like the one Hershey proposed.

However, Hurricane Greta destroyed most of the tall old trees on September 18, 1978. 'It made some of our ideas obsolete,' Trout says. 'It made the farm look like a plucked chicken. Anyone in his right mind would have walked away and asked the insurance company, "What will you give us for this?"'

Fortunately, the hurricane did not kill many of the small seedlings in the nursery. There were a couple of blocks of trees the proper size, three to four meters, which survived.

The trees lost had been three times that height.

Hershey's botanist, Gordon Patterson, prefers cocoa trees about the size and shape of peach trees for optimum production. Planting density, he feels, should be about 1,125 to 1,250 trees per hectare.

Hummingbird-Hershey's production goal is 1,200 kilograms per hectare, compared to the national average in Belize of 400 kilograms per hectare or output of 750 to 800 kilograms per hectare in a top growing nation like Brazil or Ivory Coast.

There was no source of improved seed or planting material in Belize. 'We needed to find one that was close enough to transport the delicate seeds; that resembled Belize as much as possible in climate, pests and diseases; and that actually had surplus seed to sell,' Patterson says. 'The only place that fit all those criteria was Costa Rica.'

POTENTIAL REWARDS

It was unlikely that any of the major cocoa producing nations would object to the Hummingbird-Hershey project: prices were high; there were plenty of buyers with good demand; supply was low; and even if Hummingbird-Hershey were wildly successful, it would produce only a minute percentage of the world's cocoa supply. The United States imports 180,000 MT annually. Even if Belize were to produce 4,500 MT, it would still be only 2.5 percent of US cocoa requirements.

But the establishment of Hummingbird-Hershey was not intended as a short term rapid solution to the problem of the quantity and quality of world cocoa bean production. The ultimate objective was, and is, to show that growing cocoa beans on traditional small farms can be financially rewarding and that bean quality can be enhanced. As Glenn Trout noted, 'This is conceived of as being a demonstration farm to showcase good agronomic practices, good hardheaded farming, using the best planting material, good fertilization and good shade technology.'

Matlick emphasized the economic aspects: 'We're doing it to prove that this particular size farm can be commercially profitable.' Accomplishing that objective has meant that Hershey has had to learn about growing other crops besides cocoa.

Hershey was able to combine the cocoa plant's need for shade with profit by utilizing a shade planting which also a second cash crop. First Hershey grew plantains, a cooking banana, and later used pigeon peas, a soil-enriching legume which is high in protein. Both crops can be marketed locally, and pigeon peas are also used as an export crop. In addition, on approximately 12 hectares of land which was not suitable for cocoa production, marsh white grapefruit was planted.

For the small farm, the combination of these various cash crops adds up to good economics and land utilization, as well as good agronomy.

Hummingbird-Hershey's first trees are fruiting now, and the 1978 planting will give a harvest worth taking this year for the first time. At present, 400 hectares are in rehabilitated trees. An additional 80 hectares of trees will be out of the nursery in another year. The best tracts have been planted; those remaining are the less desirable land. Hershey is consolidating its position, taking the best possible care of the trees it has growing, and reviewing its current position.

Although the future of Hummingbird-Hershey will be determined by Hershey's top management, some of the innovations on the farm are being watched carefully by world cocoa growers. 'But so far the local farmers are taking it slowly; they have no experience to judge us by, but they are watching us. We must make money to impress them. That is our intent,' Trout says.

Local growers have responded well, however, to buying Hummingbird Farm seedlings from the Belizean government, which purchased them and has offered them to farmers at a subsidized rate.

'I predict Hummingbird is going to be the most widely visited cocoa farm in the world,' Matlick concludes.

It promises to be a worthwhile stop for anyone interested in upgrading cocoa production, in closing the gap between textbook technology and on-farm production.

SAVING GHANA'S COCOA INDUSTRY

Providing a stable supply was a key concern in developing Hummingbird Farm. Most of the world's cocoa has traditionally come from Ghana, but that country is now faced with massive problems. While theoretically able to produce 800,000 MT of cocoa annually, Ghana's output will probably reach only 250,000 MT this year.

Farmers in Ghana are asking, 'Why bother growing cocoa if I can't get it to market?' While low prices and smuggling are problems, the major difficulty is transportation. Much of last year's crop remains locked up in villages. The road network in Ghana has deteriorated so that trucks cannot reach the harvested crop. Meanwhile moths and humidity are destroying the crop's quality.

In an effort to overcome this logistics problem, the Ghana Cocoa Marketing Board is searching for solutions. One of the most unusual was proposed by the Ghana Cocoa Fruit Processing Company (GCFPC) several years ago. The chief purpose of GCFPC is the commercial exploitation of an entirely new system for the collection, transport and processing of cocoa pods. The GCFPC system involved an industrialized transport system for the pods using an enclosed pipeline to carry the pods 100 to 120 kilometers to a processing facility at Tema.

GCFPC believed that a system using a pipeline to carry pods to a central location and then splitting them would improve both the quantity and quality of cocoa beans, compared to the traditional system.

A further advantage of this scheme was that with centralized processing, a large volume of byproducts would be available. The byproducts of the cocoa pods make up 85 to 90 percent of the pod by weight. These consist of the sugary, gelatinous mass around the seeds and the fibrous husk or shell. Potential uses are in cattle feed, organic fertilizers, building materials, furfural manufacture and alcohol.

The proposed pipeline promised to be an expensive and technically complicated affair. The GCFPC approached a leading US investment banking firm for assistance. The firm insisted that to raise the millions of US dollars needed to finance this project, a financial and economic feasibility study would be necessary. Six leading agribusiness consulting firms were contacted and asked to submit proposals. After a California firm apparently won the bidding, it was informed that the project would not go forward.

Today both the pipeline and Ghana's cocoa industry continue to languish. Since 1978, Ghana has no longer been the world's leading cocoa producer; this honor now belongs to Ivory Coast.

24 Contract growing of flue-cured tobacco in Jamaica

ROBERT G. LEWIS

One of the world's outstanding success stories in the transfer of agricultural technology to a developing country has been achieved in the island nation of Jamaica.

Last year Jamaica produced 80 percent of the Virginia-type (flue-cured) tobacco that was used in the manufacture of cigarettes, which supplied almost its entire domestic demand and a small but growing volume of exports.

Less than a decade ago, more than 80 percent of its requirements were imported. The first small hectarage of Virginia-type tobacco was harvested there only 28 years ago.

For several centuries, international tobacco industry experts had generally accepted the notion that Jamaica could not grow the world-renowned 'Virginia-type' tobacco leaf, the world standard for making quality cigarettes. In disproving that conventional wisdom, Jamaica's tobacco industry also countered a dismaying down-trend in the country's overall agricultural production.

Jamaican farmers have been plagued by multiple problems during recent years. Adverse weather has brought floods, droughts and hurricanes. A chronic lack of foreign exchange has created shortages of imported inputs, including fertilizer, pesticides, farm and transport machinery, and spare parts. The weak internal distribution and marketing system continues to deteriorate. Disease and pest problems have afflicted coffee and coconut, as well as tobacco.

In 1980, overall agricultural production in Jamaica was down by ten percent from its 1978 peak. The leading export crops were hardest hit: sugar production declined by 35 percent and coffee by 30 percent from the levels of five years before. Banana exports fell to an all-time low of 33,000 tons, down from 77,000 tons five years before, and were barely one-fifth of Jamaica's export quota to the United Kingdom. The country's total agricultural export earnings, despite higher prices, were down nine percent from five years before.

IMPORT SUBSTITUTION

Jamaica's contrasting tobacco success story was initiated in response to the government's mandate to expand domestic production to substitute for imports so as to conserve scarce foreign exchange. As the country's financial condition worsened during the 1970s, this motivation became increasingly urgent.

Two kinds of tobacco are of primary importance to Jamaica's economy, and both were affected by the national effort to improve its foreign exchange position.

Most tobacco consumption in Jamaica is in the form of cigarettes. The goal here was to substitute domestic product for the costly imports of Virginia-type leaf, which had been used almost exclusively to supply the growing domestic market.

The other type is air-cured dark leaf, used for making cigars for both domestic and long-established export markets. Here the goal was to increase foreign exchange earnings by expanding export sales of Jamaican-produced tobacco, particularly in the form of manufactured cigars, but also as unmanufactured tobacco.

The Virginia-type tobacco used for making cigarettes is the more important economically in Jamaica, as it is in the world. No Virginia-type tobacco was grown in Jamaica until 1954. There was no previous experience nor capability with the distinctive technology for producing this type of tobacco in Jamaica at that time. Progress was slow at first: by the end of eight years, annual production had reached only 225,000 kilos of cured leaf.

Thereafter, spurred by the growing urgency of the nation's financial crisis and encouraged by preliminary successes, production increased swiftly, approximately doubling every three years. The 1981-82 crop, estimated at about 1.35 million kilos, is a six-fold increase over the crop of nine years ago.

From complete dependence upon imports of cigarettes and unmanufactured Virginia-type leaf 28 years ago, Jamaica now supplies about 80 percent of its total consumption of cigarette tobacco. Although some imports have continued to be necessary for blending with the domestic product in order to maintain taste standards, the industry aims eventually to become 100 percent self-sufficient in all qualities of cigarette tobacco.

The impact of Jamaica's drive for self-sufficiency in Virginia-type tobacco upon its imports from the United States illustrates the program's contribution to the country's foreign exchange balances. During the five years 1974-78 inclusive, annual imports from the USA averaged 720,000 kilos. In 1981, imports of US leaf were only half that much - 373,050 kilos. Jamaica's imports of US-made cigarettes also declined during the period, from a five-year average of 35 million to only two million in 1981.

The apparent saving in foreign exchange resulting from this successful substitution of domestic for imported leaf and cigarettes reached approximately US$5 million in 1981. Foreign exchange benefits have been achieved also by the increase in domestic production of cigar-type leaf, but the amounts are smaller.

A concerted effort to increase production of the dark air-cured type of tobacco was started in 1969. It is now being intensified after a set-back during the last half of the 1970s due to disease and other problems. Production averaged only 203,400 kilos annually during the past five years. The 1982 crop of an estimated 337,500 kilos represents a substantial increase.

CONTRACT FARMING

How were these successes achieved? How were the difficulties usually associated with transferring advanced farming technology to developing countries overcome? How could the tobacco industry cope relatively so well with the economic and financial problems that beset the national economy?

The credit clearly must be given to the introduction of a production system known as 'contract farming.'

Few Jamaican farmers had any previous experience with the use of modern technology in growing tobacco. In the case of growers of the Virginia-type, almost none of the present growers had ever before grown tobacco of any kind, by any method.

In the contract farming system, individual growers enter into contracts with a central authority having the capability to provide all of the financial resources, production inputs, and technical knowledge required to develop and apply modern production methods. Growers are obliged to accept strict supervision of their farming practices, and are provided with systematic training and precise instructions in approved methods. The contractor selects and provides the seeds (or seedlings) best adapted to produce the desired qualities of the product; advances funds needed during the production, harvesting, and curing processes; and provides the production inputs required to produce a crop of the desired characteristics and qualities. The cost of these services and inputs is charged to the grower's account and deducted from the value of the crop at the end of the season, when the contractor takes possession.

Theoretically, the contractor in such a system may be either a private-sector company, usually a manufacturer or processor of the crop to be grown, or a governmental or quasi-governmental agency. In the Jamaica tobacco program, both kinds of contracting agencies are present.

The Cigarette Company of Jamaica Ltd. is the contractor for almost all of the Virginia-type tobacco grown on the island. The government-sponsored Tobacco Industry Control Authority (TICA) is the main contractor for the cigar tobaccos. The Jamaica Tobacco Company, one of the island's four cigar manufacturers, also contracts with growers.

The Cigarette Company of Jamaica is now the sole manufacturer of cigarettes in the country. In recent years imports have been negligible, and marketed almost exclusively to the tourist trade, placing the company in an extremely strong position in the domestic market.

The Cigarette Company of Jamaica is an affiliate of Carreras Group Limited, which in turn is associated with Carreras Rothman Limited, the internationally-known British firm. The cigarettes manufactured in Jamaica are all filtered and of English-type blends.

Nine of the internationally-known Carreras Rothman brands are produced in Jamaica, including Craven 'A', Rothmans King Size, Carreras #7, Consulate, Dunhill International, Piccadilly, Benson and Hedges 'special filter' and 'special mild,' and Mattahorn. According to Hugh Hart, the Carreras Group's Chairman, the association with Rothmans ensures that the company's Jamaican cigarettes 'meet the high quality standards required of international brands.'

The company owns or leases eight large tracts which had previously been used for growing sugar cane. Although only marginal for sugar production, the sandy soils of these tracts have proven to be ideal for tobacco.

All of the contract farmers are trained from the very fundamentals to produce tobacco. Growers are selected from the farming and working communities of the particular area. Some have worked for other farmers, while others may have been company employees. Choices are made after consultation with a committee of existing growers, and production contracts are offered either on their own land, if available, or as sub-tenants on land leased by the company. Each farmer averages eight-tenths hectare of planted tobacco.

Contracting with a company is highly popular with farmers. Tobacco yields more income per hour of labor 'than any other legal agricultural commodity on the island today,' remarked John Hall, Managing Director of Cigarette Company of Jamaica. 'On the usual yield of 1,334 kilos per hectare, the farmer will clear US$1,410 per hectare,' Hall said. 'That's a good return for a 17-week crop.'

The planting is spread from September to mid-January so as to permit maximum use of buildings and facilities for curing and handling the crop. Machinery for land preparation and tillage, facilities for curing the leaf, and irrigation facilities and services, are furnished by the company in a pool for joint use by groups of farmers. In addition to providing and financing all purchase inputs and advancing funds for hired labor until the crop is harvested, the company provides up-to-date technical guidance to the producers. The company relies upon Biological Consulting Associates of Raleigh, North Carolina, USA, for consulting services.

GROWERS' COMMITTEES

The company encourages the formation of growers' committees elected by the farmers in each farming project, and works with them in training programs, administration of the project activities, and consultations on technical and operating problems as they arise.

In interviews with a group of growers and company officials at tobacco farms in the Cheateau-Rock River region near May Pen, it became apparent that the elected growers' committees function as informal growers' communication and negotiation associations. Ainsley King, the company's senior farm manager, and George Johnson, manager of the farms in the Cheateau-Rock River region, described the growers' participation in decisions affecting management, training, operations, and pricing of the products as a positive and constructive feature of the system.

As the growers present nodded in agreement, King described the annual consultations preceding the determination of prices to be paid for the crop.

'We lay out all the facts on the table,' King said. 'Everyone reviews the data, and the growers can judge the fairness and accuracy on the basis of their own knowledge and experience. It reduces the procedure to a negotiation of the payment to be received per hour for the labor required to produce, harvest and cure the crop.'

During the off-season, growers are restricted from planting specific crops which might transmit or incubate insect or disease infestations to which tobacco is vulnerable. But off-season crops which are permitted – including sweet maize, red peas, red kidney beans, African red beans, pumpkins, and some others – may be raised for market or home consumption. A small charge is made by the company for off-season use of its tobacco land.

The dark tobaccos grown for commercial cigar manufacture also are produced under contracts similar to those used by the Cigarette Company for Virginia-type. TICA, the government-sponsored agency, controls about two-thirds (194 hectares in 1981) and Jamaica Cigar Company the other one-third (101 hectares in 1981) of the commercial hectarage.

Carl A. Leighton, TICA's deputy manager, explained that growers are guaranteed a minimum price before planting. Payment is made within about two weeks after delivery of the leaf by farmers. The cost of advances for production requirements is deducted from the payment. When TICA's marketing success warrants, proceeds in excess of costs and the initial payments are distributed later to growers. TICA had 54 growers producing cigar tobacco and six producing cigarette tobacco in the 1981-82 crop.

TICA markets cigar tobacco to the four other cigar manufacturers in Jamaica, and for export as unmanufactured leaf. Its growers' cigarette tobacco is sold to the Cigarette Company of Jamaica. Jamaica Tobacco Company manufactures most of the leaf produced by its own contract growers.

The structure of trade in cigar tobaccos is different from that in cigarette leaf in that suitable specialized leaf for wrapper and to some extent binder and filler probably will continue to be available only from import sources. Consequently, the volume of imports of manufactured cigar-type leaf is likely to need to rise in proportion to the rise in total cigar production. Therefore it is the export volume in manufacturing cigars that offers the main hope of foreign exchange benefits to the Jamaican economy.

This hope is being realized. Cigar exports are estimated to reach 29 million pieces in 1982, up 89 percent above five years ago.

A SUCCESS STORY

The Jamaican experience with tobacco indicates that when the proper circumstances are present, the contract farming system can transfer and apply modern agricultural technology successfully in a developing country, even when its farmers at the start lack skills, training and experience. The vital conditions are that the contractor have ample financial and organizational resources, highly-trained technical personnel,

187

and support from the government in permitting foreign exchange to be used to import essential materials, equipment, and consulting services.

The Cigarette Company of Jamaica is an example in which these conditions are met fully. The company's technical and managerial staff members are highly educated, and margins in its almost captive domestic market are sufficient to ensure ample financial resources.

To its credit, the company pursues enlightened and creative policies in its relations with the contract growers. The technically-trained management people are respected, warm, and considerate in their work with the growers. The encouragement and recognition given to the growers' participation through elected negotiating committees conform to the best principles of modern participatory management. The morale of growers seems to be high.

However, the gains and successes won by the contract farming system must be regarded with some caution.

For one thing, tobacco production is a relatively small part of Jamaica's agriculture. In the 1981-82 crop, no more than a thousand contract growers were affiliated with the three contractors - less than one percent of the total number of farmers.

The land area devoted to the commercial tobacco crop is likewise very small, well under one percent of the country's total of 'good' and 'fair' cropland.

Nor do the contract growers account for the total tobacco industry. The number of traditional 'backyard' tobacco producers in Jamaica is unknown, and their significance in the economy appears to be greater than once believed. But these traditional producers seem sure to be left behind technologically, and probably will disappear in the long run as the urban culture and its products displace their traditional markets.

25 Puerto Rico's Agricultural Diversification Program

JOHN FREIVALDS

After years of delay, Puerto Rico's first rice mill is about to be completed, but at this time, only about 100 hectares of rice are under cultivation on the island. When the project began in 1978, 5,000 hectares were scheduled to be planted by 1982. 'When this mill is completed, we will only have enough domestically produced rice to keep it running for one hour!' complains one critic of the island's US$25 million rice project.

What has happened to Puerto Rico as it has tried first to industrialize, then to diversify its agriculture, is symptomatic of what some developing countries encounter in moving too fast to industrialize, neglecting their agriculture. Once self-sufficient in food production, Puerto Rico is now almost totally dependent on food imports. Every year Puerto Rico imports around 190,000 MT of rice alone plus other foodstuffs for a total cost of US$1.2 billion. Even the famous Puerto Rican rum is now made from molasses imported from the Dominican Republic.

Puerto Rico's agriculture is in disarray. Sugar cane yields are only half what they were 25 years ago, and the State Sugar Corporation set up in 1973 (the owner of the majority of the sugar land and seven mills) has run up a debt of US$450 million. A government study found that the cost of producing sugar in Puerto Rico was four times that of Hawaii, 2.6 times that of Florida, and twice that of Louisiana.

The rice mill and the lands surrounding it were to be a

catalyst for revitalizing agriculture, but problems have plagued the efforts. The mill has experienced numerous delays and design changes, and rice cultivation was delayed by severe storms, disagreement on land preparation methods, the death of a key manager, the total restructuring of the project's financing, and conflict over the management contract arranged with a US rice milling company.

'We might serve as a horrible example to any underdeveloped country that wants to move too quickly,' says Jose Vicente Chandler, author of Puerto Rico's agricultural modernization program.

OPERATION BOOTSTRAP

A major economic development program was begun in the 1940s to bring industrialization to Puerto Rico, a Caribbean island 160 kilometers long and 56 kilometers wide with an area of 8,900 square kilometers. Industries were attracted from all over the world, and people left the countryside to work in the newly created jobs. Farmland disappeared at the rate of 1,600 hectares a year, dropping to 60 percent of the island in 1981 from 90 percent twenty years previously. The agricultural workforce represented 38 percent of the population in 1950, but only five percent by 1981.

Farming became not a respectable occupation. Sugar cane, citrus, tobacco, coffee and banana plantations and farms were slowly abandoned. Whereas ten million MT of cane were ground in 1950, only 2.2 million MT were processed in 1980. Rice imports grew at a particularly alarming rate. Some critics complained that while it was bad enough to import rice, it was insulting that the rice was polished and talc added to produce a shiny kernel. The talc then had to be washed off before the rice was cooked.

While there were new industrial jobs, the massive exodus from the farms created unemployment. The commonwealth status of Puerto Rico enabled many to immigrate to the United States. Today there are more Puerto Ricans living in New York City than there are in San Juan, Puerto Rico's capital.

GETTING AGRICULTURE MOVING

The government realized that something had to be done. Should it try to rejuvenate the declining sugar industry or diversify into new areas?

Sugar was the mainstay of the island's economy, but a worsening export market and higher production costs kept eroding sugar's competitiveness. By 1978, the Puerto Rican

190

Sugar Corporation ('Corporacion Azucarera') was US$350 million in debt. Puerto Rican consumers paid US$0.15 more for a kilo of domestically produced sugar than had it been imported.

A consensus grew that the solution would be to keep only the best sugar cane lands and processing plants in operation, and to retrain cane workers to produce vegetables and rice.

The advantages of rice cultivation were touted by most decision makers: rice would be the catalyst to develop local agriculture; it would have an assured market; it would compete favorably with imported rice and reduce imports; freight costs would be cut; two harvests would be possible; and the straw and bran byproducts could be used by the animal feed industry which depended on imported feedstuffs.

A twelve year plan was created to develop 16,000 to 20,000 hectares of land capable of an annual production of 145,000 MT of rice.

Phase I of the project was to cultivate 2,067 hectares in the Manti and Vega Blanca areas on former sugar cane lands. Because a previous attempt to grow rice in Puerto Rico failed in 1975 because there was no mill to process it, a US$8 million rice mill was planned as well. The mill was to have 12 silos, each 25 meters in height with a storage capacity of 33,000 MT of rice. It was to process up to 108,000 kilograms of rice per hour and employ 70 people. Initially the mill was to be financed by a private commercial bank with a government guarantee.

Recognizing that few rice growing skills existed among local farmers, the project called for intensive extension services to the prospective rice farmers, including training on irrigation, aerial spraying of herbicides and insecticides, and custom rice harvesting and drying.

Land preparation for rice included leveling and an elaborate drainage system. The cost, US$1,280 per hectare (in 1978 US Dollars), would be absorbed by the government as a subsidy to the grower.

To aid in the introduction of new techniques, a model farm of 256 hectares was to be established. This farm would product certified seed for the entire project as well.

The necessary lands were to be acquired by the Puerto Rican government's Land Authority and then rented out to farmers selected on their ability to undertake a new farming project. The 20 farmers initially selected to farm the Phase I lands were required to put up at least 15 percent of the necessary investment.

The goal in all this effort was to provide domestic rice to the consumer for US$0.51 per kilo, instead of the US$0.64 it cost for a kilo of imported rice in 1979.

Table 25.1
Chronology of Puerto Rican Rice Project

1969	Major rice varietal trials begin to evaluate 100 varieties. It is demonstrated experimentally that it is possible to have two to 2.5 harvests of rice annually producing a total of 11.2 MT/ha. of rough rice yearly.
1973	The experiment station is given US$223,000 to evaluate the feasibility of producing rice on a commercial scale.
1975-76	US$600,000 is given to the Land Authority to plant commercial quantities of rice.
1977	US$600,000 is given to Texas A&M University (USA) to study feasibility of building a commercial size rice mill.
1978	The government announces a 12 year plan to grow 80 percent of Puerto Rico's domestic requirement of rice by the end of the 12 year period. The P.R. Agriculture Department invests US$8 million in developing land suitable for rice production.
1979	Rice mill construction begins. Projected cost, US$17.6 million. Projected completion date, April 1980.
1980	First harvest of rice. Mill now scheduled for completion in 1982.
1981	Second rice harvest destroyed by torrential rains.
1982	Mill construction to be completed in final quarter of year.
1985	Estimated time to bring 4,800 hectares of rice into cultivation so mill can break even.

TECHNOLOGY TRANSFER

Bids were let by the Puerto Rican Secretary of Agriculture for design, construction and management of the project. Specifically, the bids called for the following: design, supervision and construction of rice mill; operation of the mill; farmer extension services; leveling lands; design, supervision and establishment of irrigation system; development of a model farm and certified seed production unit; and packaging and marketing of rice.

Firms submitting proposals included Mechanized Farms International, E.E. Grosjean Rice Milling Company, Empresa Molinera, Bond Engineering, Agueybana Agro-Industrial Enterprises, Hester Engineering, United Rice Growers and Millers, and Early California Industries.

The Industrial Development Authority hired a rice milling expert to help it conduct feasibility studies and evaluate the proposals. The evaluation criteria included the degree of private financing, the technical skills of the organization, and its ability (and desire) to transfer these skills as quickly as possible.

Finally, United Rice Growers and Millers, Inc., was selected to construct and operate the mill and provide the necessary agronomic services. From the very beginning, United had problems in putting together a financial package for the project. United sent a man to Puerto Rico to tie the various pieces together, but when he died after several months work, the project stalled. 'People sometimes think that projects consist only of land, machinery, and money. The death of United's man and the subsequent delays show that people, good people, are the key element,' noted one banker.

The death of United's manager took away the project's leader and resulted in many groups becoming involved. United dropped out of the project altogether when its financial package failed. Nonetheless, the government went ahead with machinery purchases, land purchase and development and bid documents for the rice mill. From US$8 million, the mill and related facilities were now budgeted at US$17 million.

A VOICE OF CAUTION

While many favored this large, ambitious project, several legislators began to advocate a much smaller project after they visited rice operations in Venezuela, which is similar to Puerto Rico in climate, population and consumption patterns. One of the legislators cited operating costs and the high investment as the main reasons for cutting down the size of the project:

> Rather than undertake a high initial investment, we should look for the development of modules right from the beginning and reduce the initial investment in the project to the needs of these modules. Eventually we could expand, depending on the experiences of the first few years. The main flaw in the government's project was that studies and projections were prepared on the basis of the experience of California, the largest rice producing state in the US.

Perhaps due to the death of its key executive, United Rice decided to merge with a much stronger company, Early California Industries, a wide ranging agribusiness firm involved in builk wines, olive processing, agricultural chemicals and rice milling. Early's sales in 1981 reached US$190.5 million. One of its divisions, Comet Rice, is one of the five largest rice millers in the USA with 1981 sales of US$104 million. With the United Rice merger, Comet Rice took over the Puerto Rican contract.

Due to the delays since the initial contract was signed, Comet wanted some changes made to its new contract. According to the San Juan Star, Comet would be given 16 hectares of land for US$120,000, or less than US$1 per square meter. Moreover, this land was to be completely developed with all facilities for the cultivation of rice. An additional four hectares were to be sold to Comet in the southern part of the island should additional drying and storage facilities be needed.

Other features of the new contract called for the government to reimburse Comet US$1 million for a three year promotional program. Another US$1.5 million was to be paid to Comet for costs incurred during the first two years of the mill's operation.

The contract also stipulated that Comet was to be paid US$44.00 for every MT of rice under the monthly minimum of 4,545 MT needed to keep the mill operating.

MARKETING

Considerable attention was given to introducing domestic rice into the local market. Puerto Rican consumers were accustomed to short grain rice, and project officials realized that the existing suppliers would not give up their markets easily. The government was encouraged when 87 percent of 1,000 families included in a consumer test found the local rice acceptable.

The initial plantings were to be a medium grain rice, so as to be generally acceptable to consumers of both short and long grain. When the rice industry became firmly established, then both varieties would be planted.

Sello Rojo and Valencia are the two name brands of rice sold in Puerto Rico. 'Arroz de Aqui' ('Rice from here') was the initial trade name selected for the local rice, but it had to be changed when it was discovered that a private company already had that trademark. 'Conqui' (a Puerto Rican frog) was the name eventually adopted for the local rice.

The problems and delays in securing technical managers and the difficulty in having several government agencies involved led to a number of costly mistakes. Perhaps one of the most serious concerned land preparation.

A dispute arose as to whether the land should be contoured (as in southern states in the USA) or leveled (as in California), a method that produces higher yields but is more expensive. The government wanted the land leveled. 'We want to assure maximum production,' stated the Under Secretary of Agriculture. 'We want to make it perfect initially.'

The sophisticated land preparation method selected for leveling proved difficult to implement. The laser beam technology which was utilized began in the US in the late 1960s, but this was its first application in Puerto Rico. With this laser system, a computer first maps out the slopes and contours necessary to make the land suitable for rice cultivation. This information is then used to set up a laser beam which will guide the tractors and other heavy equipment as they work the land.

The leveler used for land grading is equipped with a receiver which emits a certain signal when it is hit by the beam. When the driver of the machine hears the signal from the receiver, he knows he is working the proper line. If he gets off the track, the laser beam will not hit the receiver and the driver will be aware of his error.

One critic of the project notes that the government began leveling the land before the drainage system was complete. 'The government people wanted the land planted before the elections. They had to show something to the people.'

As a result, major changes had to be made later at great cost. In fact, the slope on some fields was initially so incorrect that after they were flooded, the water ran out.

Because of these problems with land development, Comet took over this function from August 1979 to May 1980. Comet executives admit that their expertise is in milling, not in land development, but they were forced to step in due to the government's lack of organization.

Other problems arose as well. The seed rice buildings had no power because the Agricultural Development Administration (ADA) delayed in awarding the contracts for electric cables. The silos were finished before some of the equipment arrived, and it had to be fitted delicately into the top, a time consuming process. Moreover, halfway through construction, someone decided to double the storage capacity.

Other equipment arrived before contracts were let to assemble it and, as a result, suffered rust damage from neglect. Another problem developed when work on the one kilometer access road had to be halted and 260 meters of it rerouted so that it would intersect the highway at an existing traffic signal.

Adding to delays caused by these problems were hurricanes David and Frederic, which wiped out the 1980 and 1981 crops; a truckers strike; a construction workers strike; and strikes at machinery suppliers.

Finally, there were allegations of corruption in letting out the contracts for the mill and for the storage expansion, since it was apparent that it would be some time before production would even begin to fill the initial storage.

According to a Comet spokesman, the mill is to be finished in late 1982 and Comet has a contract to manage it for 15 years after completion. In addition to some start-up expenses, Comet will get a share of any profits that the mill makes.

An executive from a US company seeking to establish another rice mill in San Juan commented:

> Profits are highly unlikely. The Comet mill won't have domestic rice for years. It will be difficult to offload rice in Arecibo due to the poor harbor facilities and the ocean swells. They will probably have to import rough rice from San Juan and then truck it a distance of 80 kilometers. The Comet mill in Arecibo should have been built in San Juan; they would have saved the trucking cost, and the market for the byproduct is here.

One person close to the project noted, 'If I had to do this over again, I wouldn't have rushed the project. And I would have placed technical considerations ahead of politics. The project is still a good one, but it's going to be a long time before it's viable.'

26 The Kufra Production Project

RICHARD J. STROHL

Take a responsive oil-rich nation and add an international entrepreneur with a flair for perceiving the non-monetary needs of a developing nation. Together they can do more than just arrive at the price of a barrel of oil or the extent of drilling rights. They can find water in the desert and begin Libya's Kufra Production Project, now 8,000 hectares of sprinkler irrigated wheat, barley and alfalfa in the middle of the Sahara, a landmark in desert reclamation and agricultural development for Africa and the Middle East.

Started and sustained by the vision of green fields in the desert and the desire for the social and political benefits of self-sufficiency in food, the Kufra project is an effort, financed by oil revenues, to turn barren sand into productive farmland. But most of all it is an experiment in technology and management. While modern agronomy and sprinkler irrigation technology have been successful in producing high yields of cereals and alfalfa in the desert sand, central government direction and control, divorced from the realities of the project, have hindered progress. Personnel policies of an innovative nature have also proven counterproductive. Nevertheless, this is only the twelfth year of a project which still has hundreds of thousands of hectares to claim from the desert and thousands of wells to drill.

The beginnings of the Kufra project date back to 1964 when the Libyan government engaged the US Agency for International Development to conduct a hydrological survey. Hydrologists working in southeastern Libya found evidence of a large subterranean reservoir of water in an area called Kufra (25°N.22°E.), 1,000 kilometers south of Benghazi.

Two years later, in 1966, Occidental Petroleum Corporation came to Libya hoping to get in on the oil bonanza. Perceiving the Libyan desire to increase food production, Dr. Armand Hammer, Chairman of Occidental, sweetened the negotiations for an oil concession by agreeing to put five percent of the profits from the sale of Libyan oil to work in developing Libyan agriculture. Libya accepted these terms and in so doing got more than money for its oil. It also captured part of Occidental's managerial ability, talent, organizational capacity, and access to information.

Oxy-Libya moved quickly to honor its commitment. Albert Frick, an agricultural manager of international repute, took charge of the agricultural development effort. Frick surveyed the possibilities for expanding agricultural production along the Mediterranean Sea where most of Libya's farming is carried on. Realizing that expansion in that area would require dams with very short lives because of severe erosion on closely grazed mountain slopes, he turned to the desert. After studying the geological maps, noting the locations of the oases, and listening to old tales of a huge lake under the Sahara, he became convinced that there was, in fact, water there.

The first wells at Kufra were drilled in 1968 and hit water at 100 meters. The drill then dropped through 300 meters of saturated sand. This reservoir of water, the Nubian Aquifer, underlies a large part of southern Libya as well as parts of Chad, Sudan, and Egypt. The volume of water stored there by some ancient river is enough to irrigate one million hectares for 400 years. As a bonus, the water quality is excellent.

Oxy-Libya decided to begin with sprinkler irrigation on a few hundred hectares and experiment with several crops. Five additional wells were drilled to supply these trial farms and three wells were drilled to provide water for traditional agriculture near the oases. Field work began in September, 1968, and by the year's end, alfalfa, barley, wheat, potatoes, radishes and several other crops were growing in the sand, watered by a classic hand-set irrigation system. A pilot project of 500 sheep was also implemented.

The results were encouraging. Crops grew well but had to be fertilized frequently because the sand, as expected, had almost no nutrients. A feasibility study of agricultural production in Kufra concluded that there were no insurmountable agronomic obstacles. Consequently, the Libyan government asked Oxy-Libya to expend the project to 1,000 hectares using automated center pivot irrigation.

In addition, the government demanded that demonstration farms be maintained and an agricultural extension service provided for traditional farmers. The objective of the project was twofold: to develop commercial farming and to improve traditional farming through training local farmers in modern agricultural techniques.

However, in September, 1969, King Idris I was replaced by the regime of Colonel Qadafi and expansion of the project was temporarily halted. But Qadafi almost immediately realized the benefits to be reaped from the project, and ordered that more wells be drilled. Between 1968 and 1973, 101 pivot machines were installed bringing into production 10,050 hectares (100 machines x 100 ha. and one machine x 50 ha.). In 1970, Libya's new regime nationalized the Kufra complex, retaining two Oxy-Libya managerial employees.

PROBLEMS ARISE

Two major problems have had a negative effect on the project. The first involves mistakes in the design of the wells, pumps and center pivot machines due to miscalculation of water requirements. The 100 deep wells at Kufra are 40 centimeter gravel packed wells drilled 300 to 400 meters deep. Four to four and one-half meters of water per minute are pumped from each well to supply the irrigation system which pivots around the pump (well head) for up to 7,000 hours per year. When the project was planned, this flow rate was expected to irrigate adequately 100 hectares, but that did not prove to be the case. To resolve this problem, the center pivot machines were shortened by 20 hectares each. The present total area of the project has been reduced to 8,050 hectares. Production remains at the previous levels due to the increased water available to each hectare.

Management also has remained a problem at Kufra. The lack of systems management throughout the entire project impedes development and, specifically, mismanagement reduced the number of sheep from 110,000 in 1974 to 20,000 in 1980.

Personnel policies mandated by the government have proven counterproductive. Virtually all employees received the same pay; therefore, it was impossible to give anyone a monetary incentive for more accomplishment. Better positions came to mean those jobs that required less effort and less responsibility. In addition, employees could not be terminated for any work-related reason. Consequently, permanent employees would not perform many of the less pleasant tasks, like cleaning sheep pens. Those who became skilled on the project learned that they could make more money in the private sector, so they left. Those who were highly skilled had no interest in seeking employment on the project.

SOME TECHNICAL PROBLEMS

Other problems which have arisen at Kufra have yielded to technical solutions. The water in the Nubian Aquifer has a high concentration of carbon dioxide. Under pressure in the irrigation system, the carbon dioxide (CO_2) combines with water (H_2O) to form unstable but very corrosive carbonic acid (H_2CO_3). The first 30 center pivot irrigation systems installed at Kufra were not adequately protected against this acid and were severely corroded by 1972, after only four years of operation.

Inspired to solve this corrosion problem by the prospect of a large sale, Lockwood Corporation of Gering, Nebraska, USA, envisioned lining standard irrigation pipes with stainless steel tubing, giving the pipe a design life of 200 years. Kufra management accepted this method and contracted with Lockwood for 40 such units. Lockwood then installed 200 mm O.D. x .5 mm stainless steel tubing in the standard irrigation pipe and expanded the tubing to a pressure fit with the pipe by detonating an explosive charge in the stainless steel tubing.

Another problem at Kufra is the hardpan which forms 10 to 20 centimeters below the soil surface. The soil particles or sand particles are like ground glass and when moved about by the wind and settled by irrigation water over the course of a year or two, form a hardpan which cannot be penetrated by crop roots. This restricts the soil volume from which roots can get water and nutrients, thereby reducing plant growth and crop yields.

Subsoiling corrects this problem and has become the standard practice for breaking the hardpan, even though it must be repeated every year or two. Attempts to break down the hardpan with aggressive, deep-rooted plants such as alfalfa and clover have not been successful.

FERTILIZING THE DESERT

Without the addition of plant nutrients, particularly nitrogen and phosphorus, many plants fail to thrive on desert soils, even when adequately watered. The water must be accompanied by fertilizer in order to turn the desert green. Much of the fertilizer used at the Kufra Project is applied through the pressure irrigation system which keeps application costs low and allows for repeated small applications. This limits leaching losses in the sandy soil while meeting a crop's requirement for nutrients at all stages of growth.

However, once adequately fertilized and watered, crops do quite well at Kufra. Alfalfa yields are from 10 to 20 tons of dry hay per hectare from ten cuttings. Wheat yields from three to five tons per hectare. Even the date palms which are getting water from the deep wells are producing more dates, probably because of the high quality of Nubian Aquifer water.

Alfalfa, barley, and wheat are the main crops grown at Kufra. Alfalfa, grown for the sheep flock, is grazed directly with the remainder cut and baled. Several varieties of non-dormant alfalfa, semi-dwarf wheats and six-row barleys also yield well. Numerous other crops have been successfully grown on a trial basis, including maize, grain and forage sorghum, cotton, sudangrass, grapes, lettuce, broccoli, and asparagus. Apparently, the desert climate of Kufra is at least as conducive to crop growth as the desert climates of the USA in southern California and Arizona where agriculture flourishes.

THE BOTTOM LINE

Merchandized agriculture has spearheaded the development of Kufra. This transfer of technology took place without the cost of investment in roads, railroads, airports, housing, or education. However, the project has had to pay the costs of the lack of infrastructure.

Lack of roads or railroads to service Kufra resulted in transportation costs of US$325,000 just to bring drilling equipment across the desert for the first wells. Similarly, high ground transportation costs are paid for everything that must be brought across the desert, such as heavy equipment and fertilizer. The alternative to these high costs is to make a large investment in roads and railroads.

For the rapid transportation of personnel and urgently needed parts and supplies, an airport has been built and air service is maintained. No doubt it is needed, but it adds significantly to the production costs for each hectare.

A large investment in housing, sanitation facilities, and community amenities also had to be made at Kufra in order to attract and keep personnel. In addition, men have had to be trained to operate this new technology. The alternatives are to pay the high cost of trained personnel from abroad or suffer the high cost of allowing men to learn by experience only.

Approximately US$120 million had been expended on the Kufra Project by the end of 1973: US$15,000 per hectare. Total cost to date is estimated at US$200 million.

OUTLOOK

In spite of the various problems, the project goes on, albeit at much less than its potential. The most modern equipment continues to be imported and maintenance contracts with the manufacturers are made in order to keep the irrigation system operating. Obviously, if that system is operating, more than half the battle of growing crops in the desert is won.

The desire to create more and more green fields in the desert is also sustained unabated. In another oases area 350 kilometers northeast of Kufra, the Sarir development project was started in 1974. The goal there is 125,000 hectares of irrigated farmland and already nearly 40,000 hectares are being irrigated.

Perserverance, modern technology, and a lot of money have begun a process in the Libyan desert which cannot be stopped. The challenge to make the desert bloom has been taken up by many men in many nations and they will continue each day to encroach on the desert wherever they can find water.

27 The Kenana Sugar Project in Sudan

R. J. A. WILSON AND TONY DORAN

Thirty kilometers southeast of the small Sudanese town of Rabak lies the largest integrated sugar project in the world. Located between the White and Blue Nile Rivers, the cane planted on the rich, virgin Blue Nile clays, the sugar factory and the township sited on a convenient firm gravel ridge, Kenana stands out in the desert as an icon to man's idolatry of gigantism. Impressive it certainly is.

As you circle the Kenana airstrip preparing to land, the mass of verdant green surrounded by the lifeless browns of the desert leaves a lasting impression, and the factory at night stands out like some space-age monster, its shining steel and aluminum form brightly lit by spotlights. Yet doubts and questions hang over the whole project, both in regard to the wisdom of its inception and the feasibility of its future productive life.

ORIGINS - A POWER GAME

Kenana dates back to 1971 when Tiny Rowland, anxious for Lonrho, the British conglomerate, to diversity in the Middle East, and Dr Khalil Osman, head of Gulf International, conceived the massive scheme. The feasibility study carried out by Lonrho between June 1972 and October 1973 led to an 840 hectare experimental pilot project in May 1974, but Kenana had to wait until February 1975 before it received official government approval.

Of the original equity base, 61 percent was held by the Sudanese Government (51 percent of which was paid by Lonrho), 12 percent by Lonrho and 17 percent by the Arab Investment Company, with Gulf Fisheries and the Japanese Nissho-Iwai also having small shares.

After a power struggle in 1977 between Lonrho and the Kuwaiti Foreign Trading, Contracting and Investment Company (KFTCI), the Kuwaitis took over the main financing of the project, which remains the position to date. The Japanese still have a small interest as, in fact, does Lonrho, but the financial interests are very much controlled from Kuwait.

Kenana was born in a time of high world sugar prices, and, with optimism abundant, three Sudanese sites were initially considered. The Kenana site was chosen for two reasons. First, the presence of the fertile Blue Nile soils, washed down from the volcanic highlands of Ethiopia, made the Kenana site attractive. But, more importantly, Kenana offered a gravel ridge above the clay soils on which to build the factory, administrative buildings and general social infrastructure of houses, schools, a hospital, fire station, and social amenity buildings. The absence of such an infrastructure was not, at that time considered disadvantageous, nor even were the non-existent communication lines thought to be a major obstacle. Yet filling in such huge gaps has proven to be an enormous drain on resources, and has led to problems which have not as yet been resolved.

Why such a large project? The geography of the area was a key factor in determining the size. The only possible site for the sugar factory was on the gravel ridge - it would have been difficult and much more expensive to attempt to build a factory on the clay soils below. Had there been several smaller schemes instead of one large project, the factories would have had to have been located on the ridge in any case. In addition, the flat lands around the ridge lended themselves to extensive irrigation, an abundant supply of Nile water being available.

Moreover, the founders and financial supporters were keen on the idea of a grandiose, highly visible scheme, and the Kuwait and Arab Funds were favorably disposed toward a showpiece project to offer as evidence of Arab solidarity.

AN AGRICULTURALIST'S DREAM

The agricultural side of the project is a tremendous success story, with Keith Rhodes, the Acting Agricultural Manager, rightly claiming, 'We're growing the best cane in Africa.' Planting started in mid-1977 and by the end of 1979 had reached 13,500 hectares. By July 1980, 22,000 hectares are planned to be under cane, with the planting target of 34,000 hectares completed by July 1981. Three seed varieties are being used, the principal one being CO527 taking up three-quarters of the hectarage, with NCO310 and NCO276 taking up the remainder. The planting rate is averaging 40 hectares a day and with three of the five cane areas now growing, it seems likely that these targets will be met.

The yield figures are very encouraging indeed, with 212 tons per hectare having been recorded, more than double the yield originally envisaged when the project was started. Keith Rhodes is understandably proud: 'I defy anyone, anywhere in Africa, to better this cane. We're growing it at the rate of 12.5 tons per hectare per year and those figures compare with the best in the world.'

As we pulled up alongside one of the growing areas, Rhodes continued:

> Look at the height of that cane. You won't see that anywhere else in Sudan, and we don't suffer from any leaning problems. It's growing tall, and it's growing straight. The thing with sugar cane is to stick to good cultivation practices. Within a week of cutting, we've fertilized and irrigated to be ready for the next ratoon (the regrowth of the cane). Other estates in Sudan are taking up to six weeks before they irrigate.

The success story is the result of several elements, the first of which is the fact that the agricultural teams have kept the site virtually weed and disease free. Smut, the main cane disease, is no problem yet, and the use of herbicides, applied by tractor-drawn sprayers, has prevented weeds which might restrict cane growth.

Perhaps, though, the irrigation system more than anything else accounts for the phenomenal success of cane cultivation at Kenana. After planting the first 3,000 hectares using standard irrigation procedures, it became apparent to Graham Lester, then the agricultural manager, that Kenana had problems. The water was flowing too quickly along the subsidiary ditch and the fields were consequently receiving insufficient water. A new irrigation system was designed and implemented - an example of the management flexibility so vital to the success of large scale projects such as this.

The agricultural manager designed a revolutionary new system and, against the advice of the consulting irrigation engineers, insisted on its installation.

In the new system, the subsidiary ditch is parallel rather than at 90° to the main channel. More startling, however, is the fact that the furrows are between 1,000 m and 2,500 m long instead of the usual 300 m, an innovation which dramatically reduces the number of furrows to be irrigated.

There are other benefits. With fewer turnarounds at the end of furrows, the most time-consuming element of mechanical harvesting is reduced, yielding large savings in harvesting time. Additionally, the agricultural labor requirement is reduced 75 percent.

The irrigation system is so successful that it is being closely monitored by Sudan's other sugar projects. And at nearby Assalaya, it is being copied.

The expertise of the agricultural management team is what is making Kenana succeed. The hard-headed African-experienced expatriate farmers who have had success in Malawi, Kenya and Rhodesia are the driving force that makes the whole agricultural machine tick. After two or three days with them, you become aware that they have the experience to sort out problems as they arise. Yet the Sudanization of what are at present expatriate posts is already planned. This process must be carried out smoothly and over a sufficiently long time period, otherwise the cane yields will most certainly fall.

THE FACTORY - A DESERT MONSTER

The other side of the Kenana story is the sugar factory itself, and as an affirmation of the technological age, it stands unsurpassed. It is the largest integrated sugar plant in the world, at capacity capable of producing a massive 330,000 MT of sugar a year. To look at it is awe-inspiring. To comprehend that it has been built in less than four years in the middle of a roadless desert is not possible. Yet built it has been and that fact alone is sufficient justification for the project in the eyes of Kenana's Contracts Manager, Basil Wiles. Describing himself as a 'troubleshooter', he states with pride:

> If you told me five or six years ago that you could build this sugar plant here, I wouldn't have believed it. The men that have built this factory have performed a miracle. Every part of that plant down to the last bolt has had to come in through Port Sudan and then on through the desert. Kenana has its critics, people who don't believe in the project, but I say just to construct this factory here is the most wonderful achievement I've seen in thirty years of worldwide engineering.

You can question Basil Wiles' logic, but certainly not his enthusiasm.

The factory is in fact two factories in one, the one being the mirror image of the other. Half of the plant came into operation in February 1980 (Phase I); the other half is to open in November 1980 (Phase 2). During the first season, it is hoped to crush 700,000 MT of cane and so produce 70,000 MT of sugar, with output of sugar stepping up in the second season (1980/81) to 200,000 MT as the second phase comes into operation, and capacity of 330,000 MT being reached by the season 1982/83.

Consulting engineers for the factory were Arkel International, a United States firm. The sugar making plant and equipment were supplied by Technip of France, and the UK firm of Capper Neill actually carried out the erection.

The power source for both the factory and the township will be bagasse, the waste material from the crushing of cane. As Wiles explained:

> The bagasse will be used to fuel the Japanese four-turbo generating plant. The generator is capable of producing 40 megawatts, and since we estimate the factory, township and irrigation system are only going to require 36 megawatts, we expect to export electricity to the Sudanese Public Electricity and Water Corporation.

The factory has yet to produce sugar, but with the testing stage complete, the Kenana management team is more than optimistic. The relief that all is going well produced a light-hearted bag testing experiment that consisted of Sudanese laborers hurling 50 kg bags of sugar around the factory manager's office.

The consulting engineers are going to run the factory for the first two years while Sudanese operatives are trained to take over. At present, selected Sudanese are being trained abroad and others will undergo on the job training once the factory starts to crush cane. The factory manager explains: 'We plan for a vertical integration of Sudanese personnel. They're going to have to work their way up on ability and the phasing down of expatriate staff will be orderly, and of course, a core of expatriates will be required for some time.'

Maintenance work on the factory is planned to take place each year during the five month rainy season from July to November when cane cannot be crushed. Management feels this will provide more than sufficient time.

So the agricultural side of the project is going exceptionally well and the factory is finished, but doubts about the feasibility of the whole scheme still remain. Those

207

doubts center on three principal areas: the transport system both for cane into the factory and for sugar from Kenana to Khartoum and Port Sudan; the need for highly technical staff and the policy of Sudanization of personnel; and the financial viability of the whole scheme.

A PROBLEM IN TRANSPORT LOGISTICS

German Magirus Deutz semi-trailer trucks are being used to transport the cut cane to the crushing plant. Each truck pulls two containers holding together 25 MT of cane. For the factory to work to its capacity - production of 70 MT of sugar an hour - 700 MT of cane an hour will have to be tipped onto the rotary elevators that feed the plant. This means that a truck load of cane must be turned around within two to three minutes, every two or three minutes. There is doubt that this will be possible.

Added to the loading problem is the fact that the trucks are traveling over unsurfaced roads that must in time deteriorate. Given Kenana's African setting, there will be maintenance problems for the vehicles. Under these conditions, the capacity output figures would seem to be target rather than probable production levels.

Transport of refined sugar out of Kenana presents even more uncertainty. At present, Kenana's only links with Khartoum and Port Sudan are a single track of narrow gauge railway and the airstrip. A road is under construction, but is as yet uncompleted. The management plan is to transship the sugar by rail and road. Fifty percent of the sugar is destined for Khartoum. From there it will be distributed for domestic consumption. The other 50 percent, headed for the Arab market, must go through Port Sudan.

As to the capability of the rail link, there are conflicting views. A contracts engineer on site was quite categorical when he stated: 'If you commandeered every piece of rolling stock that Sudan Railways owned, you still wouldn't have sufficient capacity to move the amount of sugar this factory is going to produce.'

When asked about the competence of Sudan Railways to move the factory output, the factory manager was adamant in his conviction that the railways can cope: 'In building this factory, our only link was Sudan Railways and they got the stuff here - all of it. I have every confidence in their capacity to transport the sugar to Khartoum and Port Sudan.'

Perhaps the most balanced view on Sudan's rail network was given by Hunting Technical Services' Chris Howse, an administrator who has been in Khartoum since 1976:

The railways here are using twenty year old rolling stock and are obviously having difficulties with maintenance and parts, especially with the country's shortage of foreign exchange. As to the future, though, I'm sure the rail situation will improve. Three years ago 90 percent of port traffic was by rail; now, as more roads are completed, it is only 50 percent. Sudan's road program must ease the situation for the railways.

Nevertheless, despite recent communications improvements, the 130 km road remains uncompleted. Will it be finished in time? Factory Manager Colin Kritzinger is confident: 'The relevant date isn't February 1980 when the factory opens, but November 1980 when we open the second half of the plant, and the road will be finished by then.'

Distribution problems are also exacerbated by the port facilities. Every manager in Khartoum has his own Port Sudan story - of supplies that do not come through, of interminable delays, of mishandled cargo - and Kenana itself has undergone a critical fuel shortage because of diesel held up at the port. The views of Barry Skinner, a consultant surveyor helping to plan port expansion, are to the point:

> There are fourteen berths at the port and we're putting three more in, but the problem isn't capacity so much as the lack of skill of the cargo handlers. A lot of materials are damaged, and a lot of shipments are delayed simply because the work force doesn't have the necessary training, skill level and job experience.

On the distribution front, Kenana will certainly have headaches.

SKILLED MANPOWER - THE MISSING LINK?

Labor issues are the second area where stiff questions are being asked. At present Kenana employs 10,000 personnel of which 700 are expatriates, with the employment projection being 14,000. Of these, 7,500 will be engaged in agricultural practices, 1,500 in the factory and the remaining 5,000 in engineering, construction, administration and finance. As regards the top management team, the managing director, Mohamel El Wagie, is following board policy in the Sudanization of staff, but Kenana's administrative manager, Brian Blatch, sees this as a limited process:

This project can't do without foreign technical experts. Technologically this is a very advanced scheme. If we used just Sudanese manpower, we'd need all of the trained personnel from every other sugar factory and plantation in Sudan.

The critical question, however, is the timing of handover from expatriates to Sudanese. At present, Kenana has top men who have gained their experience from sugar plantations all over the world. Replacing them will be a very precarious task indeed.

As to technicians and skilled tradesmen, Kenana is undergoing a massive training program. Brian Blatch explains:

The mechanization in this scheme is enormous. Ninety-five percent of the cane is machine harvested with an extensive transport system to move the cane to the factory. We've set up a separate training department to develop both inservice courses and on the job training. The courses vary from one year training programs abroad in Hawaii and the United States, to the training of Sudanese in the use of mechanical harvesters by Claas, the manufacturers in Germany. We even have two-week typing courses on site.

In a skill-impoverished country such as Sudan, Kenana's management has no option but to try to impart industrial, agricultural and mechanical skills to the work force. Given the amount of mechanical hardware on site, it is equally clear that if Kenana is to succeed, the training program must succeed first.

There have also been problems in obtaining unskilled agricultural labor. Brian Blatch explained:

The location of the project away from major towns and sources of unskilled labor has meant that housing and social infrastructure have had to be provided. In pushing on with the project, these basic amenities have taken a new priority to prevent high turnover of Sudanese labor. The reduction, though, in agricultural labor requirements through the introduction of the new irrigation system has eased the labor shortage situation tremendously.

FINANCE - DOES THE MONSTER EAT CANE OR CASH?

On the financial side, there have been serious cash-flow problems. Although the initial feasibility study put the estimated cost at US$125 million in 1973, it had increased to US$530 million in 1976, and has now escalated to over US$700 million. With the drop in sugar prices from their high levels of the early 1970s, Kenana can never justify its existence in terms of sugar production. The need to build the whole social infrastructure has proved an enormous drain on resources and the Kuwaitis are certainly drip-feeding their 'desert monster' with respect to cash.

Kenana's agricultural stores manager, visiting Khartoum because of a drastic parts shortage, explained: 'We're suffering a dreadful shortage of cash at the moment. The Kuwaitis are very reluctant to hand over additional money and are monitoring every spending item individually. They insist on sending over an inspection team to check on the need for each cash request.'

Presumably once production starts, the cash flow situation will ease, but one would need a very long time horizon before one could contemplate a payback period. The recurrent cost escalations have meant constant revisions. To cover only fixed costs, a price of US$450 per MT for at least ten years would be required; fifteen years is the probable time span for break even to be achieved, including running costs. These prices must be viewed, however, against the guaranteed market which the scheme's backers are offering. Sudan's existing smaller sugar schemes, designed exclusively for the domestic market, do not have that advantage, and are all experiencing losses.

MARKETING PLANS

The present plan is to market half the sugar output within Sudan and to send half for export. The sugar marketed domestically will be sent to Khartoum, where the Sudan Sugar Corporation, which handles sugar from the smaller existing schemes, will take charge of distribution to retailers. As communications have improved in Sudan, new markets have been opened up for agricultural products, especially in the south of the country.

The sugar exported will be sent to Port Sudan. From there it will be shipped to nearby Jeddah in Saudi Arabia (about 300 km across the Red Sea), and also to the Gulf ports, including Kuwait and Dubai. Almost all refined sugar consumed in the Arabian Peninsula at present is imported from Europe at considerable cost; this will be replaced by sugar from Kenana. The Kuwaitis and the Saudis, who are the chief financial backers for Kenana, have guaranteed free access to their markets, which is, after all, in their own self interest. Many basic commodities are subsidized in Saudi Arabia as part of the government's attempt to keep down prices, and Kenana sugar may qualify for this subsidy.

There are some worries about the quality of the refined product from Kenana. High standards must be maintained so that it will be acceptable to consumers on the Arabian Peninsula who are accustomed to pure white European sugar.

The byproducts of the sugar making process will be utilized in at least two ways. The bagasse will be used to fuel the on-site electric generators, while the molasses will be sold off, mostly within Sudan, but also across the Gulf in the Arabian Peninsula.

Recently there has been some discussion about establishing a distillery on site for making alcohol from the molasses for use as a fuel-stock. Although these plans are still at a very early stage, there is obviously considerable potential.

With the scheme only just starting to produce sugar, it is perhaps too early to draw out any lessons. Still, there are salutary points worth emphasizing. To build a technologically complex plant and surround it with a highly mechanized agricultural production process necessitates the continued use of highly skilled manpower. To do so in a country that does not possess its own supply of such skills must mean imported manpower and a very slow transition to the use of local staff.

Secondly, to locate a project in the middle of a desert lacking both transport and social infrastructure has meant the absorption of a very large part of the initial outlay in providing that infrastructure. Since Kenana has weathered that drain on resources, it is hoped that Kenana succeeds in solving the remaining obstacles.

Basil Wiles expressed an optimistic view of the outlook for Kenana:

> This project has sown two very important seeds for the future. We've built the infrastructure here and that's going to make it so much easier for other agricultural projects to set up in this area. And secondly, with the present energy crisis, it's not only possible but probable that in ten or fifteen years, this cane will be producing fuel, not sugar. And we've got a lot of cane here.

28 Starting a feed industry: the crucial ingredients

DR. EVERETT BLASING

While some people believe that modern feed technology can be transferred overnight, the feed industry in most developing countries must be developed from its very beginnings. Just this year, one small producer in Egypt was still using a cement mixer to formulate feed, while in the Dominican Republic a liquid feed business began four years ago with one company mixing liquid feed ingredients in a small swimming pool.

No matter how humble the beginnings, the principles of feed formulation and the importance of an animal feed industry remain the same. In developing countries, there is always the need to upgrade the quality of the human diet through meat, milk and eggs. Through animals fed on formulated feed, agricultural byproducts are converted into high protein human food.

The feed industry in developing countries often starts as an export-oriented business. For example, when the Chilean economy was depressed in the early 1970s, most of the wheat milling and sugar processing byproducts were exported. International firms rushed in with pelleting and export handling equipment.

When the economy improved, however, people demanded more meat, which meant increased demand for animal feed. At present the domestic feed market in Chile has pushed the price of byproducts so high as to make them noncompetitive in world markets most of the time. The pellet mills and export handling

213

Table 28.1
Animal Feed Usage

	Mixed feed used (million tons)	Population (millions)	Ratio
United States	110	220	1:2
EEC	80	240	1:3
Japan	20	100	1:5
Mexico	5	60	1:12

equipment stand idle.

This phenomenon has occurred in countries as diverse as Iran, Morocco, and Haiti. Only the least developed countries like Zaire and the People's Republic of China still export their byproducts, but it is these countries that present the best long term opportunities for the feed industry.

ROOM FOR GROWTH

The potential growth of the animal feed industry in developing countries can be demonstrated by comparing animal feed usage to population in different countries. (See Table 28.1.)

Most developing countries have feed/population ratios similar to that of Mexico. However, many technical analysts believe the ratios will soon approach those of the developed countries. 'They have no choice,' notes one government official. 'Countries have to find the quickest and most efficient way to provide high quality food to the populace. Developing an animal feed industry, particularly for chickens, seems the most rapid method.'

A great deal of progress is possible. In Indonesia, for example, bad weather, disease and poor feed have kept yields low, with an average annual output per chicken of 150 eggs, compared to 240 in most developed countries. With ruminants, one estimate has it that increased world population and buying power will create demand for 74 percent more milk, 82 percent more beef and 90 percent more sheep and goat meat in the year 2000 than were consumed in 1970.

As with any industry in a developing country, care must be taken to make a product acceptable to the local culture. In a thriving part of Panama, one US feed manufacturer erected a feed plant to serve the local broiler industry, but the chickens that received this feed did not sell well. The local population was accustomed to a tougher, more pungent meat, but the balanced, high quality feed ingredients with little roughage made for bland tasting birds by local standards. Eventually, the assistant plant manager, a Panamanian, convinced the expatriate manager to try something different. More roughage was added to the birds' rations; the gains were lower than with the previous feed, but so was the cost of the new ration. Birds fed on the new feed received much greater acceptance.

Although the feed industry has a long history in many parts of the world, it is virtually unknown in others. That is another reason why cultural differences become so important. In one Caribbean country in 1976 the poultry industry - and the feed companies that supplied it - underwent a severe setback when a rumor began circulating that female hormones were being included in poultry feeds. Reportedly, when chicken fed with this feed was eaten by males, it caused feminine tendencies. As the rumor advanced, sales of chicken meat fell by 60 percent as the men sought to protect their 'machismo.' The market is only now returning to normal.

THE ESSENTIAL INGREDIENTS

An animal feed must emphasize nutrition and economics. A complex mixture of protein, energy, mineral and vitamin sources, it is balanced to meet the nutritional requirements of animals and poultry for economic production. Nutritional requirements, plus a safety factor, must be met at 'least cost.'

Figure 28.1 shows how unbalanced single ingredients can be. Soybean meal, fed alone, has twice the protein that would be found in an equal amount of balanced feed, yet it is lacking in energy, minerals and vitamins. Maize, on the other hand, has excessive energy, but is deficient in protein, and almost completely lacking in vitamins and minerals. The components of a typical complete feed are set forth in Table 28.2.

The feed industry, to a great extent, utilizes byproducts of agricultural processing, including flour and cereal milling, oil seed processing, and the sugar, fishing and animal slaughtering industries.

Oil meal byproducts (with a heavy emphasis on soybean meal) provide the protein, supplemented by animal byproduct meals and fish meals. The energy sources are the cereal grains, primarily yellow maize, although other grains and carbohydrate sources may be used, based on economics. The major minerals are calcium, phosphorus and salt. Trace minerals, vitamins and other additives are incorporated in very small amounts, and although they do not add greatly to the cost, their function is critical to an efficient feed.

Feed manufacturing involves advanced technology in selecting

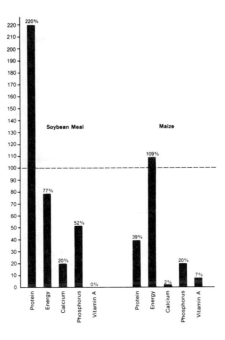

Figure 28.1 Soybean Meal and Maize Composition expressed as
Percentage Requirements of a Balanced Feed

the best blending process. This requires careful mixing of
bulk ingredients in large quantities with vitamins and trace
minerals at the level of parts per million. Furthermore,
because there is great variability in the composition of the
bulk ingredients, a careful quality control program is
essential. One need only recall the damage done to the feed
industry in the USA when a fire retardant was mistakenly added
to a dairy formula instead of the similarly packaged magnesium
oxide.

A key control of quality is the feed formula specifying the
amount and mixing order of each ingredient. A typical formula
will be produced from up to 18 ingredients, each with varying
amounts of up to 60 nutrients. To produce a least-cost formula
with ten ingredient restrictions and 16 nutrient restrictions
requires the use of a computer.

ESTABLISHING A FEED INDUSTRY

The problems in starting a feed industry in a developing
country include inadequate infrastructure, low food prices,

Table 28.2
Components of a Typical Complete Feed

	Percent of total weight	Protein	Energy	Calcium	Phosphorus	Vitamin A
				Percent Contributed		
Maize	62.97	24.6	68.8	1.0	12.0	0
Soybean Meal	25.03	55.2	19.3	5.0	13.0	0
Super Concentrate	10.0	20.2	6.3	94.0	75.0	100.0
Fat	2.0	0	5.6	0	0	0
	100.0	100.0	100.0	100.0	100.0	100.0

lack of technology and training, inadequate marketing facilities, and problems with procurement of raw materials and in relations with the government.

Transportation is a key element for the success of a feed industry. Road, rail and water transport are all involved in moving ingredients to the feed mill and finished product to the farm. Often rural roads are deficient and rail and water transport unreliable. Communication is important so that orders may be processed efficiently; frequently radio communication must be used. Often a stand-by power facility must be provided to assure a reliable energy source.

Government food policy to maintain low consumer prices often conflicts with expeditious development of the feed industry. The problem in establishing beef feeding enterprises in developing countries has always been the inability to get a higher price for fed cattle than for range cattle. The market makes no distinction in most cases.

There are some exceptions. The Rubiyat, a very popular restaurant in Brazil, serves baby beef fed in its own feedlot. By marketing its beef this way, it can afford to feed the cattle. In Iran under the Shah, a two-tiered beef pricing system existed to allow feedlot beef to capture a higher price from those willing to pay for it. At the same time, range-fed beef prices were controlled for mass consumption.

The feed industry in many countries is well organized to fight for incentive prices. In Mexico, for example, the feed industry for a number of years got subsidies for imported ingredients. Unfortunately, this served as a disincentive to domestic production of ingredients.

Another potential problem concerns the indigenous animals and poultry which may not have high productive potential. It may be necessary to import semen and basic breeding stock of high genetic potential. Although indigenous livestock in the Tropics may be well adapted to the environment, part of this adaptation has probably been achieved by a natural selection against productivity. Disease must be controlled through adequate diagnostic facilities and drugs and vaccines.

Extension training must be provided to assist feeders in proper husbandry practices. In Brazil, broiler producers accused feed manufacturers of producing poor feed which made their chickens sick. When the feed industry sent out veterinarians to check, poor hygenic practices were found to be causing most of the problems. When the feed industry in Brazil was faced with high costs and low margins, it dispatched management help to its customers. 'If we make them more efficient, they can become better customers,' one mixer noted.

As a result of this training effort, many feed manufacturers end up selling not only feed but also veterinary supplies and management services.

INDIGENOUS RAW MATERIALS

Supply of raw materials is often a problem. Feed requirement is constant but the raw materials supply is variable due to weather, government policies, transportation and other factors. Since raw material costs can reach 75 to 80 percent of the farm cost of compound feed, the availability and price of adequate supplies is a key factor in the success of a feed project.

In many developing countries, it is sometimes necessary to use unconventional ingredients for which there is little analytical information. Problems in getting foreign exchange have led many a feed manufacturer to develop local sources of raw materials.

There has been considerable progress in developing feedstuffs from tropical crop byproducts, such as coffee pulp, surplus bananas, and coffee mask (from instant coffee manufacture). In Senegal, a diet containing 40 to 50 percent groundnut hulls is being used with undecorticated cottonseed, sorghum bran and molasses to obtain average daily gains of one kilo in cattle. In Kenya, pyrethrum marc (the waste remaining after the extraction of insecticides from pyrethrum flowers) can be used at levels not exceeding 50 percent of the total ration in feed for sheep and dairy cattle. Table 28.3 shows

Table 28.3
Extraction rates for byproduct feeds derived from
crops grown in the humid tropics

	Byproduct feed	Byproduct feed as % original crop by weight
Castor	Castor meal	50
Cotton	Cottonseed meal	47
Maize	Maize bran	10
	Maize germ meal	19
Groundnut (unshelled)	Groundnut meal	43
Rice (paddy)	Rice bran	10
	Broken rice	4
Sesame	Sesame meal	80
Soybean	Soybean meal	78
Sugar cane	Green tops	7
	Molasses	3
Babassu nuts (kernels)	Babassu kernel meal	35
Cocoa beans	Cocoa shell meal	11
Coconuts	Coconut meal	
	hydraulic press	34
	expeller press	35
	primitive press	42
Illipe nuts (kernels)	Illipe nut meal	60
Oil palm (fresh fruit bunches)	Sludge (dried)	3
	Palm kernel meal	22
Rubber seeds	Rubber seed meal	50
Sago (trunks)	Coarse sawdust	60
	Crude wet sago	40
	Unrefined sago flour	21
	Sago refuse	19

Source: Proceedings of the Conference on Animal Feeds of Tropical and Subtropical Origin, Tropical Products Institute.

some tropical crops that have feed value.

MARKETING THE FEED

Adequate marketing facilities are essential since, as one commodity merchant pointed out:

The work of the nutrition scientist in utilizing the available raw materials is of no use if other management skills are not available to ensure that the right quality of product is available to the livestock farmer at the time, with regularity of supply and at the right price to ensure that he can operate profitably.

Not only does the feed manufacturer have to get the product to his customer, he also has to convince the customer of its value. Thus the feed manufacturer should assist the livestock producer in developing recording systems to appraise the efficiency of his livestock enterprise. Without records, the livestock producer can assess a compound feed only in terms of its price per ton. With records he can evaluate the feed in terms of cost per unit of output.

In Haiti, small farmers had bought bags of wheat milling byproducts for years and were accustomed to a certain price per bag. When a small feed operation began which charged twice the amount for a complete feed, the farmers were suspicious. The new feed mixer had to prove his feed was worth the extra money.

GOVERNMENTAL RELATIONS

The government in most developing countries takes an active role in the food system and any feed operation will have to work with it. One English feed manufacturer noted governmental problems usually arise in four areas: raw materials; quality control; relations between the feed industry and academic institutions; and relations with government extension services.

The whole livestock industry must emphasize to government planners the importance of continuity of supply of all raw materials. It may not be possible to guarantee the full requirements of the industry, but at least the minimum needs of the industry should be featured in government planning.

Problems with quality control arise when government officials take standards from developed countries and try to apply them to their own countries. However, if the feed manufacturer cannot obtain the appropriate quality of raw materials, strict standards for the finished product will be impossible to meet.

In one country, for example, the government accused a feed manufacturer of cheating on weights. What really had happened was that the substantial weight losses in transport were due to the hot climate.

Finally, the feed manufacturer must maintain close ties with extension services and scientists. As one planner noted, 'Without this effort, a feed industry cannot play its full role in a coordinated livestock development program.'

PART OF A SYSTEM

In discussing how the feed industry fit into his country's food plans, one Nigerian official noted:

> The establishment of the compound feed industry does not automatically lead to the wider availability of livestock products to a greater proportion of the population. Only if the agricultural and general economic background of the country are right can the feed industry help to speed up the wider availability of livestock products.

Due to the integrated nature of the feed business, it is not surprising that new feed operations are of an integrated nature. When Central Soya, a large US feed manufacturer, wanted to get into the feed business in Jamaica, it did so as a joint venture with a broiler grower. With undependable local feed supplies, the company set up a grain import system using an aluminum export pier. Similarly, when Ralston Purina set up a feed mill in Korea, it also started a poultry operation at the same time.

Continental Grain Company and Chia Tia Investment Company have announced that they will invest US$30 million in an integrated feed and livestock operation in China. The feed mill will initially produce 80,000 MT of feed, gradually expanding to 360,000 MT. To the extend possible, Chinese feed grains will be used. To create demand, it will sell hog breeding stock and day-old chickens from its livestock operation to Chinese communes, as well as to Hong Kong and other Far East markets. Taking integration one step further, the venture will consider building pork and poultry processing plants if necessary.

'A new business in a developing country is often a chicken and egg situation,' commented one Latvian feed executive. 'Do you build the mill first and hope business develops, or do you concentrate on building up animal numbers?' Increasingly, many organizations choose to do both simultaneously.

29 Jamaica's attempts to develop its dairy industry

THOMAS CRAIG

Milk is the perfect food, according to some nutritionists. It is also one of the most political foods as consumers the world over want to buy it at the lowest possible price. And because there are always more consumers than farmers, they often succeed at keeping milk prices low.

The Jamaican dairy industry is in poor health, at least partly because of consumer pressure on the government. One study shows, however, that its condition varies at different stages of the commodity system. At the consumer level, the system works relatively well: milk is normally available either in fluid or condensed form at acceptable prices. The processing sector, although inefficient, is able to supply adequate quantities of milk most of the time. Work stoppages and breakdowns in the distribution system (trucks and coolers) are the most frequent causes of supply interruption.

JAMAICA'S PROBLEMS

The principal failure of the Jamaican dairy system is in milk production and the relationship between farmers and processors. Jamaica has become increasingly dependent on imports to satisfy its dairy needs. Farmers complain that they are ignored by processors, while processors complain that it is unprofitable and burdensome to use local fresh milk. Much of this problem stems from deficiencies in pricing.

Demand for dairy products has been strong in Jamaica. In 1980, total milk consumption in fluid equivalents was estimated at 101 million liters (ml), up from 67 ml in 1975.

Increased demand was satisfied largely by imported milk solids which rose by the equivalent of 24 ml from 50 ml in 1975 to 74 ml in 1980 – an increase of 48 percent. In the same 1975-1980 period, estimated domestic fluid milk production rose by 9.5 ml (56 percent) from 17 ml to 26.5 ml. Consumption of processed dairy products such as ice cream has increased rapidly in recent years and contributed significantly to demand for imported milk solids. Increased demand for these products is evident in the number of newly opened ice cream parlors throughout Jamaica.

PRODUCTION AND PROCESSING

Milk in Jamaica is produced by a comparatively small herd of 18,000 milking cows on about 1,200 farms. Production is relatively concentrated with 400 commercial farms owning over 80 percent of the lactating cows. The remainder of the herd is owned by small farmers, most of whom sell their milk locally or consume it on the farm.

In the past, small farmers have been encouraged to keep milk cows. There has been a prevalent philosophy that all farmers, regardless of size, have the right to participate in commercial dairy. Processors, notably Cornwall Dairy, have had to collect small quantities of milk (as little as five liters per pickup) from these farmers. Although few analysts question the appropriateness of the policy to encourage small farmer participation in dairy, most agree that promoting sales into commercial marketing channels has increased costs and created friction between small farmers and processors, neither of whom thinks the other has performed well.

The government has established two milk grades, Grade A and Grade B. To qualify as Grade A, a farm must have proper chilling and storage equipment. Grade A milk can be extracted by hand as long as it meets normal quality specifications. Grade B milk is sent to the condensary. Currently, the price for Grade A milk is set at US$0.48 per liter, while the price for Grade B milk is set at US$0.34 per liter.

Milk processing is performed by seven companies in Jamaica. Fluid milk is retailed by stores with refrigeration facilities, notably supermarkets in the major urban areas. Condensed milk is found in most stores throughout the country.

An understanding of how prices are set throughout the dairy system helps in understanding the nature of Jamaica's milk pricing problem. Farm and processor prices are set by two different organizations, a factor which complicates coordination of the industry.

Since milk is a 'Schedule B' commodity, farm and processor selling prices are set by the government. Retail prices are not regulated, although a recommended price is published. The local price of milk solids is also established by the government-operated Commodity Trading Company. Thus, the government has control over price throughout the dairy system, an opportunity it has not used effectively.

The price of milk to the farmers is reevaluated annually by consultation between the Jamaica Livestock Association and the Ministry of Agriculture. Prices are set by prorating capital costs, operating costs and a return on investment over milk production of a 'typical' farm with 50 milking cows, each producing seven liters per day.

Processors' margins are set by the Ministry of Industry and Commerce based on actual costs plus a return on investment, except for the condensary where the selling price is indexed to the farm price. Cost items included in the calculation of processors' margins include raw milk prices, packaging, wages, factory expenses, pickup, selling and distribution costs, administrative costs and a profit margin.

Current prices to the dairy farmer are US$0.48 per liter. Of this, US$0.11 is paid by the Government as a subsidy and US$0.37 is paid by the processor. The processors' selling price for whole milk to retailers is US$0.62 per liter. The recommended retail price is US$0.71 per liter. Prices and margins for whole milk are summarized in Figure 29.1.

Pricing policy has not been coordinated to stimulate milk production by promoting procurement relationships between processors and farmers. The root of the pricing problem is that it is significantly more costly for processors to use domestic fresh milk than imported milk solids. The Commodity Trading Company's price for standard grade milk solids is currently US$1.52 per kilo. At a yield of one kilogram of powder for 6.3 liters of milk, the cost to the processor is US$0.24 per liter equivalent. Assuming that all delivery, storage and handling costs for fluid milk and powder milk are the same, the processor who buys fresh local milk at US$0.37 per liter suffers a cost disadvantage (or opportunity loss) of US$0.13 compared with powder milk.

To the processor, therefore, the local dairy farmer has been an undesirable high-price supplier. Processors buy local milk out of social obligation, government pressure, or to hedge

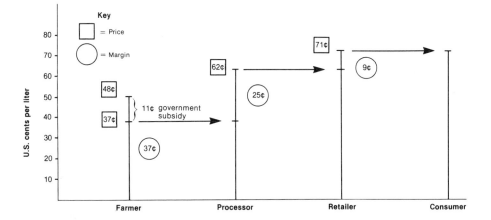

Figure 29.1 Prices and Margins in the Jamaican Dairy System
(liter equivalents)

against unavailability of milk powder. The problem is aggravated since processors cannot charge more for fresh milk despite the evidence that there is a consumer segment willing to pay a premium. Processors' enthusiasm for fresh milk is further diminished by the growth of higher margin markets such as ice cream and flavored drinks, which compete for the same factory facilities.

Critics of the processing sector refute processors' complaints about their price-cost squeeze by pointing out that current processing margins are equal to a hefty 40 percent of the US$0.62 per liter selling price to the retailer. Processors respond that although in theory these margins are fair, as calculated by the Ministry of Industry and Commerce, several hidden costs are not included. The most important of these are returns of spoiled milk mishandled by retailers, and pilferage. Industry estimates indicate spoilage can equal ten to 15 percent of sales, while pilferage can reach five to seven percent. Since profit margins for fluid milk are low compared to other products even under the best circumstances, these losses present yet another deterrent for procuring local milk.

GOVERNMENT OBJECTIVES

The Jamaican government has stated that its objective is to become self-sufficient in milk. Its principal reasons are to conserve scarce foreign exchange spent on imported milk

225

solids; a strategic concern that milk solid surpluses in the developed world may eventually disappear; the desire to demonstrate that developing countries can develop their dairy industries; and national pride.

Most government efforts to stimulate the industry have focused on the farm level. Support prices have been increased to give farmers an attractive return; resources have been committed to research into pasture development and tropical dairying techniques (although there has been little success in getting this information to the farmers); and a pedigree program has been started.

The critical problem in developing dairy, however, has been a failure to view the industry as a system where the perspectives and needs of all participants - farmer, processor, retailer and government - are balanced. It is clear that attractive farm prices for milk are ineffective as a stimulus to production if processors do not want to buy it.

CORNWALL DAIRY

Cornwall Dairy provides an interesting case study of the problems Jamaica has encountered in its attempt to build an integrated dairy system. Cornwall Dairy, located in Montpelier in western Jamaica, is owned by the Jamaican Government. The facility was built in 1972-73 as part of a program to develop the dairy industry. Originally begun in 1970 as a farmers' cooperative by a local dairyman, the project was taken over by the government in its early stages. The Swedish government provided aid for its development.

The facility uses the Ultra High Temperature (UHT) process (packaged in Tetrapak) to produce long-life milk. Although UHT is a sensitive process for a developing country, it was chosen in an attempt to provide whole milk to Jamaicans living in areas without refrigeration. Cornwall handles less than one ml of locally produced milk, much of which is sent as Grade B milk to Jamaica Milk Products for processing into condensed milk.

The factory was built as part of an integrated development plan which included sale of dairy cows to farmers, a network of milk collection points, a processing facility, and a marketing system. The system has never worked well because of poor coordination in its implementation, politics, and shortages of working capital. The factory has been plagued with problems since its beginning. The plant has never made money and has been losing about US$580,000 per year, according to informed sources.

Cornwall Dairy has been surrounded by a continual debate over the appropriateness of its location (far from the country's largest markets), its procurement system, the choice of the UHT technology, the fact it was managed from Kingston rather than Montpelier, plant design and shortages of working capital.

As part of the Government's divestment program, the factory has been offered for sale to private investors. Several bids have been received - including offers from US companies such as Land O'Lakes, and Beatrice Foods - but none has satisfied the Jamaican government. Alcan, the aluminum company, has agreed to manage the plant in the interim.

A SYSTEM THAT WORKS FOR EVERYONE

Developing a healthy domestic dairy system depends on structuring prices so all participants find it in their self-interest to work toward the same goal. The primary objective of the farmer, processor, and retailer is to make an adequate return on investment, whereas the primary goal of the government is to conserve foreign exchange and assure the availability of milk.

Assuming foreign exchange considerations are paramount to the government, one must compare the foreign exchange cost of importing milk with the cost of domestic production. Incremental domestic production will be achieved primarily through increased feeding of imported concentrates.

Figure 29.2 presents a simplified analysis of the foreign exchange costs of locally produced milk compared to imported milk solids. Foreign exchange is valued as its shadow price on the parallel market (black market). This analysis shows that the incremental cost of producing a liter of milk is J$0.23 while it costs the country about J$0.54 for imported solids (this assumes the landed price of milk solids is J$0.22 below the Commodity Trading Corporation's selling price, and that there are no other foreign exchange costs to producing milk domestically). At the margin, the country therefore loses J$0.31 on every liter of milk produced with imported milk solids. The government thus has an interest in creating incentives for processors to use local milk.

There are two principal ways to induce processors to buy local milk. The first is to make the availability of milk solids conditional upon buying a certain quantity of local milk. The second scheme is to equalize the price of domestic and imported milk by subsidizing local fresh milk or increasing the price of imported powder.

The first scheme would create a stronger incentive for processors to take action since access to milk powder, which will continue to account for a majority of production for the foreseeable future, would be conditional upon developing

227

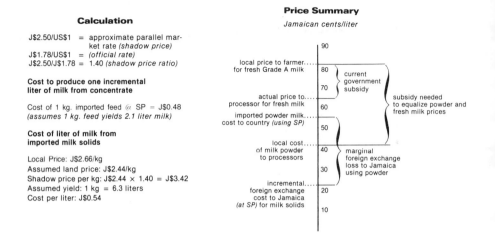

Calculation

J$2.50/US$1 = approximate parallel market rate *(shadow price)*
J$1.78/US$1 = *(official rate)*
J$2.50/J$1.78 = 1.40 *(shadow price ratio)*

Cost to produce one incremental liter of milk from concentrate

Cost of 1 kg. imported feed @ SP = J$0.48
(assumes 1 kg. feed yields 2.1 liter milk)

Cost of liter of milk from imported milk solids

Local Price: J$2.66/kg
Assumed land price: J$2.44/kg
Shadow price per kg: J$2.44 × 1.40 = J$3.42
Assumed yield: 1 kg = 6.3 liters
Cost per liter: J$0.54

Price Summary

Jamaican cents/liter

	90
local price to farmer..... for fresh Grade A milk	80 — current government subsidy
	70 — subsidy needed to equalize powder and fresh milk prices
actual price to..... processor for fresh milk	60
imported powder milk..... cost to country *(using SP)*	50
local cost..... of milk powder to processors	40 — marginal foreign exchange loss to Jamaica using powder
	30
incremental..... foreign exchange cost to Jamaica *(at SP)* for milk solids	20
	10

Figure 29.2 Foreign Exchange Costs of Locally Produced Milk

procurement relationships with farmers. The second scheme is less direct since it only removes the negative economic consequences of procuring locally while providing little incentive to change existing dependencies on powder.

The second alternative carries a heavy cost to the government if one examines total costs rather than just foreign exchange costs. At the full local cost of US$0.48 per liter, local milk is US$0.24 more expensive than powder at US$0.24. Current government subsidies on domestic fluid milk are US$0.11 per liter. If the government decides to equalize prices by subsidizing domestic milk the full US$0.24, it will double its subsidy payments. This conflicts with the new policy to reduce involvement in the country's economy.

Two other actions will help stimulate production. The first is officially allowing processors to price fresh milk at a premium to reconstituted milk, something already done unofficially by at least one processor. The second is to encourage processors to integrate into milk production, something they have been discouraged from doing in the past. This gives processors benefit from potential profits in production and will increase incentives to build strong and predictable procurement systems.

30 Eggs for Haiti: poultry project brings modern technology to peasant farms

DAVID TOHT

Like the tethered goats and pigs, scavenger laying hens are common on every Haitian peasant farm. They're lean, quick, and lay about an egg a week - if it can be found. But in the area surrounding the village of Fermathe, Haiti, mountain peasants like Madame Charisil raise modern hybrid layers that each average five to six eggs per week. Madame Charisil's hill-hugging stone henhouse contains 80 brown egg layers. They significantly supplement her income as a roadside vendor and have added eggs to her family's regular diet. Her laying flock is the result of a small but effective poultry project that has brought modern poultry technology to 75 rural Haitian families.

Because modern hybrid layers are often thought of as suitable only for the hothouse environment of technologically advanced 'egg factories,' it is assumed that they will not produce well in more primitive circumstances. In fact, the stress that total confinement places on layers has caused breeders to respond with layers that are not only highly productive and feed efficient, but exceptionally hardy and disease resistant as well. The Fermathe project - begun jointly by a religious volunteer group and Farms International, Inc. - has successfully developed a program that enables Haitian farmers to utilize small hybrid layer flocks.

EARLY PROBLEMS

When George Bisbee, a retired poultry specialist and present administrator of the project, arrived in Haiti in 1976, the Fermathe project was already underway. Its primary purpose was to provide Haitian families with their own backyard source of eggs. Another goal of the project was to use as many inputs of Haitian origin as possible and to encourage self-sufficiency by requiring farmers to pay their flock costs through egg sales. At the beginning, several small floor houses were built, each equipped with a raised droppings area, hanging feeders and waterers, and wooden nesting boxes. Each held 20 to 50 leghorn layers.

'The houses were actually too good,' says Bisbee. 'They saddled the people with an unreasonable amount of debt. They became discouraged.' Worst of all, a miscalculated feed ration was starving the layers and holding production down to a trickle.

'I recommended that in all but two flocks the best thing they could do would be to butcher the birds - although they were pretty thin,' says Bisbee. 'I thought maybe they could at least be made into soup.' Word spread that the chicken project was a failure.

Thus from the outset the project had to overcome three major problems: an inadequate layer ration, an expensive and inefficient housing system, and local farmer perception that the flocks were not profitable.

FEED FORMULATION

Hybrid brown egg layers were chosen both because of the Haitian preference for brown eggs and because the hens are full-bodied enough to be a good meat source after their productive lives are finished. However, for optimum production such layers demand carefully formulated feed. The first step in developing a new feed was to carefully choose a ration base.

'We tried to discover what ingredients were available at a reasonable price and go from there,' says Bisbee. 'We tried to use a minimum of items which are used as human food.'

They aimed for a ration of 17 to 18 percent protein. Because wheat middlings (flour offal) were available locally and were relatively inexpensive (US$66/MT), they were chosen as the ration base. The resulting feed was formulated as follows:

315 kg. wheat middlings (local milling byproduct)
 90 kg. ground maize (imported)
 45 kg. 44 percent concentrate (imported)

```
45 kg. cottonseed meal (local byproduct)
34 kg. calcium (local)
 1 kg. salt
```

This ration proved both adequate and inexpensive. At first, truckloads of whole maize had to be hauled down to Port-au-Prince for grinding and then mixed with the other ingredients using a scoop shovel on a concrete floor. Later the project acquired a small hammer mill and mixer. After mixing, the feed was packaged in 45 kg. bags which could be carried by the farmers to their flocks. Today the cost of 45 kg. of feed is only US$8.05 - less expensive than comparable quantities in many parts of the United States.

CAGE HOUSING

Housing for the flocks had to be inexpensive and yet incorporate as many of the appropriate features of modern housing systems as possible. Bisbee decided to change over to battery cages.

In a country where the annual per capita income is less than US$300, it might seem inappropriate to ask peasants to spend US$2.00 per bird for a cage and feeders. But for the layers to produce up to their ability, adequate food and water were essential.

Bisbee said:

> There's a definite psychological advantage to keeping the hens in cages. If the chickens are on the floor or running out in the yard and the farmers see them pecking around, they figure they're getting something to eat. But if the chickens are up in cages, they can see that the birds aren't going to get anything to eat unless they feed them.

Importing expensive ready-made cages was out of the question. Instead, rabbit cage clips and galvanized fencing mesh were used to make cages with compartments 35.5 cm. high, 30.5 cm. deep, and 40.5 cm. wide - large enough for two chickens. To get the eggs out from under the hens, the floor was inclined and extended beyond each cage front. The front-most edge was bent up to catch the eggs as they rolled out from under the hens. A hinged mesh door at the top of each cage provided access to the compartments.

Because sheet-metal feeders and waterers rusted quickly, Haitian-manufactured PVC pipe was used to make inexpensive, durable feed and water troughs.

The resulting housing system was inexpensive and

long-lasting. Because the feed and water troughs were placed on the outside of the cage they could be easily filled and cleaned. An added benefit was easy manure removal. The manure, when composted, was a boon to the ubiquitous Haitian vegetable gardens. In some cases it was even fed to swine.

A SECOND TRY

With an adequate ration and a workable housing system in place, it was time to give the project a second try. Dou Dou Paul, a Haitian farmer who had previously participated in the project, agreed to convert his floor house to the cage system. After Paul's 21-week-old pullets had a chance to settle in, Bisbee paid a visit to see how the birds were doing.

Recalling that first visit, Bisbee said:

> Dou Dou said that he had gotten twenty eggs that day. Well, that seemed impossible - he only had twenty chickens. But when I checked his egg count for the previous four days, it was there in black and white - eighteen eggs, nineteen eggs, then two days of twenty eggs.

By selling his eggs in the local market, Dou Dou was able to pay off the cost of his hens and equipment in three months. He soon increased his flock to 100 birds. With Paul's success, a few other farmers were encouraged to give the project a second chance. Because the farmers were supplied with ready-to-lay hens, the advantage of the new system was quickly apparent. Soon there was a waiting list for more hens.

FROM HATCHERY TO FARM

Although the potential of hybrid layers is dramatic, they cannot simply be dropped in a farmer's lap as day-old chicks. It is axiomatic that a layer is only as good as the way in which it is grown. Good growing necessitates proper 'brooding' (those crucial early weeks when hooded gas jets provide the chicks with all the warmth of a brooding mother hen); adequate feed and water; proper vaccination; and uncrowded, sanitary growing conditions.

Upon arrival at the Francois Duvalier International Airport in Port-au-Prince, the day-old chicks have logged about 3,000 kilometers on their way via Miami from a commercial hatchery in Quakertown, Pennsylvania USA. At the hatchery the chicks receive a vaccination for Marek's disease, a form of avian cancer. Because chicks draw the egg yolk into their bodies before hatching they are relatively well prepared for long travel at day-old. To date, no chicks have died in shipment. Mortality by three weeks of age is under two percent. Very few are lost after that. Cost of the DEKALB-Warren Sex-Sal-Link chicks, including airfreight from Pennsylvania is about US$.57 each.

Replenishing the project's flocks requires about 1,400 grown pullets four times a year. Bisbee oversees the brooding and growing of the pullets from day-old to eleven weeks of age. The pullets are raised in open floor houses with hanging, nonmechanized feeders and waterers above a raised droppings area. The floor area is covered with wood-chip litter which is cleaned out between flocks.

At 11 weeks of age, the pullets are transferred to the growing houses of two Haitian growers. One grower receives US$.50 for each finished hen. He supplies the housing and labor; the project supplies the cages, feed, and any necessary medication. The other grower buys the 11 week old pullets for US$1.50 each with the understanding that the project will assist in placing the mature layers. He supplies all the necessary inputs: housing, cages, feed and labor. When the pullets are moved from the project's brooding house, they are vaccinated for pox. Chicks are also vaccinated for Newcastle-bronchitis via drinking water at four days, four weeks, and four months of age. No medication is added to the feed. Amprol is used to treat coccidiosis as needed.

EXPERTISE GIVEN

As administrator of the project, Bisbee performs several functions. Most importantly, he provides the technical expertise necessary for growing the pullets properly and, through periodic flock visits, helps Haitian farmers adhere to the fairly intensive discipline of raising confinement livestock. In addition, he purchases the feed ingredients and raw materials for the cages and waterers. He works closely with each farmer to schedule new flocks. Bisbee makes farm visits to book future hen placements, to troubleshoot production problems (he insists that every poultry keeper maintain daily egg production records as a means of monitoring disease or husbandry problems), to assist in fitting out new houses, and to help move in a new flock.

New flock owners are encouraged to start small - usually with 20 hens - to limit the risk of an unsuccessful experience. Even experienced poultry owners are limited to 100 hens to encourage diversification and spread the benefits of the layers among as many people as possible.

A new flock owner is usually responsible for constructing

his own henhouse. Houses are built of native limestone and roofed with raw timber beams and corrugated sheet metal. Care is taken to include ample window area for adequate light and ventilation. Wire mesh (often second-hand or scavenged, as is the roofing in many cases) covers the windows to keep out predators and disease bearing wild fowl. The cages are hung from the roof beams. This arrangement provides an added benefit.

'During hurricane Allen in 1980,' recalls Bisbee, 'most of the henhouses came through undamaged because the cages hanging from the roof beams provided enough weight to keep the roof from blowing off.'

The unique feature of Bisbee's chicken project is that it touches individual Haitian families directly, enabling them to improve their standard of living. The Fermathe project is not a give-away program. The cost of all the ingredients is paid for by the farmers: the hens, the feed, the cages, the feed and water troughs, and building materials. Only Bisbee's time and knowledge, and a short term loan to get started, are given free.

'If we gave the pullets away, they wouldn't take enough interest in them,' says Bisbee. 'That's true not just of Haitians; it's true of anybody. If something comes too easily, you don't take any interest in it.'

ECONOMICS

Favorable economics have certainly helped the poultry project. A dozen eggs sell for US$1.05 wholesale, US$1.25 retail — substantially higher than in most developed nations. Feed costs average US$0.55 per dozen eggs.

The most striking economic factor is the high value of a spent hen. If the farmer chooses to butcher and market the hen himself, he can recoup his entire pullet cost of US$3.50. That means he can replace his flock every twelve months at virtually no cost once he has paid off his original flock. Though hybrid hens can usually lay profitably until 78 weeks of age, the high spent hen value in Haiti makes it advantageous to replace the flock earlier. Start-up costs for a 50 bird flock include US$150-$250 for a 3 m. x 4.5 m. limestone and mortar building, US$175 for fifty 22-week-old layers (at US$3.50 each), and US$100 for cages.

Start-up funds are financed through a modest 'revolving fund' at no interest. The loan must be paid back within the first year. A small desktop computer is time-shared to lend some order to the project's accounting system and keeps track of loan payments, feed and equipment purchases, and farmer's individual 'deposits' or savings accounts. For many of the

Table 30.1
Layer Project Expense/Income
(basis: 50 layers for one year)
(US Dollars)

FIRST YEAR

Expenses
Henhouse	$ 150.00
50 Hens at $3.50 each	175.00
Cages, troughs	100.00
Feed (at 45 kg/6 days)	517.05
Total	$ 942.05

Income
Egg sales:
  Assume: 250 eggs/bird, $1.05/doz.

250 x 50 - 12 x $1.05	$1,093.75
Net Income	$ 151.70

SECOND YEAR

Expenses
Henhouse	$ -0-
50 hens at $3.50 each	175.00
Cages, troughs	-0-
Feed (at 45 kg/6 days)	517.05
Total	$ 692.05

Income
Sale of spent hens	$ 175.00
Egg sales	1,093.75
Total	$1,268.75
Net income	$ 576.70

farmers, this is their first experience at saving sizeable sums of money and it has enabled them to purchase small tracts of land to add to their farms.

UNEXPECTED BENEFITS

Although the poultry project was first intended to supplement the diets of peasant families - not to be a source of cash income - it is arguable that the Haitians have benefited more

235

from the discretionary income provided by egg sales than they have by the simple addition of eggs to their diet. Income generally goes for dwelling improvement, land purchase, education, and medical expenses. After the first year, families begin to eat the cracked eggs that otherwise would be sold at a discount.

Aloes St. Juste is an example of a farmer helped by the project. His initial success with 50 layers allowed him to double his flock. Profits from hens allowed him to buy a piece of land for US$420 on which he grows market vegetables. His children carry two hard-boiled eggs with them to school each day and Aloes has set aside some money for unforeseen medical expenses.

This evolution toward selling the eggs, rather than consuming them, was possible only because a successful marketplace had already been established within the project area to offer an outlet for farmers' vegetable crops. The market had a good reputation among those in Petionville and Port-au-Prince able to afford the drive into the mountains up Fermathe.

Without such an outlet, the entire nature of the project would have changed. Most likely it would have more directly fulfilled its original goal of supplying eggs directly to peasant families. However, in doing so, it would have provided a less dramatic boost to the local economy. The market serves the consumers that are usually the first to benefit from advanced agricultural technology - the wealthier professionals who can afford to buy the end products. These are the traditional beneficiaries of modern turnkey poultry operations.

But in the case of the Fermathe project, the profits go not to a few entrepreneurs but to 75 individual Haitian families. Clearly, the project gets the benefits of advanced agricultural technology where they are most needed.

An individual like George Bisbee is essential to the success of such a project. He would be the most difficult element of the project to replicate. Bisbee is self-supporting (through his own retirement funds), content to work without any monetary incentives, an expert in poultry husbandry, and willing to patiently nurture a project of modest scope. He is not an administrator in an air-conditioned office. Every day he pounds down the road in his beat-up red Subaru station wagon to visit flocks and growing houses. Frequently he must drive as far as he can and then hike into the abrupt eroded mountains to reach remote flocks.

Today, the extent of the Fermathe project is limited only by Bisbee's ability to administer the project. He feels he cannot personally handle more than 75 families and hopes to train someone - preferably a Haitian - to duplicate his role.

One dramatic benefit of such a project is its role in stabilizing the movement of the rural population. The Fermathe area has shown less migration toward Port-au-Prince than comparable areas. Much of this stabilization has been attributed to the success of the Fermathe poultry project. The project provides Fermathe farmers with some moderate upward mobility, stemming the flow of rural poor toward the endemic poverty and unemployment of Port-au-Prince. The Fermathe poultry project has shown itself to be an effective source of farm income and animal protein in a country starved for viable grassroots enterprise.

31 Protein for Panama: financing cattle production

JOHN FREIVALDS

Few places are as beautiful as Rio Sereno, Panama. Located near the Costa Rican border at an elevation of 1,000 meters, Rio Sereno has warm days and cool nights. The volcanic soil is rich and almost everything flourishes. The pangola grass pastures are lush and nutritious for cattle. It was — and still is — the 'Wild West' of Panama. But for Rio Sereno and the rest of Chiriqui province to prosper, credit was needed, in addition to such crucial items as transport and extension services.

Government agricultural programs have been almost non-existent in the area. In fact, local people say they see government officials only before elections are held. Few officials make the effort to leave the paved Inter-American Highway for the dirt farm-to-market roads that are impassable during the rainy season. To get to their upland 'fincas,' Panamanian ranchers cross the border into Costa Rica where the roads are better, head up into the mountains and then drive back into Panama. And it is not surprising to find Costa Rican state veterinarians attending cattle in Panama.

Yet as remote as Chiriqui province is from Panama City, it served as the starting point for a pioneering agricultural credit program by the Chase Manhattan Bank from its regional office in David, the provincial capital. Now thirty years old, the program has taught Chase a great deal about credit for livestock, and for agriculture in general. Every Chase branch in Panama now has an agribusiness loan department.

In 1950, the Panamanian cattle industry was in a very primitive state. Breeding on many of the farms was completely unmanaged. Bulls ran continuously with the breeding cows and the rest of the herd. Little attempt was made to cull animals and even less to select breeding stock. Most of the cattle were a criollo-Brahma mix.

Calving was often unattended, with consequent calving losses. Once the calf was weaned, no major difference existed in the feeding of the animal through the remaining production phases. Growing, finishing, and fattening were all accomplished on pasture, with minimal supplemental feeding and no segregation of animals in the various development stages. As these operational patterns would indicate, buildings, fencing, corrals and handling equipment were absent from many ranches.

Disease was also significant, with brucellosis and cysticercosis not uncommon, as well as parasitic diseases such as neonatal diarrhea and enteric fever. 'Some of the open sores on the cattle were so bad, they looked like they had been shot with a gun,' one bank officer recalls. Effects of disease included reduced meat production, reduced reproduction rates, stunted development in the animals and rejection of meat at the abattoirs.

Salts were the most commonly used input, but even their use was not universal. The use of medicines varied. Although many of the more experienced ranchers could perform preventive medical practices themselves, the limited availability of medicines in more remote areas was a handicap. During the rainy season, just getting to Rio Sereno, 65 kilometers from David, could take 14 hours and once you got there, there was no refrigeration.

Pastures were native in most instances and except for a few scattered and experimental attempts, lime and fertilizers were not applied to pasture or forage crops. Overstocking and overgrazing were major problems on many ranches, resulting in general pasture deterioration and reduced carrying capacity.

Cattle moved to market in several ways. Proximity to killing centers and the condition of roads determined whether the cattle were driven or trucked. If driven down to David, they often lost ten percent of bodyweight.

As a result, when the Chase program began in 1950, Panama imported 20,000 steers yearly to satisfy the limited demand of its 600,000 inhabitants with an annual consumption per capita of 12.5 kilos. In contrast, Panama exported in 1978 some 2.25 million kilos and regularly exports breeding heifers to Nicaragua, Venezuela and Ecuador. In 1977, 25,000 breeding heifers went to Venezuela alone.

In 1950, the Chase Manhattan Bank started thinking seriously about utilization of the resources of the private sector to encourage agricultural development in Panama. It was guided by the basic economic principle that a commercial bank receives deposits from different sectors of the economy, and by lending these deposits to the less developed sector, it brings about a general benefit in the economic and social life of the country. By this practice, a commercial bank offers security to the depositors, helps the borrowers, increases the general commercial activity by stimulating the productivity and purchase power of the neglected rural sector of the country, and in the long run new sources of deposits are generated.

The bank was convinced that the prosperity of its urban clients depended greatly on the creation of a stable market in the rural sector, less influenced by fluctuations caused by international events.

Guided by the premise that rural credit must be practiced in the field, a branch in David, Chiriqui, was established in 1950, to offer to the most important agricultural province in Panama the same services that the bank had rendered for several years to commercial and industrial activities in the cities of Panama and Colon.

Agricultural loans made by the David branch focused primarily on mortgage loans and warehouse advances to coffee producers and millers, lines of credit for discounts to dealers of fertilizers, farm machinery and equipment, chattel mortgage loans for grass feeding of steers, and breeder cattle loans to increase and/or improve the breeding herd. During the initial year of this first rural branch, all loans were based exclusively on the moral standing, financial statement and the available physical guaranty of the applicant.

Every bank has its own way of evaluating loan requests. The Bank of America frequently mentions the '5 C's of Credit':

1. Character. Honesty and integrity are the most valuable assets, yet the most difficult for a banker to measure.
2. Capital. In determining the financial strength of the borrower, measures used to evaluate capital include balance sheets and profit and loss statements from several years.
3. Capacity. The ability to repay the debt requested and the capacity of management to handle the operation are examined.
4. Conditions. The economic climate of the industry and the country as a whole are evaluated.
5. Collateral. Liens can be placed against property in order to secure the loan.

The moral standing of the applicant was quite important. Principles of accounting and financial statements were generally unknown to the ranchers. It was estimated that 90 percent of the Panamanian cattle ranchers did not keep any kind of records and accounts, and 70 percent of them had not received an education higher than elementary school. Therefore, the bank decided to concentrate mostly on cattle loans secured by steers, advancing 75 percent of their market value for a term of eighteen months. The cattle ranchers of the area were very enthusiastic about this first source of commercial cattle credit in the history of the country.

STEERS FOR SECURITY

The original concept, with cattle loans based on the number of steers presented by the applicant as collateral, proved faulty. It appeared to be more harmful than beneficial for the normal development and progress of the cattle industry. It soon became apparent that smaller ranchers were selling their breeding stock - for slaughter or to larger ranchers. They had concluded, correctly, that to enjoy the services of the Chase, they needed steers. The bank did not accept breeding cattle or pasture-land as security.

Those involved in the program were concerned with the effect of this situation on the cattle industry in Panama. Some of the breeding stocks were falling into the hands of a few strong ranchers and the rest were being slaughtered; the proceeds were then invested in purchasing more feeder steers, which in turn were pledged to the bank. The ultimate effects were easily foreseen - a monopolistic situation, reduced breeding stock, and inflated prices for feeder steers caused by demand-fueled speculation. With steers required for security, Panama would once again need to import 20,000 steers a year to satisfy the national demand.

NEW CREDIT PRINCIPLES

Fortunately, the collateral problem was detected early, and Chase immediately decided to establish a comprehensive cattle credit program based on general principles adapted from cattle financing practices in the USA. The credit decision and recommendations were based on 'personal merits, financial situation, managerial ability, productive capacity, and purpose of the loan.' Accordingly, the repayment schedule and the term of the loan were planned to enable the borrower to meet his obligations with the least effort and the most benefit.

Mortgage loans were made for a maximum term of five years; breeding cattle and/or pastureland were used to secure loans for breeding purposes and/or improvement of pastures. Annual lines of credit were established for short term loans and for loans secured by steers for a maximum term of eighteen months. However, the application and practice of the new approach did overcome the problems that surfaced during the initial period. The early experience showed that farm credit can either be beneficial or harmful, depending on how it is recommended and used. It is preferable not to have credit at all than to have a poorly planned credit program. Fortunately, in Panama, a change in credit procedures at the beginning of the program averted problems later on.

The basic principles of a modern agricultural credit system needed to be taught and encouraged. Most of the cattlemen were unfamiliar with a balance sheet, an inventory, or keeping records and accounts of any kind. The more advanced cattlemen did not keep records because they were afraid that the government could use this information to tax them. On the other hand, when they were asked verbally how many head of cattle and how many hectares of land they owned, invariably they would understate the real figure. They were afraid to supply accurate information because they did not believe in confidentiality. In a small country like Panama, very few things are confidential; it is not surprising that the ranchers did not trust a newcomer who wanted to know about their private business in detail.

In consideration that reliable information was essential for the success of any program, it was necessary to convince key ranchers in certain communities of the importance of supplying correct information to help them and to help the bank. By using examples and by observing a strict code of never talking or commenting to anybody about somebody else's business, they developed a great confidence in the bank.

VERBAL APPLICATIONS ACCEPTED

To make the program as simple and as attractive as possible to the medium-sized cattle ranchers, Chase accepted applications made verbally to the managers of the cattle credit program. Through this verbal information, the preliminary feasibility of the loan was determined. If further study of the loan was advisable and the bank did not have information about the moral standing of the applicant, the loan officer consulted with old customers living in the vicinity of the applicant. This way, it was possible to get reliable, verbal references about the applicant. Credit ratings in banking and commercial circles were also investigated.

242

If the applicant proved worthy from a moral point of view, then a detailed physical investigation was undertaken by an Agricultural Technician visiting the ranch. The technician arrived early in the morning to appraise and make a detailed, classified inventory of the herd, including the number of cows, heifers, calves, breeding bulls and steers, as well as their brands. This classified cattle inventory enabled the technician to judge the condition and type of the cattle, to appraise them according to class and type, and to determine the ratio between cows and breeding bulls. Questions were asked about deaths of adult cattle and calves, about births of calves, and about preventive sanitary practices, such as spraying and medication for the control of external and internal parasites and diseases. This information was used to make recommendations to correct faults, to improve conditions and to increase productive efficiency of the herd. The bank, said some, had a better extension program than the government. 'Yes,' retorted one Panamanian official, 'but the bank also paid their people more than the government could.'

When the cattle inventory was complete, a rapid inspection of the ranch was done to determine the topography of the land, the type of soil, the condition of pastures and fences, the approximate area of improved and partially improved pastures, brushland and/or woodland. In the drier sections of the country, the water supply was carefully checked.

Finally, the maps and titles of the properties were studied to verify their areas and to make sure that they were properly recorded in the name of the applicant. Land without title was assumed to be controlled by possessory rights. This information was used to calculate the present carrying capacity of the ranch, to estimate its maximum potential when completely improved, and the cost of improvement.

Other general financial information was ascertained (such as other sources of income, other assets and liabilities) to facilitate reaching a sound decision concerning the loan. Before making a decision about the amount of the loan, a complete budget was worked out with the rancher to compute the required amount of credit to fulfill the necessary purposes, and the repayment of the obligation as scheduled without difficulty.

LEGAL REQUIREMENTS FOR SECURED LOANS

Under the program all loans for terms exceeding a year are secured. In loans secured by steers, the cattle are identified by the brand of the bank and the brand of the client.

In loans secured by breeding cattle and pastureland, the legal procedure is similar to the one used for steers.

Breeding cattle are not branded with the bank's brand in consideration that most of these loans are repaid in a three-year period. Traditionally, cattlemen do not want a strange brand to remain on their cows and heifers with no outstanding obligation. They do not mind branding their steers because they are to be slaughtered, but breeding cattle will remain on the ranch for a long time. Understanding that this point could handicap the acceptance of the program, program officers agreed to a new policy - identifying the breeding cattle by the client's brand and by branded numbers, instead of the bank's brand. This decision had the general acceptance of the cattlemen and it encouraged them to pledge breeding cattle, thus providing the bank with a more ample field of operations. The mortgage loans secured by improved pastureland were similar to other mortgage loans.

RESULTS OF THE CATTLE PROGRAM

The success of the Chase Manhattan Bank cattle finance program is reflected in the fact that the Panamanian cattle industry in 1950 was made up of 600,000 head of inferior cattle, and 30 years later it is comprised of four million head of much improved cattle owned by 31,000 ranchers. Once a beef importer, Panama now exports beef produced mainly by the small and medium-size ranchers.

Beyond the improvement in the size and quality of Panamanian herds, certain other more intangible changes have taken place. The rural population has been educated in the use of credit. The people have learned to cooperate with the bank in supplying the minimum necessary information to work out a credit program. They meet their interest and amortization payments as scheduled.

The value of rural agribusiness investments has been recognized. The cattle finance program has proven that rural loans are as good and as reliable as urban loans, if properly planned, used and supervised. Ranchers received the benefits of financial and technical assistance, a lower interest rate, and credit according to their abilities and needs.

Since 1950, Chase has lent over US$200 million to cattle ranchers, and sixteen other banks have also entered this field. Sr J. Pedro Barragan of the Chase Bank in Panama City notes, 'During all these 30 years, our charge-offs in this program have not exceeded US$115,000, which speaks highly of the borrowers.

The economy of the rural area has flourished and grown in importance. Ranchers are able to sell their cattle in the free market. The greater commercial activity and the increase in purchasing power of the region has created a new potential market for many goods.

Expansion and improvement in cattle raising have taken place among the bank's clients. Ninety-five percent have increased their cattle inventories by four times. The cattle have been improved by selection and introduction of better breeds.

A social and economic service has been rendered to the country by creating new and better job opportunities in the rural areas. This has helped to slow rural to urban migration.

The moneylenders who charged exorbitant rates of interest to cattle ranchers in need of credit have disappeared. Some lenders had charged as high as 36 percent per annum for small loans secured by most of the properties of the borrowers.

The experience acquired by the bank in Panama resulted in the establishment of similar rural credit programs in other countrres. In 1963, a cattle credit program was begun in the Dominican Republic, and in 1964, a poultry credit program was begun in Trinidad. The bank has also assisted its affiliates in Brazil, Colombia, Venezuela and Honduras in organizing similar programs.